The Cuban Revolution

The Cuban Revolution

Past, Present and Future Perspectives

Geraldine Lievesley
Senior Lecturer in Politics, Manchester Metropolitan University, UK

First published 2004 by
PALGRAVE MACMILLAN
Houndmills, Basingstoke, Hampshire RG21 6XS and
175 Fifth Avenue, New York, N. Y. 10010
Companies and representatives throughout the world

PALGRAVE MACMILLAN is the global academic imprint of the Palgrave Macmillan division of St. Martin's Press, LLC and of Palgrave Macmillan Ltd. Macmillan® is a registered trademark in the United States, United Kingdom and other countries. Palgrave is a registered trademark in the European Union and other countries.

ISBN 0–333–96852–2 hardback
ISBN 0–333–96853–0 paperback

This book is printed on paper suitable for recycling and made from fully managed and sustained forest sources.

A catalogue record for this book is available from the British Library.

Library of Congress Cataloging-in-Publication Data
Lievesley, Geraldine.
    The Cuban Revolution: past, present, and future perspective/Geraldine Lievesley.
        p. cm.
    Includes bibliographical references and index.
    ISBN 0–333–96852–2 (cloth) – ISBN 0–333–96853–0 (paper)
        1. Cuba–History–Revolution, 1959. I. Title.

F1788.L537 2003
972.9106′4–dc22   2003062244

10   9   8   7   6   5   4   3   2   1
12   11   10   09   08   07   06   05   04   03

Printed and bound in Great Britain by
Antony Rowe Ltd, Chippenham and Eastbourne

This is for David

'Con los pobres de la tierra quiero yo mi suerte echar'
(*Guatánamara*, written by Jose Fernández and based upon *Versos Sencillos* by José Martí)

'I have lived marvellous days'
(Che's farewell letter to Fidel)

Contents

List of Abbreviations

ANAP	Asociación Nacional de Agricultores Pequeños (National Association of Small Farmers)
CAME	Consejo de Ayuda Mutua Económica (Council for Mutual Economic Assistance)
CDRs	Comités de Defensa de la Revolución (Committees for the Defence of the Revolution)
CTC	Confederación de Trabajadores de Cuba (Confederation of Cuban Workers)
FAR	Fuerzas Armadas Revolucionarias (Revolutionary Armed Forces)
FEU	Federación Estudiantil Universitaria (University Students Federation)
FMC	Federación de Mujeres Cubanas (Federation of Cuban Women)
ICAIC	Instituto Cubano del Arte e Industria (Cuban Institute of Art and Industry)
PCC	Partido Comunista de Cuba (Cuban Communist Party)
SDPE	Sistema de Dirección y Planificación de la Economía (System of Direction and Planning of the Economy)
UBPCs	Unidades Básicas de Producción Cooperativa (Basic Units of Production)
UNEAC	Unión de Escritores e Artistas de Cuba (Cuban Union of Writers Artists)

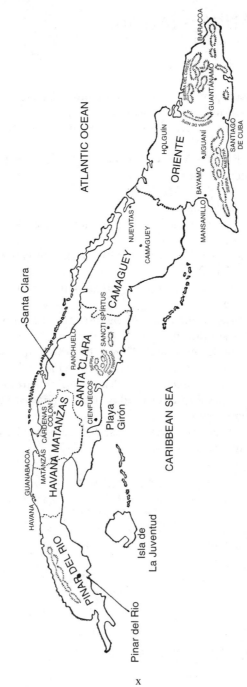

x

1
Introduction

There is considerable interest in contemporary Cuban politics as the present leadership ages; as Cuba experiences tremendous changes in its economic life which have had a significant impact upon its social and political processes; and as commentators speculate about the nature of the political transition which the island has embarked upon. There have been many books about the Cuban Revolution, many of them written by North Americans and frequently by authors with Cuban origins or family backgrounds. Much of the literature upon Cuba is driven by ideological preoccupations. I felt there was an opening for a book which takes a more reflective perspective upon what the Revolution has meant and the influence it has exerted upon diverse groups. These groups would include the Cubans themselves, leaders and people; the states of Central and Latin America (particularly left-wing parties and popular movements); the United States (the political establishment, public opinion and the Cuban émigré community); the old Soviet Union; other states such as Canada and the countries of the European Union and Africa; and academics and activists. This is a political process which has remained fascinating to many and, as Dick Parker has observed, shown 'a surprising capacity for survival'; such capacity, I will argue, has been founded more upon legitimacy than coercion but it has been a legitimacy which has had to be constantly recreated and revitalized if the Revolution was to endure.[1]

This is not a straightforward history; rather, I discuss significant themes (amongst which will be the politics of identity, ideology, state and civil society) and illustrate my argument with reference to specific events and processes. The objective is to explore the nature of the Revolution through examination of the complex interaction between the commitment to socialism and a strong sense of national independence; its

1

achievements and weaknesses, and the relationship between the political leadership and Cuban society. It is important to understand why a country which has experienced such a prolonged state of siege has managed to maintain an open, internationalist approach towards the rest of the world. The US government began constructing its punitive blockade in 1960, completing it with a total prohibition on trade in 1962. The consequences for Cuba of this economic quarantine would be enormous. In this book, I will be using the word 'blockade' rather than 'embargo' because the US does not simply decline to do business with Cuba but directly interferes in Cuba's sovereign relations and political contacts with other countries.

My personal interest in Cuba goes back to strong memories of the news coverage of Che Guevara's death in October 1967. After my first degree in politics, I did doctoral research on Peruvian Marxism and embarked upon a journey of understanding of the nature of US imperialism in Central and Latin America and the long history of resistance to it. Che and Cuba have played an iconic role in that resistance and the symbolism of 1959 continues to have great resonance in the region and elsewhere in the Third World. My travels in Cuba have had the effect of only increasing my fascination with the place as well as confirming my belief that Cuba *does* matter. For someone of my generation and political leanings, the Cuban Revolution generated tremendous interest and debate but its experience has also continued to attract later generations. The universal appeal of Guevara is intrinsic to this interest. Let us consider just one example, that of the 1994 rebellion of the Ejercito Zapatista de Liberación Nacional (EZLN – the Zapatista National Liberation Army) in the southern Mexican province of Chiapas. Whilst linking their struggle to that of another revolutionary icon, Emiliano Zapata, the *zapatistas* have been clear that Che's memory is close to their heart. For Subcomandante Marcos, Che is 'still around and alive thirty years on from his death ... all rebel movements in Latin America are the heirs to Che's rebellion'.[2] Marcos accepted that their tactics were different but contended that the EZLN took from Che '... the human part ... a *guerrillero* who went, against all odds, to raise a dream, a utopia ...'.[3] Cynics might say that this was Marcos engaging Che's memory in the process of myth-making but it is certain that Guevara remains an enduring icon throughout the Americas.

Many commentators and activists who witnessed the Revolution or who followed its progress in subsequent decades will have experienced moments of profound disquiet (for example, Cuban approval of the Soviet invasion of Czechoslovakia in 1968) interlaced with an underlying support. My major problem with the way that political life has been shaped in Cuba since 1959 has been the official equation of criticism of government policy with counter-revolutionary intent. There must be a place within a revolutionary process for constructive discourse. The fact that the Revolution has had more than its fair share of enemies who have wished to demonize its leaders and engineer its destruction should not have led to the state imposing boundaries upon debate and attempting to induce conformity.[4] Any political process which seeks the legitimacy that authentic popular support imparts and which operates in difficult domestic and external circumstances – which the Revolution has since those heady days of January 1959 – needs to recognize its own shortcomings and be receptive to new ideas and modes of behaviour. I return to this issue in a number of ways throughout the text.

There is a huge literature upon Cuba and none of it is neutral.[5] The problems with the demonologists has been that their views have had an invidious influence upon US foreign policy makers. Anti-Castro commentators have excoriated domestic fellow travellers for emasculating Washington's Cuba policy. Opponents of a more muscular policy comprised hippies, left wingers and bleeding heart liberals within the political establishment. Thus the National Security Council (NSC), under Carter and Clinton, represented the 'old anti-communist Left of the 1960s' in its arguments for relaxation of the blockade. To Radu's mind, the 1995 refugee agreements which followed the *balseros* raft crisis of 1994, tolerance of private organizations' funding of projects in Cuba and the relaxation of travel restrictions were all products of the work of NSC fifth columnists.[6] He was heartened, however, by the hardening of the blockade engineered by the Torricelli and Helms–Burton legislation and was confident that conservatives at the State Department were making the right decisions again.[7] Ratliff argues that Fidel Castro destroyed Cuban dreams of national independence when he became a Soviet puppet and manipulated foreign journalists (from Herbert Matthews, whose articles in the *New York Times* in February 1957 began the creation of the myth of the heroic guerrillas, onwards) into believing that he was leading a democratic movement.[8] The level of analysis in such texts is unsophisticated and vitriolic but what is more worrying for those who believe that the Cuban Revolution has a right to exist is that such sentiments have often been at the core of US Cuba policy.

In recent years, the major preoccupation for Cuba watchers has been the question of what will happen when Castro either retires or dies and what kind of transitional regime will follow that event. During the difficult period following the demise of the Soviet bloc, many regarded the Cuban Revolution as a political dinosaur, isolated from the modern globalized community by its commitment to what was an antiquated and defeated ideology. The Cuban government, refusing to follow a Gorbachev-style strategy of *perestroika*, instead proclaimed its Special Period and reiterated its commitment to ¡*Socialismo o muerte*! Many observers were certain that this would be a final bravura performance. The largest march in Cuba's revolutionary history took place on 12 June 2002 in defiance of such views. The popular referendum held that month saw 98.9 per cent (some 8 million people) of registered voters supporting a constitutional amendment declaring socialism 'irrevocable'. Detractors argued that this was a manipulated and thus invalid endorsement but for its adherents, it represented yet another example of Cuba's determination to remain independent.

Its history is intrinsic to understanding Cuba's present circumstances and its experience of imperial domination is particularly pertinent. Spain was interested in Cuba because its geographical position allowed it to be used as a base of operations to exploit other American territories. Cuba was the last country in Latin America to gain independence. The Cuban oligarchy had been a willing partner in the maintenance of imperial structures of domination and, in particular, the institution of slavery. However, it was swimming against the tide of history in that the plantation system facilitated 'Cuba's integration into the world market ... and created sources of wealth that enabled ... the rise of a very advanced intellectual core that would become the architects of the national ideology'.[9] Over time, opinion within Cuba split between those who saw survival through retaining union with Spain, others who looked to incorporation by the United States and those who desired an as yet ill-defined nationhood. The anti-imperialist nationalist tradition was best represented by José Martí (1853–95), the creator of the idea of *Cuba libre*. However, after three wars of independence in the nineteenth century, Cuba found itself in a neo-colonial relationship with the United States, an arrangement which was codified in the 1902 Platt Amendment to the Cuban Constitution. This justified future US intervention in Cuban affairs in order to maintain order and protect US interests. Washington felt no compunction in pursuing what it regarded as an imperial right. Thus, a few years after Platt, President Theodore Roosevelt pronounced himself 'so angry with that infernal little Cuban republic that I would like to wipe its people off the face of the earth'.[10]

The subsequent economic, political and cultural penetration of Cuba replicated the ways in which the US established its hegemony throughout Latin and Central America. Such domination stimulated anti-imperialist sentiment which often provoked a violent American response. When the 26 July Movement guerrillas led by Fidel Castro began armed struggle in the Sierra Maestra in December 1956, they 'challenged core American values and sought to topple the ... alignment of Cuban foreign policy with US policies and ... protection for US trade and investment'.[11] This is precisely why the US has pursued aggressive policies towards Cuba since the Revolution in 1959, policies which included blockade, invasion and the promotion of terrorism against the Cuban state. Even after the end of the cold war and an implicit acceptance that Cuba no longer posed a security risk (if it ever had), US administrations have shown little willingness to rethink their policies in response to 'the major shifts in Cuban foreign and domestic policies that [have] occurred since the late 1980s'.[12]

Despite Washington's best efforts, in the 1960s Cuba embarked upon a programme of structural changes which sought to transform the lives of its people and which 'embodied the aspirations and captured the imagination of Latin America's masses as no other political movement had ever done'.[13] The Revolution was conscious of drawing upon a historical tradition which included Bolívar, Martí, Zapata and Villa, Mella, Sandino and Touissant L'Ouverture in its pantheon. It was a tradition which combined internationalism and anti-imperialism, the pursuit of social justice and the creation of a higher form of human sensibility. These aims caused 'the waters of revolution' to pour 'over the dam, submerging Latin America in political and social ferment that threatened the very foundations of the established order'.[14] Its triumph offered optimism to compensate for the pessimism which had fallen over the left generally in the light of the disclosures about the Stalinist regime at the Twentieth (All-Party) Congress of the Communist Party of the Soviet Union (CPSU) in 1956; it influenced subsequent experiments in socialist construction in Chile and Nicaragua and national liberation movements in Africa and Asia and inspired countless popular mobilizations for human rights. However it also aroused the ire of Latin American authoritarian elites and their military establishments and stimulated a bloody backlash which ravaged the countries of the region and contributed to the creation of a hostile backdrop against which the Revolution developed.

As with all revolutionary processes, Cuba has undergone many changes, made mistakes and also encountered problems. Thus, it swapped dependency upon the US with dependency upon the Soviet Union; attempted to marry the instincts of Cuban nationalism with a commitment to building a Cuban socialism and tried to find a way to resolve the obstacles of underdevelopment. It experimented with various forms of economic management and searched for ways to combine strong political leadership with public accountability and popular participation. It also needed to represent the voices of all Cubans, a task which has not always been successful. Margaret Randall has written about the importance of the Cuban people retrieving control over their history after so many years of oppression, but regretted that 'this new history is most often told from a male perspective, and although it sometimes includes *more* women, it is rarely from a feminist standpoint'.[15] She talked of witnessing profound efforts to 'rout institutionalized racism. I saw the profound changes in the lives of women ...' but criticized the Revolution for not doing enough to improve the daily experience of Cuban women and Afro-Cubans (and I would wish to add, gays and lesbians) and to prevent the continuation of prejudice and discrimination. The Cuban government has used state power 'to dismantle the pillars of racial segregation ... [its] radical policies of redistribution resulted in significantly lower levels of social and regional inequality in general, and of racial inequality in particular'.[16] Nevertheless, in contemporary Cuba, *santería* is used as a tourist attraction and the sparse presence of Afro-Cubans within that industry suggests that double standards persist.[17] The state also made race visible in international politics and culture both in terms of its links with African-American radicals and African national liberation movements and its celebration of the African roots of Cuban music and dance. There is a danger here of making blackness symbolic and in so doing, ignoring the ongoing problems which Afro-Cubans face.

After a woeful approach by the state in the 1960s, by the 1990s greater toleration towards Cuban gay men and lesbian women appeared to be symbolized by the enormous success of the 1993 film, *Fresa y Chocolate* (*Strawberry and Chocolate*, directed by Tomás Gutiérrez Alea and Juan Carlos Tabió). In one sense this offered a simplistic love triangle but what was exceptional by Cuban standards was that its central character was gay. Diego is not a typical *loco* [mad person – one of the official derogatory terms attached to gay people] in that he does not flaunt his sexuality, is cultured and literate and although sometimes effeminate is so only in pursuit of what he desires. As a person, he compares favourably with Miguel, the dour young communist for whom all things foreign are to be distrusted. Diego loves everything Cuban – music, literature, *santería* – but also appreciates Western luxuries such as whisky. He is finally forced to leave Cuba because he is regarded as antisocial but he continues to support the Revolution despite his condemnation of its intolerance and its view of art as serving the ideology of the state. *Fresa y Chocolate* is a flawed film. There is no direct attempt to address the reasons for 'revolutionary homophobia' and the film replays 'the clichéd equation of homosexuality and bourgeois decadence' but, nevertheless, it presented ground-breaking subject matter to Cubans and did offer a critical perspective upon public sensibility.[18] As Jorge Perugorria (the actor who played Diego) maintained: 'Maybe now we don't persecute homosexuals, but we still haven't achieved the political maturity to give equal opportunity to everybody regardless of political, ideological, or other differences. . . . The film argues for the reconciliation of all Cubans.'[19]

In his analysis of the economic prospects facing Cuba at the end of the twentieth century, Ken Cole admitted that 'although there is general agreement on the seriousness of Cuba's economic predicament, there is no unanimity as to the causes, consequences or solutions'.[20] This statement aptly summarizes general views on the Revolution: there is no unanimity but, instead, multiple perspectives upon its development and its future and all are politicized viewpoints. Mine is clearly not a neutral view although I have tried to avoid both demonization (which I wholly disagree with) and hagiography (which is an unhealthy condition). Many who have been sympathetic to the Revolution have hesitated to offer criticism in case it fed into the anti-Cuban lobby. This is understandable but unhelpful in that the result was a silence which did not and can never benefit Cuba.

Chapter 2 discusses how the Cuban Revolution was received by international opinion and, most particularly, by the United States. Chapter 3 offers an analysis of the formation of Cuban national identity as it evolved in the nineteenth and twentieth centuries before 1959. Chapter 4 begins with an examination of the ideological underpinnings of the Cuban revolutionary tradition and concludes with an account of the heroic period of the 1960s. The discussion in Chapter 5 of domestic and foreign policy in the 1970s and 1980s provides a companion text for the examination in Chapter 6 of the nature of the relationship between the Cuban state and civil society. The issues it deals with include questions of popular participation, civil liberties, the status of women and Afro-Cubans and censorship in the arts. Chapter 7 begins with an account of the difficult decade of the 1990s and then develops into an inevitably open-ended consideration of Cuba's future.

2
Encounters with 'the Monster' and Others

> I have lived in the bowels of the monster and I know him well; my sling is David's. [José Martí, 1895. The 'monster' was the USA][1]

The Cuban Revolution has had a profound and enduring influence upon world politics, an influence which belies its status as a small, poor Third World country. The underlying concern of this book is to investigate and appraise the very diverse and different responses which the Revolution has engendered and this chapter hopes to advance this objective by considering the role of Cuba in the world in the early years following its 1959 triumph. Later foreign policy processes and relationships between Cuba and Latin America, the rest of the Third World, the Soviet Union, Western Europe and, most importantly, the United States are discussed in subsequent chapters. An analysis of the international role Cuba has constructed for itself, how it is situated within the international political economy and the reaction that this has stimulated in other states is one aspect of my intention; the other is to understand how Cuba has perceived this role and how it has viewed its place in the world. The complexity and variability of the ways in which the Revolution has been received and the meanings that have been constructed around it were succinctly demonstrated by Alistair Hennessy when he argued that:

> It challenged orthodoxies of the left; it extended the Cold War to the Americas; it popularised a new revolutionary strategy of armed struggle in which the rootless would be leaders; it energised the concept of Third World solidarity ... by equating it with resistance to U. S. hegemony.[2]

Since 1959, Cuba has continued to perceive itself as a significant international actor despite the restraints upon it imposed by its own economic vulnerability and the policy positions of both the United States and the Soviet Union. For Jorge Domínguez: 'Cuba is a small country, but it has the foreign policy of a big power.'[3] Over time, it has offered support for guerrilla struggles in Latin America, been a significant player in the Non-Aligned Movement, sent expertise and aid to Third World states and attempted to initiate trading and diplomatic openings with European countries. This ambitious strategy frequently led Cuba to overextend itself both in terms of its financial possibilities and by overplaying its political hand and so aggravating relations with other governments. At times the government's international priorities had clear costs in terms of welfare. As Castro said in late 1978: 'in Cuba ... there is a need to build schools, but we are, nevertheless, building schools in Jamaica and Tanzania. ... We still have a shortage of hospitals, but we are, nevertheless, building a hospital in Vietnam.'[4] Domínguez contends that 'Domestic constraints have had little effect on the patterns of Cuban support for revolution. ... Two of the periods of greatest Cuban support for such movements – in the late 1960s and in 1979–80 – were also times of deteriorating domestic economic performance.'[5] It is clear that Cuban consideration of self-interest has differed from the norm; whether this is seen as altruistic or self-destructive will depend upon one's perspective upon politics. The motivating factor behind Cuba's actions on the world stage has been and remains its strong commitment to internationalism. This international perspective has been tempered by the restraints imposed by Cuba's most defining relationship – that with its near neighbour, the United States. The historical roots of this relationship are examined in the following chapter, but here I wish to consider Washington's reactions to the political situation in Cuba prior to the Revolution's triumph on 1 January 1959.

Revolutionary struggle in Cuba: the 1950s, Batista, Castro and the Americans

Fulgencio Batista dominated Cuban politics between 1934 and 1959. However US confidence in his ability to maintain order and prevent political unrest began to dissipate following his coup of 1952. The symbolic beginning of growing opposition to his rule was Castro's abortive 26 July 1953 attack on the Moncada Army Barracks in Santiago de Cuba whilst armed rebellion began in earnest with the *Granma* expedition which landed in Cuba from Mexico on 2 December 1956.[6] The United States was extremely concerned because there 'was uniform hostility ... to the idea of a successful antidictatorial movement dominated by radical nationalists'. Morley argues that 'American hostility to Castro before 1959 is central to an understanding of the US response to the Cuban Revolution after 1959'.[7] Thus, there was policy continuity rather than a new initiative on Washington's part after 1959. There were strong US military and intelligence links with Batista's regime and a heavy flow of military *matériel* ranging from guns to rocket launchers was orchestrated by the Military Assistance Advisory Group. Such aid was supposedly regulated by a mutual security agreement and was intended to be used for 'hemispheric defense' but the US turned a blind eye to the fact that it was being used to repress domestic critics rather than external enemies. The US also maintained a continued physical presence in Cuba due to its possession of the Guantánamo Naval Base. Under the Platt Amendment, the US leased the land around Guantánamo Bay on the south-eastern end of the island. The Guantánamo base has long been regarded by nationalists as a blatant violation of sovereignty and since 1959, the Cuban government has refused to accept what it regards as blood money.[8] Batista could also count upon US assistance in a more shadowy form through the Central Intelligence Agency's support for the Buró Represión de las Actividades Comunistas (BRAC, the Bureau for the Repression of Communist Activities). In Cuba, as elsewhere in the Third World, the US and its allies defined 'communist' in a highly elastic manner as anyone who was challenging the conservative political status quo, endangering their economic investments or championing the interests of the poor.

US policy makers held divergent views on the resilience of the Batista regime and the political potential of the opposition. These views were characterized by varying degrees of ignorance and self-delusion and reflected, in the main, a simplistic world view which took Manifest Destiny and the notion of the 'backyard' as a given. Official observations about Castro and the 26 July Movement (named after the 1953 attack), and other opposition groups tended to be couched in the language of imperialist hegemony and rested upon an infantilization of Cubans generally. In early 1959, CIA Director Allen Dulles told the National Security Council that the Cubans 'had to be treated more or less like children ... they had to be led rather than rebuffed. If they were rebuffed, like children, they were capable of almost anything.'[9] The supremacist thinking which dominated American attitudes was fuelled by negative images of *latinos* generally and of Cubans in particular: 'One nice thing about Cuba', however, *Houston Post* editors smugly wrote in 1956, 'is that she can have a revolution any time hotbloods get in the mood without adding to world tension.'[10]

The most uncomprehending US witnesses to the revolutionary struggle which unfolded after 1953 were frequently those closest to the action. Thus, Ambassadors Arthur Gardner and Earl E. T. Smith, both Republican loyalists, 'took the Batista point of view and never fully plumbed the depths of Cuban discontent', although other diplomats, such as Park F. Wollam, the American consul in Santiago who successfully negotiated the release of prisoners kidnapped by Raúl Castro in summer 1958, held more nuanced views.[11] Meeting only the top echelons of Cuban society, not speaking Spanish and lacking any semblance of political astuteness, Smith's response to Castro's victory was to argue that it had been engineered by liberal subversives in the State Department. Ambassadorial myopia was compounded by lack of interest further up the executive ladder. President Eisenhower gave little time or attention to Cuban affairs, delegating decision-making and failing to grasp the wider picture. It was left to journalists such as Herbert L. Matthews to give Washington food for thought with respect to the danger the rebels might pose whilst US business pressed for action, mindful of the burning of sugar-cane fields and attacks upon United Fruit warehouses, the Texaco refinery and Nicaro nickel plant in Oriente province.

Not all US officials lacked the ability or the desire to appreciate what was happening in Cuba. Thus, William Wieland, head of the Office of Middle American Affairs at the State Department, believed that the United States should act as an intermediary between Batista and his opposition, convincing the former to end the killing and torture and call free elections. A role for the Organization of American States [OAS] as honest broker was also envisaged. If such a compromise were not reached, Cuba could fall into political chaos. Some members of Congress, such as the Democratic Senators Mike Mansfield of Montana, Hubert H. Humphrey of Minnesota and Wayne Morse of Oregon (all of whom sat on the Senate Foreign Relations Committee) were also well informed about Cuba. They advocated a policy which would offer Cuba economic rather than military aid and which, in nurturing development, would forestall political radicalization. Ranged against them were the Joint Chiefs of Staff who argued that any suspension of arms shipments to Batista would benefit the spread of international communism.

As 1958 progressed and it became evident that Batista refused to introduce reforms and moderate his repression, opinion within the Eisenhower administration shifted with the aim of distancing the United States from his regime (even cutting back on arms supplies) and urging the formation of a third-force government, one that would exclude Castro and would be amenable to US concerns. This demonstrated a failure to grasp that there were *no* viable alternatives and that the insurrection had a broad and popular base as well as the simple fact that the guerrillas were winning the war. When Washington finally decided to abandon Batista in late 1958, it had no options left. Fidel was unacceptable to it, ex-President Prío was discredited and other notables were either in jail or exile. No other politician or group could challenge the support that the 26 July Movement and the urban resistance commanded. This did not prevent members of the same political elite later blaming the US for the indecisiveness of its policy towards Batista and inferring that it had actually helped Castro into power. In his memoir, Nestor T. Carbonell recounts how his father and two other former senators met with Batista in August 1958 in an attempt to persuade him to step down: 'Their relationship with Batista, although strained since the coup, went back many years and enabled them to engage in frank and open discussions' but progress was stymied by Washington's tentativeness.[12]

Washington's myopia about political realities in Latin America prevented it realizing that the Cuban Revolution was not as exceptional an event as it supposed if viewed against the backdrop of the toppling of dictatorships in Argentina, Peru, Columbia and Venezuela between 1956 and 1958; the emergence of Christian Democratic parties and the embrace of nationalist programmes by the Brazilian and Peruvian militaries.[13] The US certainly consistently underestimated the pervasive anti-Americanism in the region. It should have learnt from Vice President Richard Nixon's May 1958 tour where he encountered fierce demonstrations in Venezuela and Peru.[14] Washington has never understood authentic popular movements fuelled by political exclusion and social deprivation. Thus it failed to appreciate, until it was too late, the power vacuum which surrounded Batista as the final revolutionary military offensive gained momentum through the autumn and early winter of 1958. Attempting, belatedly, to manage events, Eisenhower sent William D. Pawley on a mission to urge Batista to resign and pave the way for the establishment of a third-force government (Pawley would later help organize the Bay of Pigs). The conventional wisdom behind this initiative was that Castro could be ignored, cajoled or forced to cooperate with the US government. The latter did not understand that Castro was committed to challenging US hegemony and to destroying the power structure which it had shored up since the Spanish–Cuban–American War and the Platt Amendment. The US did not understand that it 'had aligned itself with a flawed, weak, corrupt, ineffective, and unpopular regime it ultimately could not control'.[15]

Nationalist opposition to Batista was linked in the minds of many Cubans with a desire to repudiate the conspicuous display of US financial and military might and to reduce dependency upon US consumerism and its cultural manifestations on the island. Castro once remarked to Herbert Matthews. 'You Americans keep complaining that Cuba is only ninety miles from your shore ... I say that the United States is ninety miles from Cuba, and for us that is worse.'[16] Paterson contends that the error made by the United States, born out of its huge arrogance, was to believe that 'every Cuban leader had his price and any Cuban government that wished to survive had to respect the United States and its interests'.[17] For Morris Morley, Cuba's 'profound integration into the U.S. agro-industrial complex and its thorough vulnerability to American economic integration', led Washington policy makers to believe that their initiatives would 'weaken the island economy, erode the Castro regime's social basis of support, and substantially strengthen the position of the United States and its social-class allies in Cuba. They were wrong.'[18] By introducing retaliatory measures such as economic sanctions – a fairly conventional manifestation of state power – Washington believed that Cuba would back down: 'Castro, however, was not intimidated. Every American step elicited a progressively more radical countermeasure, as when Fidel responded to the American oil refineries' refusal to refine Soviet crude by confiscating the facilities.'[19] Cuba was determined to break with historical precedent and pursue its independence.

The Cuban Revolution engages with the world

Since 1959, Cuba has tried to operate as a player on the world stage, pursuing its own policy objectives and attempting to avoid being used as a pawn in Great Power struggles. However, inevitably, in the 1960s it found its international agenda being 'largely dominated by its dealings with the world's two superpowers'.[20] The three major crises in the first revolutionary decade were the abortive Bay of Pigs invasion and the imposition of the trade blockade in 1961 and the Missile Crisis of the following year. From the late 1960s, the US was increasingly preoccupied with events in South-East Asia, particularly its involvement in Vietnam and the aftermath of this which saw American public opinion turn against future foreign interventions. Its obsession with Cuba had to take a back seat. This gave Cuba the opportunity to develop its own initiatives in the Third World, particularly within the Non-Aligned Movement (NAM). It was committed to a restructuring of the international system in order to empower the poor states of Latin America, Africa and Asia. Here Cuba encountered a problem. The closeness of its relationship with the Soviet Union may have given Cuba the security to undertake such a role but it also made many states suspicious of the aims of Cuban foreign policy.

Cuba and the Soviet Union in the 1960s

During the armed struggle against Batista, Moscow periodically made somewhat perfunctory condemnations of the dictator as a 'Yankee stooge' but offered little help to the Cuban communists, with whom it only had tenuous links, and was highly sceptical of Castro and the 26 July Movement, making disparaging remarks about their lack of a coherent political programme. It was slow to engage with the new revolutionary government and when Castro declared the Revolution to be Marxist-Leninist, 'the Soviets [were] surprised and embarrassed by the declaration. . . . It was to tie them to a wayward ally who until 1967 pursued an independent *via armada* line of guerrilla strategy which ran counter to the official policy of Latin American communist parties.'[21] The relationship was an extremely wary and often testy one during the 1960s and there were periodic breakdowns in subsequent decades. Havana did not join the Soviet bloc in a quiet or submissive manner for it was resolved to maintain its independence in all its international relations. Sometimes it appeared that Castro went out of his way to antagonize his ally. Thus, at the Havana Conference of Latin American Communist Parties held in November 1964, his proud retort of 'We do not need the brains of other people' implied that Cuba could think for itself and did not relish getting received wisdom from Moscow or elsewhere.[22] However, Cuba's defensive concerns in the context of the US trade blockade, Cuban émigré invasion and assassination plans and its expulsion from the OAS meant that it had to come to terms with Soviet policy in the Americas (which was actually far more conservative and tentative than many simplistic Western analyses suggested given Moscow's embrace of peaceful coexistence) and to enter into practical relations with the erstwhile reviled communist parties. This was made easier once Guevara had left Cuba. Although initially close to the communists, Che had become increasingly concerned about Moscow's influence over the Revolution.

Following Guevara's death and the defeat of the Latin and Central American guerrilla movements, Havana drew ever closer to the Soviet bloc. Thousands of Soviet technicians, military personnel and their families arrived in Cuba (although there was little contact between them and ordinary Cubans) and Moscow began to count the cost of its huge economic investment in the island. The reconciliation appeared cemented in 1972 when Cuba became the first non-European nation to be accepted as a full member of the Consejo de Ayuda Mutua Económica (CAME, the Council for Mutual Economic Assistance). However, Moscow remained anxious about its idiosyncratic ally. As the relationship evolved in the 1970s and beyond, it became ever more complex, oscillating between collaboration and confrontation. Whilst conservative commentators wished to view Cuba as no more than a Soviet puppet, others highlighted the differences in Soviet and Cuban policy positions and the tensions these generated.[23] For Robert A. Pastor, the Cuban connection required far more adept handling by Moscow than did its relations with most of its Eastern bloc satellites: 'The Soviets do not tell the Cubans what to do, but they let the Cubans know what they cannot do and the Cubans accept that.'[24] Jorge Domínguez has located the core of the relationship as a 'combination of Soviet hegemony with Cuban autonomy'. Moscow sought the upper hand by imposing limited sanctions such as slowing down petroleum supplies, arms and technical assistance. By the 1970s, there was an 'asymmetrical concentration of power in Soviet hands' but 'the retention of much client autonomy to formulate and implement foreign policy'.[25]

The Latin American response to the Cuban Revolution

Ernesto Guevara anticipated that support for and emulation of the Revolution in Latin America and, indeed, elsewhere in the Third World, would stimulate a fierce response from the dominant world powers and particularly from the United States for 'imperialism has learnt its lesson and will not be taken by surprise again'.[26] He accepted that: 'Each time that an impudent people cries out for liberation, Cuba is accused; and it is true in a sense that Cuba is guilty, because Cuba has shown the way. . . . This Cuban example is bad, a very bad example.'[27] Indeed, 1959 inaugurated a historical period only ended by the electoral defeat of the Sandinistas 30 years later. After the Revolution, five key dates charted the progress of the left: 1959 itself;

the murder of Che in Bolivia in 1967; Pinochet's coup against Allende's Unidad Popular (UP, Popular Unity) government in Chile in 1973; the revolutionary triumph of the Frente Sandinista Liberación Nacional (FSLN, the Sandinista National Liberation Front) in 1979 and its departure from government following the 1990 elections in Nicaragua. Of these, the Cuban Revolution was by far the most important. For Jorge Castañeda, it was the 'Revolution within the Revolution'.[28] For the Latin American left, the Cuban Revolution was extraordinarily important in that it represented a decisive historical moment, one which would hopefully inaugurate a continental process of nationalist, anti-capitalist struggle which might develop into the establishment of socialist governments across the region. The revolutionary victory seemed to bring to an end the pessimism which had been endemic within the Latin American left (and the left in Western Europe, the US and elsewhere) following the death of Stalin in 1953 and the revelations of the CPSU Congress in 1956. Cuba also posed a fundamental threat to the political orthodoxies espoused by communist, Trotskyite and Maoist parties because of the nature of its revolutionary process and the strategies the Cubans and Ernesto Guevara advocated.

The core of the Cuban revolutionary message can be encapsulated by the following statements. The Latin American revolution would be hemispheric in scope and socialist in character. It would be achieved through armed struggle led by a vanguard of the enlightened middle classes who would stimulate the political consciousness of the popular sectors. Vanguard parties should ally only with revolutionary forces and not with the national bourgeoisie, existing governments, populist parties and corrupt trade union bureaucracies. This injunction constituted a frontal attack upon the strategy of communist parties and was a provocative assault upon Soviet ideological hegemony. From the Cuban perspective, communist parties were no longer authentic revolutionary organizations. The key alliance was that between the peasantry and the revolutionary vanguard and the armed struggle would be waged in the countryside before a final assault on the cities through the means of a general strike. Underpinning these premises was a theoretical perspective which emerged in ad hoc fashion but would come to be known as dependency theory. It embraced a recognition of the neo-colonial nature of the world economy; the division of nations into metropolitan and satellite states and the unequal distribution of power which resulted from this and the necessity to break these ties of dependency and pursue a socialist model of development. The Cuban 'model' would stimulate a wave of armed struggles throughout Latin and Central America during the 1960s and early 1970s, some of which would be decimated rapidly and others which would endure longer but still be defeated.

The Revolution exercised a huge influence over Latin America and yet the practical consequences of this influence, in terms of the revolutionary initiatives which followed it, were disastrous for Latin American left-wing parties and guerrilla movements and were instrumental in stimulating authoritarian reaction and the establishment of military governments. Fear of continental revolution was instrumental in Kennedy's endorsement of the Alliance for Progress and confirmed Washington's intention to remain closely involved in Latin American affairs. Cuba's foreign policy in Latin America also facilitated further confirmation for its critics that it was operating on Moscow's orders (often referred to as the surrogate thesis). In his book on rural guerrilla movements, Richard Gott quotes Ernst Halperin who, in his foreword to a 1967 book on Cuba, maintained that Cuba joined the Soviet corner not for protection from the US but because Soviet support 'opened the perspective of spreading the revolution to the Latin American mainland'. Gott comments: 'This now seems to be United States official and academic orthodoxy, and is based on a complete ignorance of revolutionary movements in Latin America.'[29] Notwithstanding the tactical and strategic mistakes made by individual pro-Cuba guerrilla movements, their emergence reflected authentic popular grievances and profound political and socio-economic inequities. They were not an artificial manifestation of Soviet imperial thrust. However, the bottom line is that the guerrillas were incapable of overturning authoritarian governments and, indeed, their existence ushered in ever more repressive regimes. Casteñada has argued that 'With the exception of Cuba, it [the Left] has failed miserably in its efforts to take power, make revolution, and change the world.'[30] This failure had consequences for both Latin and Central America's future and for the trajectory of the Cuban Revolution itself.

The Alliance for Progress

The Alianza para el progreso was introduced at the Inter-American Conference held in Punta del Este in Uruguay in August 1961. In a package which superficially resembled the post-war Marshall Plan for Europe, the US promised to lend $20 billion in public and private capital over the next ten years which Kennedy declared would be the 'decade for development'.[31] The ostensible purpose was to stimulate economic growth but the rationale behind the Alliance was a highly politicized one: 'The Kennedy administration decided to embark on a campaign to underwrite change and development in Latin America because U.S. officials feared that the region seemed vulnerable to radical social revolution.'[32] The objective was to 'immunize Latin American societies against radicalism' by increasing military aid in order to strengthen internal security and suppress left-wing insurgencies, by turning a blind eye to the overthrow of constitutional governments and by supporting the imposition of military regimes.[33] In his speech at Punta del Este, Ernesto Guevara dissected the programme, arguing that Cuba would willingly support a real alliance for progress but not one which was aimed at destroying Cuba, the 'free territory of the Americas'.[34]

Despite his earlier criticism of Eisenhower's misguided support for Batista and his recognition of the power of nationalism whilst on the stump, once in office President Kennedy projected an image of a vigorous cold war warrior who was committed to ridding Latin America of Castro's Cuba and any other potential communist satellites. In a speech in Salt Lake City during the 1960 presidential campaign, he had depicted the cold war as 'a struggle for supremacy between two conflicting ideologies: Freedom under God versus ruthless, godless tyranny'.[35] This rhetoric was symptomatic of the administration's approach to what it regarded as 'the most dangerous area in the world'; its foreign policy was conducted on the basis of little knowledge or expertise, simplistic analysis, a condescending attitude towards Latin American politicians and, on the part of the Kennedy brothers, a macho belief that family honour which had been besmirched by the Bay of Pigs fiasco had to be avenged.

The US believed that economic development and a more equitable distribution of wealth and resources in Latin American societies would act as a bulwark against popular support for guerrilla movements. This was not a bad idea (Che had himself argued that all available avenues of political activity should be explored before recourse to arms and that intelligent reformist politicians would introduce wide-ranging reforms in order to assuage popular discontent), but it failed to take account of the resistance to change amongst governing elites who wished to preserve their own privileged position within those societies: 'Eager to perform economic miracles, US officials sponsored high impact, visible projects that failed because of poor planning, institutionalised conservatism and a lack of political will.'[36] No attempt was made to address the unequal terms of trade with which Latin American economies had to contend; indeed, the US insisted that recipient countries purchase

American products as a condition of funding. The Alliance further opened up *latino* economies to US business and banks, inserting them ever more closely and adversely (in terms of their own interests) into the international political economy. This set the scene for the massive infusion of foreign loans into the region which would result in the debt crisis of the 1980s. There was little attempt to introduce structural reforms and where they were attempted, for example agrarian reform in Chile and Peru under Frei and Belaúnde, they were half-baked and ineffectual. Huge amounts of Alliance money were also directed towards the Latin American armed forces. In September 1961, President Kennedy ordered his secretary of defence to explore what steps could be taken 'to increase the intimacy' between the US and Latin American militaries; the latter needed to be taught 'how to control mobs and fight guerrillas'.[37] Under the cover of the Alliance, the US undertook to tutor the armies and internal security forces of Latin and Central America in counter-insurgency and in the torture and repression of their civilian populations.

During the 1960s, US policy was predicated – under cover of the progressive rhetoric of the Alliance – upon the need to 'save' Latin America from the world communist conspiracy. It pursued this aim both in its specific policies towards Cuba and also in its frequent interventions in the domestic politics of other countries. Washington applied considerable pressure to Latin American governments with the aim of forcing them to break diplomatic relations with Cuba and so isolate the Revolution. The 1954 Declaration of Caracas, an intellectual heir of the Monroe Doctrine, was a statement of anti-communist intent which the Eisenhower administration had forced upon the OAS in order to justify its overthrow of the Arbenz government in Guatemala in the same year. It stated that 'the domination or control of the political institutions of any American state by the international communist movement ... would constitute a threat to the sovereignty and political independence of the American states ...'.[38] US policy manifested itself in a series of incidents and relationships. Thus, it pursued gunboat diplomacy in both the Dominican Republic and Haiti. In the former, the CIA was involved in planning the dictator Trujillo's assassination in May 1961. However, its preferred candidate, Joaquín Balaguer, was then defeated in elections by Juan Bosch whom the US embassy regarded as pro-Cuba. Washington made no protest when he was overthrown by the military in September 1963 and, subsequently, President Johnson sent 20,000 troops to ensure 'stability' in the country. In Haiti, the US decided that it could tolerate the continuance in power of the brutal Papa Doc because it feared that the alternative would be a nationalist, pro-Cuban government. The US was suspicious of reforming governments, withdrawing support and undermining presidents Frondizi in Argentina and Goulart in Brazil (who fell to military coups in March 1962 and April 1964 respectively). This was despite the fact that their development programmes reflected the avowed aims of the Alliance for Progress.

Latin American states differed in their responses to US policy on Cuba. When Cuba was expelled from the OAS in January 1962 (with sanctions on trade and shipping and the severance of diplomatic relations following in July of that year), Argentina and Venezuela abstained from voting whilst Mexico, Chile, Bolivia and Uruguay voted against the US-sponsored motions. Whilst Arturo Frondizi had committed Argentina to the Alliance and was warm in his praise for the Kennedy government, he refused to adopt its cold war stance on Cuba and maintained diplomatic relations with Havana. João Goulart had warned that the US should be aware that the 'Latin American masses are instinctive[ly] on [the] side of tiny Cuba whenever it [is] menaced by [the] colossus to [the] North'.[39] Mexico infuriated Washington by keeping open its embassy in Havana as well as enjoying diplomatic ties with the Soviet Union. Other politicians competed to gain American approbation. Rómulo Betancourt of Venezuela was hailed for his vehement criticism of Castro and received massive funding from the World Bank as a reward. During the 1964 presidential elections in Chile, the US injected money into Eduardo Frei's successful campaign and conducted covert operations against his rival Salvador Allende who had condemned its aggression against Cuba (these covert activities infamously increased following the election of Allende in 1970).

The US was also active in the internal affairs of British Guiana, supporting Forbes Burnham in his struggle with Cheddi Jagan whom it saw as a Cuban ally. Its destabilization operations reduced the country to a state of civil unrest and facilitated Burnham's capture of power and the start of 20 years of authoritarian rule. President Ydígoras permitted the CIA to use Guatemalan territory to train Cubans for the Bay of Pigs but when he agreed that ex-President Arévalo could run in elections, the military overthrew him in March 1963 and the US made no complaint. Cuban-American émigrés were active in lobbying OAS governments to convince them that the Alliance for Progress should be strengthened by the addition of an Alliance for Freedom committed to military action. Although this did not materialize, there was an informal network of anti-Cuban and reactionary movements who were responsible for ongoing interventions in Latin and Central American states and who could count upon Washington's complicity.

The Alliance and the anti-revolutionary agenda it represented was instrumental in facilitating the imposition of military rule in a number of Latin American countries beginning with the Brazilian coup in 1964. Military assistance continued to expand and the US turned a blind eye to any violations of constitutionality and human rights. Convinced that the Soviet Union was not in a position to intervene militarily in the area even if it so wished, Washington's policy was posited on the vital need to maintain internal security in Latin America. Thus, it concentrated upon strengthening its military establishments and training them in counter-insurgency techniques. In 1959, Senator Wayne Morse (Democrat, Oregon) had sponsored an amendment to the Mutual Security Act that barred military aid for internal security. However it allowed for presidential exemptions. Kennedy assured Congress that large injections of money and expertise would protect Latin American countries from communist penetration but would not inhibit the functioning of democracy. Some members of the administration demurred albeit belatedly. Arthur Schlesinger – one of the architects of the Kennedy myth – subsequently castigated the US's failure to oppose military coups and argued that 'counterinsurgency was "the worst folly" of the Kennedy administration as it contributed to a "militaristic assault on democracy that disfigured Latin America in the 1960s" '.[40]

Cuba and Third World politics

Many Third World countries responded enthusiastically to news of the Revolution and the Cuban government lost no time in developing policies towards them. Cuba's early Africa policy can be divided into three phases, the first when it was preoccupied with Algeria, the second when it focused upon sub-Saharan Africa (Che's three-month trip in 1959 and the dispatch of troops to Zaire and Congo-Brazzaville) and between 1966 and 1974 when it undertook a long involvement with Guinea-Bissau. Cuban interest in Africa rose as the revolutionary tide in Latin America ebbed. Recognizing the parallels between the Algerian struggle against French rule and its own fight, Cuba was enthusiastic about helping the Algerians. Shortly after signing the 1962 Evian Accords with France, its leader Ben Bella indicated that the newly independent Algeria would emulate Cuba's example: 'We live in Algeria but our hearts are in Cuba ... the fundamental line which we have chosen is the same as the Cuban one and this will determine the proximity and the unity of our countries and our revolutions.'[41] When Ben Bella met President Kennedy in the United States, Castro hailed it as 'an act of courage in the face of U. S. imperialism' whilst the Algerian leader's visit to Cuba in October 1962 was hailed as a meeting of fraternal minds.[42] Algeria became Cuba's window on Africa and many Latin American revolutionaries sought refuge there. Cuba began an honourable tradition by sending medical aid and doctors to Algeria. For Gleisejes: 'It was an act of solidarity that brought no tangible benefit and came at real material cost.'[43] Havana also dispatched weapons and combat troops when Algeria clashed with Morocco over a border dispute in October 1963; although the Cubans did not fight, they certainly influenced the move towards a ceasefire. When Ben Bella was overthrown in June 1965, there was consternation in Cuba and relations with the new regime of Houari Boumedienne were frosty. It is evident that Cuba's decision to become involved in Algeria was not done on the orders of Moscow but was one of its assertive foreign policy initiatives.[44]

Cuba had participated in the founding conference of the NAM in 1961 but its membership was compromised by its commitment to revolutionary change as articulated by the Second Declaration of Havana in February 1962 and Che's January 1966 Message to the Tricontinental Conference. Cuba maintained that it would only ally with states which were anti-imperialist and expressed a desire to create a revolutionary axis of Third World socialist states (itself, Vietnam and North Korea) which would be free of Moscow's control. However, politically 'moderate' members of the NAM (those who remained within the US sphere of influence and those who vacillated between West and East) as well as those who saw Soviet influence behind all Cuban actions suspected its motives. As the guerrilla movements in Latin America were defeated one by one and as its rapprochement with Moscow grew ever more intimate (demonstrated by its reluctant support for the invasion of Czechoslovakia in 1968 and its grudging acceptance of the Brezhnev Doctrine which stated that the Soviet Union would not be indifferent to political developments in other socialist states), Havana's Third World revolutionary offensive was modified. It seemed willing to tolerate more diverse types of regime within the NAM although it still clearly aspired to play a leading role in its affairs.

The first post-independence premier of the Congo, Patrice Lumumba, was murdered in January 1961 on the orders of the secessionist leader of Katanga, Moise Tshombe. Civil war ensued with the intervention of

Congo's large, aggressive neighbour Zaire led by Mobutu and supported by the CIA and Western mercenaries. The US feared that the Congo could become a communist bridgehead although, in truth, Moscow evinced little interest in the struggle. Cuba followed events very closely. When he addressed the UN General Assembly in December 1964, Che argued that it 'must ... avenge the crime of the Congo!'[45] Cuban military columns were despatched to both the Congo and Zaire. In April 1965, Guevara and 200 Cuban soldiers arrived in Congo-Brazzaville to fight against Tshombe's regime. This was not a quixotic mission dreamed up by Che himself but reflected Cuba's belief that the countries of sub-Saharan Africa were ripe for revolution. The Cubans encountered a highly complex set of relations between the Congolese factions, all of whom distrusted the Cubans and particularly Che, whose charismatic authority they regarded as threatening. His relations with future president Laurent Kabila were particularly poor. The Cuban troops experienced scant logistical support and inadequate aid from their Tanzanian allies and found the Congolese troops to be poorly disciplined, superstitious, cruel to their prisoners and lacking in political conviction. The outsiders also failed to attract support from the Congolese peasants. First isolated from the military action and then in danger of being surrounded, Fidel finally ordered their evacuation. Che was profoundly depressed by what he regarded as his own ill handling of the expedition. A more fundamental criticism would be that the Cubans should not have got involved in a complex political situation of which they had little knowledge.[46]

In the mid-1960s, Cuba also made contact with the guerrilla movements fighting for independence in the Portuguese colonies of Angola, Guinea-Bissau and Mozambique. Guevara thought highly of Amilcar Cabral, leader of the Partido Africano da Independência da Guiné e Cabo Verde (PAIGC, the African Party for the Liberation of Portuguese Guinea and the Cape Verde Islands), but relations were more fraught with Eduardo Mondlane and FRELIMO (the Front for the Liberation of Mozambique). Cuba sent a military mission as well as doctors and advisers to the PAIGC's base in Conakry, the capital of Guinea, but respected Cabral's insistence that his own organization take charge of operations. Cuba's most significant involvement in Africa would be in the third colony, Angola, in the 1970s.

Cuba and Western Europe

The relationship between revolutionary Cuba and the states of Western Europe was subject to intense pressure from Washington as it attempted to impose its commitment to the destruction of Castro's government upon its allies. However, individual states resisted its efforts to control their trade policy and diplomacy. The British government had sold fighter planes to Batista but it made no attempt to prevent Leyland's 1964 deal to sell buses and trucks to the Castro government. This and the British government's willingness to guarantee the company export credit infuriated the US and stimulated difficult conversations between Lyndon Johnson and then Premier Sir Alec Douglas Home. Leyland reported excellent business relations with the Cubans and its Havana office only closed in the early 1970s following industrial restructuring in the United Kingdom. France – which, under de Gaulle, was antagonistic towards what it regarded as Washington's attempts to dominate Western European politics – was even more intent on pursuing its own policies with regard to Cuba. Although France feared that Cuban expansion in the Caribbean would threaten its own colonies of Martinique and Guadeloupe, its pragmatic handling of Algerian independence drew Havana's approbation. However, whilst de Gaulle had challenged American hegemony (vetoing the UK's Common Market entry, withdrawing from NATO and making overtures to Moscow), his successor President Pompidou was far more circumspect. Nevertheless, French banks kept credit lines open to Cuba into the 1980s. By the mid-1960s, Spain had become Cuba's most important trading partner in Western Europe. This could be explained by their shared historical and cultural traditions and also by the strange acquaintance struck between Castro and Franco. It must be said that all contacts between Cuba and Western European states were tempered by criticism of its political practice, by its closeness to the Soviet Union and by a recognition that US opinion had to be considered.

Cuba and the United States in the 1960s

The challenge to the Monroe Doctrine

> ... the existence of Cuba represents not only the hope of a better future for the peoples of America but also the prospect of a dangerous future for the ... United States.[47]

The shock of the Revolution suggested to Washington that it could no longer control Cuba and that the Cuban disease could spread to Latin and Central America, thus challenging the Monroe Doctrine which had underwritten US hegemony in the Americas since it was enunciated in 1823. President Harry Truman had reaffirmed and updated the Doctrine in March 1947 when he announced that the United States would oppose the spread of communism anywhere in the world. The opinion that Cuba had extended the cold war to the 'backyard' was predictable and uncompromising and left precious little space for informed negotiation. Ignorance and a highly circumscribed window on the world were central elements in US policy towards the region. James Nathan comments that 'Eisenhower and [John Foster] Dulles [his secretary of state] found it difficult to believe that revolutionary change in the non-Western world might be the product of indigenous forces.'[48] Nikita Khrushchev would claim that the Missile Crisis had destroyed the Doctrine, but his misplaced statement of political bravura would prove to be incorrect on numerous occasions in many Latin and Central American countries in the decades to come. The US had experienced earlier crises in Latin America – the Mexican and Bolivian revolutions, Guatemala in 1954 amongst others – but none had committed themselves to encouraging revolutions elsewhere. Washington's response to 1959 was to develop a strategy which 'concentrated on preventing future Cubas, on isolating Castro and on strengthening the political, economic and military structures elsewhere in Latin America'.[49]

Domínguez has argued that the escalation of antagonism between Cuba and the United States was as much the product of a calculated and 'brilliant' strategy (or risky and intractable depending on how you view it) on Castro's part as it was a reflection of Washington's cold war warrior stance. Given the distribution of power in the world, Cuba would have to carve out a position within that international order by dealing with both the United States and the Soviet Union. Knowing that the former would resist any revolutionary experiment in the Americas, Castro consciously undertook radical measures in order to engineer US aggression and so ensure Soviet help. Domínguez concludes: 'This independent, self-conscious, shrewdly analytical decision to practice carefully implemented deception is a paramount explanation for the success of Cuba's revolution at home and its realignment abroad.'[50] This analysis is based upon a belief that Castro was both adept enough and had the opportunity to shape events so masterfully. It underestimates the price of failure of such a strategy and does not take into account that Cuban policy making in the 1960s appears to have been far less strategic and far more improvised than Domínguez contends.

The Bahía de Cochinos (the Bay of Pigs)

In March 1960, Deputy Soviet Premier Anastas Mikoyan arrived in Cuba to negotiate a trade agreement; in April, President Eisenhower asked the CIA to begin preparing an invasion force. This decision was made before Cuba had entered into any commitments with the Soviet Union and also before it had proclaimed itself socialist. It can be argued that the US response was much more the product of the desire to reassert hegemonic control than of fear of a yet as unknown ideological challenge. The military operation which President Kennedy would inherit from Eisenhower was predicated on a series of flawed expectations and misguided judgements. Recruiting from the Cuban émigré community in Miami, training of the task force began at Fort Meyers, Florida in May 1960 whilst a command centre, known as Quarters Eye, was set up in Washington. The strategy was fourfold: to create a united 'government in waiting' outside Cuba; to orchestrate a propaganda campaign against the Castro government; to support opposition forces within Cuba (insurgents were operating in the Escambray Mountains to the north of Trinidad whilst other groups were engaged in clandestine and terrorist activity elsewhere on the island) and to create a paramilitary force outside it.

The problems began immediately. The political groups which opposed Castro were organized in the Frente Democrático Revolucionario (FDR, the Democratic Revolutionary Front). Initially led by Tony Varona, this was beset by internal divisions as *priistas* rejected Batista supporters and were themselves attacked for their corruption (the *priistas* were supporters of ex-President Prío Socorrás). The FDR was renamed the Consejo Revolucionario Cubano (CRC, the Cuban Revolutionary Council) in March 1961 as the US brought in more 'left-wing' politicians (such as José Miró Cardona, the first prime minister of the revolutionary government) in order to make it make more respectable although the right wing refused to envisage the membership of those they regarded as too radical such as the Movimiento Revolucionario del Pueblo (MRP, the Revolutionary Movement of the People) whose programme resembled that of the 26 July Movement. The CRC lacked a coherent political platform and was impeded by the fact that the CIA never envisaged it assuming leadership of the operation but intended it solely as legitimizing US involvement.

The Pentagon and the CIA also failed to appreciate that the Escambray rebels and the underground network did not have the strength to launch an insurrection and their intelligence reports communicated a false portrait of massive opposition to Castro. This became apparent at the time of the actual invasion and the popular defensive mobilization it engendered but never appeared to impinge upon official attitudes. Infiltration teams which entered Cuba were efficiently eliminated by the state security service. The propaganda war and the spread of misinformation it engendered waged against the Cuban government was orchestrated by Radio Cuba Libre (operating from an island in the Gulf of Honduras) and various radio stations and newspapers on the US mainland. However the intended psychological softening up of Cuban morale did not happen. A fundamental error made by all agencies involved in planning the Bay of Pigs was that they never seriously engaged with the idea that Castro might be seen as heading a legitimate government by a majority of Cubans.[51] Washington initially wished 'to work through groups in Cuban society hostile to the Castro government, with economic and political sanctions playing only a complementary role'. However the disintegration of those 'insiders' within Cuba compelled it 'to shift the bulk of its energies towards a dual "outsiders" strategy: political confrontation with Cuba on a regional scale and economic confrontation on a world scale'.[52]

Amongst President Kennedy's first policy decisions was to agree to the expedition which would become the Bay of Pigs invasion of 17 April 1961. This was despite the fact that several of his closest advisers (including Dean Rusk and Robert McNamara, the new secretaries of state and defence respectively) doubted its rectitude. Kennedy insisted that US involvement must be concealed and covert; if Castro's Cuba was to be invaded, it must be by Cubans themselves. There were a number of considerations behind this reasoning. One was that outright US aggression would damage its reputation as the defender of democracy and would very likely lead to anti-American sentiment. There was no consensus within the administration as to how Castro should be removed. Whilst the CIA and the Defence Department were enthusiastic about an invasion, the State Department was much cooler because of its concern about negative reactions in both Latin America and the rest of the world. Some officials argued against any involvement in an invasion force. Thus, Undersecretary of State Chester Bowles contended that an invasion would violate the obligation the US had accepted when it signed the Act of Bogotá (which had created the OAS) that no member state had the right to intervene in the affairs of another. Hawkish opinion held that Cuba had removed itself from the rules governing international behaviour by its totalitarian rule. Concern was also expressed about what the CIA would do with the émigré force if an invasion did not go ahead; the Cubans were seen as unstable and potentially difficult to control. However as time progressed, opinion within the Cabinet grew increasingly pro-invasion. It was argued that the world would see pictures of Cuban patriots ridding themselves of a dictator and receiving overwhelming popular support. For the Kennedy brothers, John Fitzgerald and his brother Robert (whom he had appointed attorney general), a successful outcome would attest both to the administration's anti-communist credentials and to the virility of its foreign policy. A defeat would represent much more than a regional setback; it would be a major triumph for the Soviet camp. Thus, above all else, the Bay of Pigs was an ideological act.

The logistics of the invasion were profoundly flawed. The *brigadistas* (the military unit was named Brigade 2506) came ashore at Playa Girón which is surrounded by inhospitable swampland and which gave them no cover when they were strafed by the tiny Cuban air force. The Americans had promised air support but Kennedy lost his nerve and rescinded the order for a second strike which would have eliminated Cuban air capacity. Even if the invaders had successfully established a beachhead, they would have found themselves far away from the bases of the Escambray rebels. As it was, they met with fierce resistance from popular militias commanded by Castro himself and many were killed or taken prisoner. The expected domestic uprisings did not materialize and, indeed, the government's retaliatory measures following the abortive invasion devastated the opposition.[53] Émigré organizations were left in some disarray with the CRC limping on until 1964 when the Representación Cubana de Exilio (RECE, the Cuban Representation in Exile) emerged. One of its leaders was José 'Pepín' Bosch, the general manager of Bacardí, who would play a significant role in émigré life over the next decades. US funding of anti-Castro military adventures diminished as its focus shifted to its involvement in the Vietnam War and émigré activity then shifted to propaganda although paramilitary groups still operated, often with deadly effect.

Following the debacle, criticism was directed at the way the invasion had been planned. A particularly damning report was delivered by the US Inspector General's office which reprimanded the CIA for becoming so obsessed with military detail that it lost sight of the necessity that any uprising must originate within Cuba itself. It had also failed to keep national policy makers 'adequately and realistically informed of the conditions considered essential for success' and its own operational and contingency planning was woefully inadequate. It is indicative of the secretive nature of Cuba policy that although long known about, this report only came into the public domain in 1998.[54] Wayne S. Smith argues that the Joint Chiefs of Staff and the CIA ignored the US embassy in Havana's appraisal of the strength of the domestic opposition and that Kennedy should have cancelled what was a suicidal mission from the start.[55] Participants at a 1998 conference who included veterans from the CIA, the State Department, Brigade 2506 and the Soviet Foreign Ministry concluded that subsequent US administrations had failed to learn from the abject failure of April 1961. Instead they continued in the same 'paternalistic, intrusive [and] imperial attitude that is implicit in it'.[56]

Operation Mongoose

After the failure of the invasion, Kennedy established a Cuba Study Group to review the errors made and plan for the future. The CIA had not lost its enthusiasm for covert activities despite the considerable criticism directed at it after the Bay of Pigs. Operation Mongoose (which was initiated in December 1961) was conceived as an extensive programme of 'black' operations which sought 'to exploit the economic, political and psychological vulnerabilities of the Castro regime'.[57] Mongoose activities included intelligence collection; sabotage attacks on economic targets; support for rebel groups; promotion of the defection of Cuban officials and defamation of Castro's reputation and assassination attempts upon him.[58] In essence, it replicated the imperatives behind the Pigs. Thus both the vigour of internal opposition to Castro and the unity of émigré groups in the United States were overestimated and the fact that, by early 1963, Castro was confident of the military leadership's loyalty was ignored. The US authorities were also having difficulty controlling the maverick émigré network although after attacks on Soviet vessels, the administration was forced to crack down, cutting funding and introducing coast guard patrols. Groups were infiltrated by the CIA and FBI but these agencies failed to bring their lawlessness to any form of legal judgement and, indeed, many agents were complicit with them. The overall picture was of 'mixed signals and inconsistency' as 'the hallmark of the dealings with the émigrés not just by the Kennedy administration but by those that followed'.[59]

Following April 1961, the belligerence of many senior administration personnel with respect to Cuba intensified. McGeorge Bundy, the president's chief national security adviser at the time, later 'argued that Operation Mongoose was a self-administered "psychological salve" on the wounded ego of the Kennedy administration' following the Bay of Pigs.[60] In the immediate aftermath, Robert Kennedy proposed that Washington propagate a rumour that Cuban MiGs had attacked the US base at Guantánamo in order to justify a military reaction to an 'act of war'. He contended that: 'the time has come for a showdown for in a year or two years the situation will be vastly worse. If we don't want Russia to set up missile bases in Cuba, we had better decide now what we are willing to do to stop it.'[61] Others cautioned against escalation. Undersecretary of State Bowles was concerned that the two advisers closest to the president – his brother and Vice President Johnson – had no experience of foreign affairs whilst UN Ambassador Adlai Stevenson feared a nuclear catastrophe and urged the president to concentrate upon diplomacy with the Russians. Washington doves were heartened by rumours circulating about clandestine proposals coming from Cuba. In a memorandum to the president of 22 August 1961, following his meeting with Che at the Punte del Este conference, Assistant Special Counsel Richard N. Goodwin insisted that the Cubans wanted to enter a dialogue with the United States in order to create a 'modus vivendi'; that the Cuban government would not give back expropriated properties but would pay for them in trade; that 'they could agree not to make any political alliance with the East – although this would not affect their natural sympathies'; they would have free elections ['but only after a period of institutionalizing the revolution had been completed'] and they would not attack Guantánamo.[62] One can only speculate whether, had he lived, President Kennedy might have pursued a more enlightened policy towards Cuba. Certainly, a senior US official at the United Nations, William Atwood, was involved in talks with Cuban politicians but his efforts were curtailed following the president's assassination. Despite its ideological bluster, Operation Mongoose was a total failure and was soon eclipsed by the far greater issue of Soviet missiles on Cuba.

The Missile Crisis (la Crisis del Caribe)

> Had there been no ... destructive covert activities, no assassination plots ... and no economic and diplomatic steps to harass, isolate, and destroy the Castro government ... there would not have been a Cuban missile crisis.[63]

The Missile Crisis highlighted the weakness of Cuba when it directly competed with the superpowers. For Norman Mailer, 'the world stood like a playing card on edge' whilst the superpowers played poker with its fate moving towards the 'cold war endgame of "mutually assured destruction" '.[64] This section does not offer a detailed account of what is a well-documented set of circumstances but, rather, offers some comments upon the consequences for Cuba. For Nathan, the early 1960s saw a waiting game as the US watched to see how Cuba would direct its foreign policy. He believes that despite the early nationalizations and the radical position the Revolution was adopting, Washington was still prepared to offer aid. However, Cuba spurned such overtures and opted for the Soviet relationship.[65] He accepts that simultaneously Eisenhower was entertaining the idea of covert operations against Cuba. In reality, Cuba was already feeling the pressure in a number of ways: these included large-scale US military manoeuvres in the Caribbean; intense pressure upon the OAS (so that by spring 1962, 15 states had broken diplomatic relations with Cuba) and constant raids on Cuban installations by émigré groups. Moscow had an ambivalent attitude towards the Castro government and was also unsure as to how Washington would react to a growing friendship with Havana and as a result '... the Soviet courtship of Cuba was slow, hesitant, and surreptitious'.[66] It is apparent that the Cuban government overestimated its importance within the triangular relationship and believed that Moscow would go to war on its behalf should Washington threaten a further invasion. Although top-level Soviet leaders such as Gromyko and Mikoyan feared US retaliation once the missiles were detected, it seems fear of an American invasion was not decisive in forming policy. Indeed, when Guevara and Raúl Castro pressed the Soviet government to make deployment of the missiles public, Khrushchev demurred. Cuba was not key to the stand-off between Washington and Moscow, merely the pretence.

What was at stake in October 1962 was not the future of the Cuban Revolution (except to the Cubans themselves) but the nature of the future balance of power between the two superpowers. The Kremlin was acutely aware of the disparity between American and Soviet missile capability particularly after Washington's deployment of Jupiter missiles on the Turkish–Soviet border, whilst the Kennedy White House was mindful of the need for a political victory over the Eastern bloc after the humiliation of the Bay of Pigs and the stand-off between Soviet and American tanks in Berlin in September 1961. Although both sides attempted to project images of decisiveness, there seems to have been a fair degree of mutual grandstanding. Thus, after Kennedy publicly acknowledged the existence of the 42 missiles on 4 September and when on the 13th of that month, he appeared to put the US on a military countdown, it appeared there was now no opportunity for negotiation. In reality, many top White House advisers were convinced that the nuclear threat was exaggerated but they needed to address the mounting rumours of the build-up in Congress and the media which belied the official view that Moscow would not dare to challenge Washington in such a manner. Whatever the posturing, it is true that the Soviet Union capitulated rapidly once an American naval blockade was announced. It is not certain if all the missiles had arrived and been installed by October 1962 but once their presence was made public, Moscow was keen to show it had no intention of using them and began withdrawal procedures.

Despite a lack of consensus as to whether the world had really been on the brink of nuclear war, there was a definite perception that the Soviet Union had lost the ideological battle and the US had triumphed. Appearances to the contrary, a compromise had thus been reached. Washington confirmed that it would withdraw its missiles from Turkey (a decision which had been made previously but was kept secret in order to avoid any idea of a 'swap') and that it would not invade Cuba.[67] There was also a move to a normalization of US–Soviet relations, one result of which was the 1963 Nuclear Test Ban Treaty. The 1962 Accord was honoured by subsequent US administrations until the 1983 Republican National Convention in Dallas when Jeanne Kirkpatrick complained that Soviet submarines were operating from Cuban ports, giving the impression that Moscow had violated the agreement. This was despite the fact that both countries had agreed that periodic submarine visits were acceptable.

For the purposes of this book, the consequences for Cuba are paramount. Despite very defiant statements at the time, by 1998 Fidel would argue that the Cubans had not wanted the missiles ('I didn't very much like the idea ... because of how it would affect the image of the ... Revolution ...') but had agreed out of respect for their Soviet allies but his anger at the time of withdrawal belies this.[68] His secret speech to the Communist Party's Central Committee in 1968 demonstrated the turbulence of the relationship in October 1962. He remembered that 'we were profoundly incensed ...' as the Cubans heard the announcement on the radio with no prior warning from Moscow. The 'hollowness of Soviet protection' had been revealed and Cuba had to come to terms with the fact that it was just a pawn in the Great Power game.[69] The Cubans had thoroughly misunderstood the relationship between Moscow and Washington and the relationship between Moscow and themselves. The essential pragmatism of Cuba's approach towards dealing with Washington came to the fore again after the Missile Crisis. Although Lyndon Johnson made no effort to begin discussions about trade or curbing émigré terrorist operations against Cuba, in his 26 July speech of 1964 Castro talked about establishing a détente based upon mutual non-intervention and recourse to international law to resolve differences. However, the US demand that Cuba break all ties with the Soviet Union before negotiations began stymied such a process as Cuba was not going to repudiate its ally, no matter how vexatious that relationship might be. The Cuban riposte to LBJ's rebuff (and, simultaneously, a challenge to Moscow) was Fidel's speech at the Tricontinental Conference when he re-emphasized Cuba's commitment to the promotion of revolutionary movements fighting in Venezuela, Guatemala, Colombia and Peru and 'even manoeuvred the ever cautious Soviets into a verbal endorsement of his tactics – however quickly [much to Castro's disgust] they disavowed them in practice'.[70]

The two Cubas

Before concluding this chapter which has dwelt upon the Cuban Revolution's place in the world in the 1960s, I wish to consider one more connection – that between Cuba and Cuban émigrés living in the United States. This latter community took a passionate interest in the development of what it saw as a struggle between good and evil, liberal democracy and communism, and many of its members participated in the numerous covert operations directed at overthrowing the revolutionary regime. Many also regarded the Bay of Pigs and the Missile Crisis as indicative of the US government's betrayal of *la causa* and its disregard for *la patria sangriente* ['the cause' and 'the bloodstained fatherland'].

There had been successive Cuban migrations to the United States in the nineteenth and earlier twentieth centuries. They were undertaken by those pursuing business and educational opportunities, by holiday-makers, artists and intellectuals and by those seeking political exile. The experience of these Cuban travellers, the communities that they formed and their interactions with North American are discussed in the following chapter. Since the Revolution, there have been five major diasporas: the immediate post-1959 departure of regime officials and the privileged; the 'freedom flights' of 1959–62 and 1965–73; the 1980 Mariel boatlift and the *balseros* crisis of 1994. I am concerned here with the early stages of this migration and its political consequences for both Cuba and US policy on Cuba.[71] The most important geographical focus for immigration was southern Florida and principally the city of Miami which had a long-established Cuban community and was also admirably suited for linkages with Latin America. The new arrivals were vehement in their condemnation of the Cuban communist state and fanatical in their hatred of Fidel Castro. Convinced that their return to Cuba was only a matter of time, they were initially disinclined to put down roots and expended their energies in the anti-Castro movement. Hailed by the US right-wing lobby as fighters for democracy, they sought government assistance for their activities.

The Cuban émigré community in the United States was never a politically homogeneous one. Early arrivals included those members of the reactionary political class who would face execution or imprisonment in the new Cuba; those who fled for fear of their wealth being expropriated; those who identified with the anti-Batista opposition and wished to return to the political system enshrined in the 1940 Constitution and those who supported the 26 July Movement but disagreed with what they saw as growing communist influence in the government.[72] Many individuals felt their own political ambitions thwarted by Castro's seizure of power; indeed, a number of leading émigrés had once been Fidel's *compañeros*. The community included people with complex political histories. One such was Eloy Gutiérrez Menoyo. A number of groups participated in the struggle against Batista's regime. One of these, the Directorio Revolucionario Estudiantil (DRE, the 13 March Revolutionary Student Directorate, a faction of the main student organization) had fallen out with Castro on the question of tactics. Its leaders, José Antonio Echeverría and Carlos Gutiérrez Menoyo, attacked the presidential palace with the aim of assassinating Batista in March 1957. Many died in the abortive attack including the two leaders. The Directorio was subsequently revived by Carlos's younger brother Eloy who later formed a guerrilla front in the Escambray Mountains. This front was one of the centres of resistance which the US hoped to utilize during the Bay of Pigs invasion. Menoyo would become one of the main leaders of the counter-revolutionary movement.

All political parties continued operating during 1959 and leaders such as Auténtico ex-President Prío publicly expressed their support for the Revolution, clearly hoping to influence the political process. However, their hopes were dashed by the government's adoption of measures such as the first Agrarian Reform Law in May 1959. Although moderate in character, it was clearly the first step in the transformation of the Cuban economy and produced a furious response from the oligarchy and the US which complained about the level of compensation for its own five large corporations. Emigration grew, encompassing not only ex-Batista officials, politicians, clergy and the professional classes but also dissidents from within the revolutionary camp. As the first conspiracies were uncovered, it was evident that the Revolutionary Government itself was not immune (thus, the first chief of the air force, Pedro Luis Díaz Lanz, was discovered to be a CIA operative in June 1959). More significant was the mutiny of Húber Matos. Born in Manzanillo to a middle-class family, he had rapidly risen in the ranks of the Rebel Army, becoming military commander of Camagüey province in early 1959. A series of disagreements with Fidel ensued, the most serious being Matos's objection to the appointment of Raúl Castro as minister of the armed forces. His rebellion was put down without violence through the intervention of Camilo Cienfuegos and Matos was put on trial in December 1959.[73] It was known that Matos had held talks with dissidents within the government and with US and British officials in Havana. The Matos affair galvanized an acceleration of radical measures by the Cuban government and also stimulated an intensification of counter-revolutionary attempts to subvert it.

The first counter-revolutionary groups were formed in the US and the Dominican Republic. The Legión Anticomunista del Caribe (the Caribbean Anti-Communist Legion) attempted the first armed invasion of Cuba under the patronage of the Dominican dictator, Rafael Trujillo. Although there is no evidence to connect the CIA to this ill-fated project, it is interesting to note that the battle plan and the intended site of disembarkation were the same as those for the Bay of Pigs. These groups represented the first examples of what would soon be a byzantine network of anti-Castro groups, involved in a multitude of conspiratorial and violent activities, organizations with high personnel turnovers, often short existences and frequently embroiled in internal disputes (it is sobering to consider what the opposition might have achieved had it been united). The United States would soon move away from groups identified with Batista, the traditional political parties and the Catholic Church and seek more dynamic allies, but the former remained a reactionary influence within the Cuban-American elite. The Movimiento de Recuperación Revolucionaria (MRR, the Movement of Revolutionary Recovery) was the first and most important of the organizations of the Catholic right wing.[74] Many individuals who began their conspiratorial activities under its aegis graduated to form other militant emigré groups.

Cuban communities in the United States became mirror images of *el Cuba de ayer* ['the Cuba of yesterday'], creating a visual time warp of a Cuba which had never actually existed.[75] Miami, whose central district was known as Little Havana, and its outlying neighbourhoods, Hialeah, Sweetwater, Coral Gables and Miami Beach, were the power-house of anti-Castro militancy. Its Cuban inhabitants aroused strong antagonisms in other residents, be they white, black or immigrants from Central America and later from Haiti. The Cubans were seen as receiving privileged treatment from the federal and municipal govern-ments and were criticized for refusing to assimilate. Massive support was provided them by the government's Cuba Refugee Program which operated an open door policy for Cubans but not for others. New immigration legislation created a fast track towards citizenship for arrivals from Cuba. Thus, the Cuban Adjustment Act of November 1966 allowed Cubans who had lived in the US for more than two years to apply for permanent residency. This proactive approach notwith-standing, many new arrivals spent years waiting to go through the bureaucratic maze of departure from Cuba and processing in the US. This problem would increase with the later waves of migration in the 1980s and 1990s. Buoyed by the Program's financial injections, a dynamic entrepreneurial spirit developed, but the dominant groups in the community attempted to impose political conformity. Those Cubans who espoused more liberal attitudes towards the Castro gov-ernment were themselves regarded as traitors and subjected to harass-ment. It was not until later that a more tolerant approach towards relations with the real Havana would emerge, albeit only amongst some sections of the community.

3
The Politics of National Identity

Introduction

The formation of Cuban national identity has been shaped by influences exerted by external forces and the response of Cubans to these. In the nineteenth century, identity and consciousness of citizenship became inextricably linked with the struggle for independence from Spain. During the post-colonial period, the main determinant in the evolution of Cuban identity was the relationship with the United States. This was a complex interaction based upon political control, economic penetration, military domination and cultural assimilation. After the 1959 Revolution – despite other important relationships that Cuba found itself involved in – the major external presence continued to be the United States. As the foreign policy of the latter has been to deny the right of the Revolution to exist and to attempt to negate Cuba's independence in the international arena, pride in national identity has assumed immense significance for those remaining on the island.

Louis A. Pérez Jr has contended that 'it is almost impossible to understand post-colonial Cuba without appreciating the multiple ways in which North American developments insinuated themselves into Cuban life'. However, he also allows that 'vast numbers of Cubans participated willingly in the very structures by which North American hegemony was exercised and experienced'.[1] In choosing to consider a wide selection of these structures and, thus, eschewing the singular and formal approaches of political economy and institutional analysis in order to appreciate the multiplicity of influences and interactions between Cuba and the US, Pérez joins a growing body of scholarly research which is concerned with the politics of identity. This is a

38

complex and fluid concept but one which can be understood as focusing upon 'the intersection of culture and power, with historical agency, and with the social construction of political life [which] are producing new questions about the nature and outcomes of foreign–local encounters'.[2]

The use of the phrase 'close encounters of empire' has been fruitfully employed in a recent collection of essays on the relationship between Latin America and the United States and the effects these encounters have had upon the construction of national identities. Joseph has defined these 'encounters' as 'the range of networks, exchanges, borrowings, behaviors, discourses, and meanings whereby the external became internalized in Latin America'. He further emphasizes that these networks are not stable structures but have been subject to historical evolution and to mechanisms of 'negotiation, borrowing, and exchange' which are 'fraught with inequality and conflict ... but *also* with interactive, improvisational possibilities'.[3] An approach based upon the politics of political and cultural identities and their interrelationship can be an important tool in understanding the development of the Cuban sense of nationhood (*cubanidad* – Cubanness) and the manner in which this has shaped Cuba's identity. This chapter seeks to examine the constituent elements (historical, political, economic, social and cultural) of *cubanidad*.

Imperial encounters

The relationship with Spain

Cuban history in the nineteenth century was dominated by the desire of many Cubans to liberate their country from Spanish imperial control. This desire was expressed in countless rebellions, both large and small; in civil discontent and alienation; in strikes on sugar plantations and, most importantly, in three wars: 1868–78; 1879–80 (known as *la guerra chiquita* – the little war) and the final struggle of 1895–98 which concluded with formal independence. The United States intervened in the third war, purportedly in defence of Cuban sovereignty and for the promotion of democracy but, in reality, to establish its own hegemony over the island. The first war of independence began with the call to arms known as the *Grito de Yara* on 10 October 1868 from his estate in the eastern jurisdiction of Manzanillo by Carlos Manuel de Céspedes and ended with the Pact of Zanjón signed by the white *criollo* (Cuban-born) rebel leadership and the Spanish commander,

Martínez Campos on 10 January 1878.[4] Cuba's new constitutional status as enshrined in Zanjón was basically of an administered territory which had received some political rights but remained subject to Spanish rule.

Although this was a somewhat muted beginning, it did constitute a transition in Cuban history. The dismantling of colonialism had begun but it was soon apparent that a number of Cubas – white and black; rich and poor; male and female; conservative and radical; collaborating with and opposing imperialism – were emerging. There were continuous revolts between 1880 and 1895. Spanish counter-insurgency tactics included brutal reprisals and the forced repopulation of many Cubans into secure settlements as bulwarks against unrest. Eastern Cuba was devastated by years of war, economic crisis and endemic rural unrest. The Cuban patriot José Martí's Partido Revolucionario Cubano (PRC, the Cuban Revolutionary Party) announced the resumption of struggle in 1895 and, despite several setbacks, by early 1896, the Rebel Army was bearing down on Havana. Ruthless Spanish repression was directed by General Valeriano Weyler. Following the blowing up of the US battleship *Maine* in Havana harbour in February 1898, an US expeditionary force landed and defeated the Spanish forces during a brief war, the landmarks of which were the naval Battle of Manila Bay, the Battle of San Juan Hill (mythologized by President Teddy Roosevelt), the siege of Santiago and its surrender on 16 July. A peace treaty was signed in Paris in December 1898 and the US occupation of Cuba lasted until 1902. Despite its significant contribution to the victory, Cuba was not represented at the Paris Conference as its part in its own liberation was rendered invisible.

For the first two centuries of imperial rule from Madrid, there was relatively little external interference and a semi-autonomous society, controlled by *criollo* commercial farmers, emerged. The brief British occupation of Cuba in 1762 encountered a rural economy based on small tobacco plantations and cattle ranches which employed a relatively small number of slaves. Within a year, Britain had inundated Cuba with slaves to work the new sugar plantations. Henceforth the Cuban economy was shaped by the foreign need for sugar. Sugar mills absorbed workers and land, artisans and peasants were dispossessed and the rural environment was devastated as forests, tobacco fields and orchards were burnt to make way for the cane fields. A 'sugarocracy' with its grandiose palaces and conspicuous consumption took over. Cuban and Puerto Rican slavery flourished in the aftermath of the Haitian revolution (1791–1804). French refugees from Haiti circulated horror stories about the 'black fear' which terrified the *criollo* planter class. Slavery was now regarded as intrinsic to the survival of the white race in Cuba and the Spanish government actively promoted the institution at the same time as its European rivals were dismantling the transatlantic trade.[5] An ailing domestic economy and growing competitiveness from a dynamic United States meant that its colonies were accorded high priority by Spain. The fact that the colonies were Spain's largest export market merged with a belief that the fortunes of its empire were indelibly linked with political developments at home. Colonialism and slavery were central to debates between conservatives, reformers and radicals within Spain as well as stimulating a discourse in Cuba. There pro-Spanish groups called for varying degrees of political and economic autonomy within the framework of a continuing constitutional relationship with Madrid, whilst others favoured annexation to the United States, arguing that it would protect the island, preserve the status quo and prevent slave revolt. Many voices within the US also favoured annexation although the abolitionist North was opposed to the addition of another slave-owning state to the Union. Those Cubans who advocated full independence failed to agree on what form the future state should take and who should be eligible for citizenship.

A distinctive Cuban culture and sense of identity were already in formation before the Wars of Independence. However this Cuban identity was a racialized one. Spain had linked the preservation of social order, implicit in which was a racial hierarchy, with the maintenance of colonial rule and encouraged white migration to the colony. Many rich planters, particularly those living in the western provinces, looked to Spain to defend both their economic livelihood and their perception of their identities as Cubans. Calls for independence were viewed as initiating the breakdown of racial boundaries. Others, intellectuals and politicians alike, called for the end of slavery in order to maintain those boundaries. Thus for José Antonio Saco 'the key to Cuban liberty and the reform of Spanish colonial rule was abolition of the slave trade and "whitening" of the slave population'.[6] He aimed to do this by encouraging miscegenation amongst European immigrants, the Cuban working class and ex-slaves. In their struggle against Spanish control, Cuban nationalists therefore had to confront the relationship between their embryonic nationhood and the issue of race. The insurgents who revolted against Spanish rule in 1868 came from the eastern province of Oriente where slavery was much less integral to the domestic economy. The western elites, whose profit margins depended upon it, responded by mobilizing paramilitary groups to defend the institution. The disparate group of eastern landowners, lawyers, writers, liberal priests and students were in agreement concerning their repudiation of colonial economic exploitation but diverged on their approach towards the abolition of slavery. The war ended in stalemate as the eastern rebels failed to win over their western counterparts to the view that Cuba was both economically and racially viable without the necessity of slavery.

The First War of Independence reflected the disenchantment felt by many Cuban progressives with Spain's failure to deliver on promised political reform. Discontent was exacerbated by the economic crisis which began in 1857 and which was created by the Spanish government's raising of tariffs on foreign goods entering Cuban ports. This was an abortive attempt to contain the growing trade between Cuba and the United States. In the nineteenth century, trading and financial contacts between the latter two increased, facilitated by their geographical proximity. The United States supplied Cuba with industrial and manufactured goods, shaping the economic profile of the island and constructing an Americanization of consumption patterns. The transfer of technology and the export of American engineers, surveyors and mining experts facilitated the introduction of steam power (1819), the railroad (the 1830s) and the telegraph (1851). The Spanish state, beset by domestic political and economic problems, was incapable of performing a similar role: 'Spanish colonialism was straining to accommodate to changes driving the Cuban economy ... Spain could not furnish adequate shipping to handle Cuban foreign trade or provide suitable markets for Cuban exports. Nor could it supply the capital to finance expansion or the technology to modernize production.'[7] It depended upon maintaining Cuba as a colony because it needed colonial revenue to safeguard its existence. However, a substantial part of the Creole bourgeoisie resented the Spanish brake on the development of the island and looked to the United States to link Cuba to world markets. Spain was attempting to keep Cuba in the past whereas the United States represented the epitome of modernity. As Pérez writes: 'Cubans perceived that colonial structures denied them the opportunity to realize their true potential', whilst Kapcia describes the situation as a conflict between 'stagnant colonialism and an assertive "New World" expansionism'.[8]

As the century progressed, the US presence on the island grew: businesses and plantations were purchased and trained personnel installed and operated the mines and a floating population of service industries emerged to administer to American needs. The Cuban middle classes reciprocated by travelling to the US on business and vacation and sending their children to be educated there. The modernization of the sugar industry through the injection of Spanish and increasingly North American capital in the nineteenth century wrought a social trans- formation as the traditional planter class disappeared and growing numbers of sugar workers, smallholders and landless peasants endured processes of marginalization. It has been suggested that the important consequence of these changes was to create 'potentially dissident, and alienated, social groups who shared an identifiable "enemy" and common interests'.[9] The enemy was colonialism and the common interest would be identified by José Martí as the fight for national sovereignty.

Cuban politics and the role of the United States, 1898–1952

> The history of U.S.–Cuban relations between 1898 and 1952 is the history of the creation and maintenance of a collaborator state serving American economic, political and strategic interests.[10]

The possession of Cuba had been an objective of US foreign policy from the start of the nineteenth century. Thomas Jefferson had de- clared that Cuba would be 'ours in the first moment of the first war' whilst in 1825, John Quincy Adams, the sixth president, maintained that 'it was a law of nature that Cuba would one day "gravitate only to the North American union" '.[11] Adams responded to 'Mexico's inde- pendence by formally warning Simón Bolívar ... not to extend his revolutionary movement to Cuba and Puerto Rico ... President Monroe was then acquiring Florida from Spain, and looking south'.[12] In his *Episodes of the Revolutionary War*, Ernesto Guevara argued that Batista's 1952 coup was the last in a series of historical interventions endorsed by the United States going back to Quincy Adams 'who ... announced his country's consistent policy toward Cuba; it was to be like an apple that, torn away from Spain, was destined to fall into the hands of Uncle Sam'.[13]

The conclusion of the Cuban–Spanish–American War in 1898 was seen as the fulfilment of Manifest Destiny. The defence of US national security interests was cited as a justification but this rationalization was overshadowed by imperialistic and racist attitudes. When the Cuban insurgents rebelled against Spain in February 1895, US public opinion, the press and many in government promoted intervention in terms of coming to the aid of the Cuban patriots. The Teller Amendment to the war resolution passed by Congress in April 1898 disclaimed any US aggrandizement towards Cuba and promised to 'leave the government and control of the island to its people'.[14] However, as the war progressed and it became very likely that Spain would not be able to quell the revolt, the Cleveland and then the McKinley administrations began to express doubts concerning Cuban readiness for self-government. Following the Treaty of Paris, the notion that it was the US's moral duty to look after the Cubans, who were at best children and at worst African savages, gained ground. Thus General William Ludlow reported back to Washington in April 1898: 'We are dealing here in Cuba with a relatively uninstructed population, whose sensibilities are easily aroused but who lack judgement, who are wholly unaccustomed to manage their own affairs, and who readily resort to violence when excited or thwarted.'[15] This attitude was exemplified by the Platt Amendment which legalized US neo-colonial control over the island. Platt prevented the Cuban government from entering into treaties with foreign powers and its Clause 3 stated: 'That the government of Cuba consents that the United States may exercise the right to intervene for the preservation of Cuban independence, the maintenance of a government adequate for the protection of life, property, and individual liberty ...'.[16]

US domination of Cuba 'exacerbated the challenges associated with nation and state building by handicapping leadership formation and national institutions, accentuating cleavages, and fostering a mentality of dependence'.[17] There were many political cleavages but the most important was that between those who tolerated or, indeed, welcomed the North American presence and those Cubans who continued to nurture the idea of *Cuba libre*, no matter how indistinct that vision remained. Cuba's acceptance of what amounted to giving Washington a free hand in Cuban affairs was the precondition for US military withdrawal (albeit temporarily). It has been argued that between 1902 and 1933, a 'Plattist' mentality dominated Cuban politics as 'a string of Cuban presidents ... competed for a place in history with a series of American overseers'.[18] With a political agenda thus determined by Washington, Cuban party politics which revolved around three factions, the Partido Republicana de la Habana (the Republican Party of Havana), the Partido Nacional Cubano (the National or Liberal Party) and the conservative Partido Unión Democrática (the Democratic Union Party), was relatively insignificant and entirely unrepresentative. The electoral system excluded almost two-thirds of the adult male population, especially Afro-Cubans and the rural working class, on the basis of property and literacy qualifications.[19] The Platt Amendment was not abrogated until 1934 and only then did Cuba attain formal sovereignty although, in reality, little changed. The proximity of the United States and the weight of its power were felt in all areas of public life.

The United States underwrote the creation of political, economic and social structures on the island, the intention of which was 'to transform Cuba ... into an American neo-colonial protectorate that would permit optimal capital accumulation, but not the emergence of a national state'.[20] The new Cuban state lacked a dynamic bourgeoisie and other institutions such as the Rural Guard (which replaced the demobilized Liberation Army), the Catholic Church and the bureaucracy (both of which remained essentially Spanish institutions) enjoyed scant legitimacy and were incapable of representing the national interest. Washington's policy was realized through direct military intervention (1906, 1909, 1912, 1917–21) and diplomatic and economic pressures as well as encouraging successive Cuban governments to develop a strong coercive capacity in order to prevent nationalist mobilization. The latter proved to be impossible. Under US economic domination, social tensions and cleavages intensified as a privileged and corrupt elite ruled over a Cuba where the displaced and the excluded sectors grew rapidly. There was disillusionment with the failure of successive governments from Estrada Palma's first administration onwards to create legitimate institutions. Ministers and politicians were tarnished by their penchant for graft and political violence and public life was characterized by *amiguismo* (cronyism) and trade in sinecures (known as *la botella*). Corruption may have reached its nadir under the presidency of Alfredo Zayas (1920–24) but even the most respected men such as Ramón Grau San Martín (1944–48) succumbed. In the late 1940s and early 1950s, the aspiring presidential candidate and radio commentator Eduardo Chibás led a one-man campaign against endemic corruption under the slogan 'Verguenza contra dinero' ('Honour against money') but it was a hopeless cause.

The 1933 Revolution and its political aftermath

Political opposition to the incumbent system emerged at the beginning of the 1920s stimulated by the collapse of the sugar industry. There was a recognition by a 'new generation of Cuban youth ... that ... social change had to be more profound that the simple overthrow of ...

dictators'.[21] Intellectuals such as Fernando Ortíz played a significant role in the reformulation of a nationalist project. Assuming the leadership of the Junta Cubana de Renovación Nacional (the Cuban Coalition for National Renewal), he attacked the degradation of public life and called for an affirmation of legitimacy and accountability by political elites. At the same time, the Cuban urban and rural working classes were mobilizing under predominantly communist leadership. The focus of their opposition was the dictatorship of Gerardo Machado (1925–33). On his election, Machado had promised reform and an end to corruption, but his rule was characterized by ruthless authoritarianism and the creation of a patronage system which linked export agricultural interests and domestic manufacturers and sought to incorporate new sectors in order to extend his base of support. Unable to control this populist project as the momentum of the Great Depression began to build, he resorted to force. Traditional political sectors failed to offer an effective opposition and it was left to workers, anarcho-syndicalists, communists and students to fight street battles against Machado's thugs. Washington's attempts to persuade Machado to leave office having failed, the Roosevelt administration abandoned him to his fate in much the same way that American support for Batista disintegrated in 1958.

The workers' and students' insurrection of 1933 coincided with the rebellion of non-commissioned officers led by Sergeant Fulgencio Batista at Havana's Campamento Columbia. The outcome was the establishment of a nationalist government led by Grau San Martín which lasted for 127 days. Its brief existence was marred by the machinations of the US embassy as it branded the government a stooge of the communists and tried to foment anti-Grau conspiracies. A volatile political situation unfolded as the students of the Directorio Estudiantil Universitario (DEU, the University Students' Directive) pressed for authentic revolutionary change, the ABC secret society opposed the Grau government because it had its origins in a military uprising and the Partido Comunista Cubana (PCC, the Cuban Communist Party) branded the president a puppet of the bourgeoisie. Although the 1933 Revolution failed, it was important in that it 'transformed the system of alliances by which the country had been governed, and centered the focus of the struggles around the agrarian issue and workers' rights'.[22] Although the Grau regime did not challenge the capitalist mode of production, it did propose wide-ranging reforms including the progressive nationalization of industry, the recognition of trade unions and the reduction of the influence of foreign capital and, thus, rapidly incurred Washington's hostility. The US welcomed Batista's coup against the Grau government on 18 January 1934.

Over the next six years, Batista was the power behind the thrones of puppet presidents (Hevia, Mendieta, Mariano Gómez, Barnet and Laredo Bru) before securing electoral victory himself in 1940. The political landscape was augmented by the creation of the Partido Revolucionario Cubano – Auténtico (the Cuban Revolutionary Party – Authentic; usually known as the Auténticos) by deposed leaders of the 1933 Revolution who hoped to capitalize on Martí's memory by taking the name of his party. Batista's rule was a contradictory combination of repression and the introduction of progressive reforms which ameliorated social conditions whilst not attacking the structural causes of poverty. Both Batista and the Auténtico administrations of Grau and Carlos Prío Socorrás adopted nationalist rhetoric in order to demobilize the popular sectors and acquire political legitimacy. Batista also entered into alliance with a surprisingly naïve PCC and its labour organization, the Confederación de Trabajadores de Cuba (CTC, the Cuban Workers Confederation). His intention was to co-opt the political and labour leadership of the working class in order to forestall any independent, revolutionary initiatives. That the communists did not have an armed seizure of power on their agenda only aided Batista's project (the political evolution of the PCC is discussed in Chapter 4). The business of government was conducted by patronage, a corrupt spoils system as political appointees enriched themselves by raiding public funds and intensifying violence (*bonchismo*).

Grau San Martín surprised political pundits by winning the 1944 election and defeating Batista's handpicked successor Carlos Saladrigas. His government's programme was handicapped by the initial absence of a Congressional majority and his tendency to attempt to rule by presidential decree. Progress was also stymied by difficult relations with the communists, the various paramilitary groups and the army and by a continuing demonstration of high-level venality. Popular opinion viewed the Grau government's record as an amalgam of criminality, ineffectiveness and moral bankruptcy; this impression was not altered by experience of public life under the next presidency, that of Prió Socorrás. Tension between the two politicians had led to the creation of the Partido del Pueblo Cubano (PPC, the Party of the Cuban People; better known as the Ortodoxos) in 1947. The PPC adopted a vague populist and anti-corruption platform and, once in office, Prío attempted to bring Grau to trial on charges of public embezzlement (that this was not successful was seen by many as evidence of collusion within the political elite). Prío also sought to crack down on *bonchismo* although his security forces targeted the left and the unions rather than more criminal elements. The political morass into which Cuba was sinking was muddied further by the influx of political exiles from Latin and Central America (particularly from Venezuela, Guatemala and Puerto Rico). Their conspiracies became embroiled with domestic political rivalries and undermined Prío's attempts to maintain control as well as provoking the US and other governments. Indeed, the OAS finally instructed Cuba to stop aiding exiles. By the time of Batista's second coup of 10 March 1952, the degeneration of the democratic political process appeared complete, with the vast majority of Cubans alienated from the system and desirous of change.

Economic encounters

Sugar

Sugar has determined the economic destiny of Cuba. Martí described the country as *la azucarera del mundo* ('the world's sugar bowl') and warned that 'a people that enlists its subsistence to one product alone commits suicide'.[23] With the seizure of Cuba and Puerto Rico in 1898 and its occupation of the Dominican Republic, the Philippines and Haiti during a number of prolonged periods in the early twentieth century, the United States became an imperial power and the Spanish Caribbean a sphere for its direct investment. A shift in global hegemony – from old European to new American – had occurred. The Cuban economy became inextricably entangled with the interests of North American capital. Reconstruction after 1898 represented a break with the colonial past as class structures and old modes of economic behaviour and social sensibility disappeared. The *criollo* plantocracy was replaced by a petty bourgeoisie which was dependent upon the United States. The Cuban economy evolved in terms of 'a monoculture dependence on one export product [sugar], lack of internal diversification of the economy, metropolitan absentee ownership, metropolitan control of shipping and economic transformation of the region under US tutelage'.[24] A gold rush of US investment deluged the island as corporations and individual investors acquired about 60 per cent of all rural properties in Cuba between 1899 and 1905; the process was most intense in the eastern provinces. This concentration of landownership resulted in the dispossession of many small farmers. The Afro-Cuban community was greatly affected with thousands moving to seek work in the cities. There was a trend 'toward an increasing racial differentiation in the rates of urbanization' with Afro-Cubans clustering at the bottom of the housing market as they also did in the employment sector.[25] Machado initially advocated economic nationalism, castigating the United States for its penetration of the Cuban economy. However, his own career as politician and businessman thrived precisely because of his close ties with US interests and over time he 'presided over the consolidation of an agro-export Cuban economy based on large inflows of foreign capital' and 'the spread of capitalist social relations of production to the countryside'.[26]

Sugar dependency ensured Cuba's continued vulnerability to the fickleness of prices and terms of trade within the world market. A prolonged structural crisis – *la Danza de los Milones* ('the Dance of the Millions') – in the sugar industry began in 1925 as a consequence of global depression, European and Asian competition and reduced demand in the US marketplace. There were various attempts to adjust tariff policies and to introduce a modicum of protection for Cuban sugar. In 1926, Machado's Verdeja Act set production quotas for individual mills and proscribed any new areas of cultivation and in 1931, the Cuban Sugar Stabilization Institute was founded. It would function as the administrative hub of the industry. However, protectionist measures adopted by the US in 1930 sent sugar prices plummeting and contributed immensely to the political crisis which resulted in the 1933 overthrow of Machado. By the Costigan–Jones Act of 1932, Cuba was assigned a sugar quotient of 28 per cent on the US market.[27] The 1933 Grau government issued a series of decrees aiming to redistribute sugar profits to Cuban small farmers (*colonós*) and encouraged their organization in order to ensure them a corporate voice in their dealings with *hacendados* (landowners). However, Grau's putative reforms were thwarted by US companies.

Dependence on the North American market was confirmed with the signing of the Reciprocity Treaty in 1934 which determined both quotas and prices for sugar exports to the United States. Preferential treatment was accorded sugar and 34 other articles in return for tariff reductions for 400 US-produced items. By 1946, 77.7 per cent of Cuban exports were destined for the United States which itself supplied Cuba with 86.9 per cent of its imports.[28] Thus Cuba was the primary producer of one item for a single market and a captive market for US goods. Although this arguably provided a greater measure of security for the sugar trade, it inhibited industrial diversification. Indeed, most of 'the principal nonsugar Cuban industries that originated in this period were in fact subsidiaries of U.S. corporations or were associated with U.S. capital'.[29] Further attempts to regulate sugar occurred with the introduction of the 1937 Sugar Coordination Law which gave Cuba greater control over production and aimed to protect the interests of the *colonós*. Ameringer argues that it 'virtually created a straitjacket for the sugar industry'.[30] In March 1941, Law No. 21 decreed that, henceforth, the industry would not function as a free enterprise system but would be run by the Cuban president. President Grau did not interfere greatly, content to see foreign ownership reduced and a partial redistribution of profits achieved. In 1946 the sugar differential stipulated that Cuba should reserve a portion of the sugar harvest (termed free sugar) to pay for commodities from countries other than the US. It was hoped that this initiative would stimulate demand as well as consolidating Cuban control.

Although there was a trend towards increasing Cuban ownership (100 out of the 161 sugar mills in operation in 1952 were Cuban-owned), Americans still controlled a sizeable part of the industry including the largest sugar company, Atlántica del Golfo, as well as 90 per cent of telephone and electrical services and dominated the railway and petroleum sectors. US banks held one-quarter of all deposits, whilst one-fifth of the national budget came from taxes paid by North American businesses.[31] These overwhelming statistics do not negate the fact that its investment in Cuba's dominant industry had been in decline for decades. Only one new sugar mill was built after 1926; investors were departing Cuba, leaving behind obsolete plant and an industry resistant to change. Despite this trend, the United States was unwilling to alter the terms of trade with Cuba. When President Truman signed the 1947 Sugar Act (which replaced the 1937 law), the quota remained essentially the same. This reneged on Washington's promise to reward Cuba 'for its excellent production performance' during the Second World War.[32] The Grau government had ignored the drafting process, making no effort to reduce Cuban dependency.[33]

Sugar companies played an important role in national and local politics as well as symbolizing the unequal relationship between Cuba and the United States. The *batey* (the mill town) experienced separate spheres of affluence and deprivation and a physical segregation of life. American expatriates lived in luxury and their Cuban employees in abject poverty, their lives stifled by monopolistic trading practices and company laws. Americans had access to the levers of power whilst Cubans were marginalized. There were few opportunities for career advancement for Cubans *because* of their nationality. Louis A. Pérez Jr maintains that 'this sense of lack of place, of not belonging, created a peculiar angst for Cubans, one of alienation and estrangement in their own land'.[34] US economic control was responsible for rapid Cuban integration into the US marketplace in terms of the introduction of a wide variety of capital and consumer goods which shaped the lifestyle and material expectations of the Cuban elite. It was also, however, responsible for the persistence of poverty and underdevelopment in an increasingly skewed internal market.

Cuban railways

The imperatives of the sugar industry stimulated the construction of a railway network which placed Cuba at the forefront of communications on a par with the United States itself as well as European nations. Cuba was the third country in the world to adopt the modern technological system of steam-powered railroads. However, the railways neither modernized nor developed the Cuban hinterland. Their function was to facilitate the relationship between local producers and their external trading partners and thus aid the accumulation of sugar wealth. Private companies controlled the system and intense speculation centred around its construction. Built by tens of thousands of indentured Chinese workers (many *culíes* subsequently joined the independence struggle), the network was concentrated in the western provinces and Havana whilst the east of the island, aside from Santiago, was neglected. For Zanetti and García 'the railroads mirrored wider developments in society: the monopolistic behavior of capitalists, the exploitative tendency of employers, and the long-suffering exploitation of laborers'.[35]

Industrial diversification and the Cuban state

Following a slow recovery in the 1930s, Cuban manufacturing, transportation and the public sector began to develop more vigorously in the 1940s. The Batista, Grau and Prío governments promoted import substitution and industrial diversification and committed the state to greater intervention in economic activity. However all this was done in a haphazard and fragmented manner under the suffocating weight of sugar and the neo-colonial stranglehold it represented. A National Bank began operating in 1950, its avowed intention being to facilitate Cuba's economic liberation. In truth, it placed the nation's resources at the service of domestic capital and US investors as well as opening up new sources of corruption. Whereas Grau's relationship with Washington had been tense, Prío proved far more favourable to a close understanding although he resisted signing a Treaty of Friendship which would have further extended American control. The Agricultural and Industrial Development Bank of Cuba began work in late 1950 with the objective of providing farmers and small businesses with credit. The economy which had been showing signs of stagnation was buoyed first by the Second World War and then the Korean War. Manufacturing output doubled between 1940 and 1950 and thousands of new jobs were created, although most were concentrated in Havana, where one-fifth of the total population lived by 1953.[36]

However, Cuban governments did not build upon these advances by further modernization of institutions and structures. Perturbed by the deadweight of sugar dependency upon the rest of the Cuban economy, Prió invited the World Bank to make an independent analysis of the economy and to recommend improvements. The Truslow Mission situated the problem in Cuba's vulnerability to shifts in demand for sugar but castigated successive governments for seeking a solution for the problem in increased state regulation of the industry. This had produced rigid management and resistance to technological innovation. It was also highly critical of what it saw as the excessive amount of workers' power: '... the wage and legal advances by the Cuban proletariat were far above what the country could afford and constituted the main obstacles to the mobilization of investment capital'.[37] Thus responsibility for Cuba's predicament lay with the state and the workers; the Mission recognized neither the quota system nor the US as contributing factors. It advised Cuba to open itself freely to foreign capital in order to integrate into the world market. This was the path to growth and modernization.

Despite the structures of exploitation into which it was locked, the economic condition of Cuba before 1959 was far superior to most Latin American countries. It ranked fourth in Latin America in per capita gross national product and first and second in the possession of televisions and radios per person. It 'ranked third in medical doctors and hospital beds per capita, and it had Latin America's lowest infant mortality ...'.[38] However a survey carried out by the Agrupación Católica Universitaria (the Catholic University Group) in 1956 found massive differences between rural and urban inhabitants. Indicators such as the facts that 91 per cent of rural dwellings lacked electricity, 85 per cent running water and half any kind of sanitary provision; that 'less than 2 percent consumed eggs ... and they rarely ate vegetables' and that

> 60 percent of the country's doctors practised in Havana province ... in the capital ... there was one doctor for every 420 inhabitants ...

in the extreme east it fell to one doctor for every 2,550 inhabitants. ... Half the children of school age did not attend school, and of the population above six years, one-third was illiterate and another third had no schooling beyond the third grade ...

reveal the appalling circumstances of the lives of many Cubans.[39]

Tourism

In sharp contrast to the conditions in which millions lived was Cuba's identity as a tourist destination. 'Cuba' had long been exoticized in the American imagination: 'The idea that Cuba existed specifically for the pleasure of North Americans took hold early. ... Havana was gendered as a seductive erotic landscape' where Americans could act out their fantasies.[40] From the early 1920s, government ministers and Cuban and American entrepreneurs combined to promote the tourist industry as an aid in development. This, however, went hand in hand with it as a criminal activity. As the flow of American tourists increased and as the construction of hotels, casinos, exclusive (and racially segregated) country clubs such as the Biltmore Yacht and Country Club which opened in 1928 and plush real estate in Varadero, Marianao and other suburbs accelerated, the Havana authorities undertook massive public works programmes which offered the potential for huge corruption. Thus, the Havana Ports Company 'became a feeding trough for political favorites', its name synonymous with scandal.[41] After 1917 when President Menocal signed a bill legalizing gambling and the Volstead Act which imposed prohibition upon the United States in 1919, organized crime moved into hotel and casino management in Cuba. Legitimate operations were used as laundering facilities for illegal monies coming from the United States.

The tourist boom withstood the 1926 hurricane and the sugar crash but was damaged by the strikes and street battles which accompanied the growing revolt against Machado and fared badly as the Depression overshadowed foreign travel. Under the auspices of Roosevelt's Good Neighbour Policy, Nelson Rockefeller's role as Coordinator of Inter-American Affairs was to encourage economic and cultural exchanges whilst the US Information Service (USIS) organized exhibitions and distributed books with the aim of attracting Cubans to the American world view. With the Cuban government promoting cultural tourism, American visitors started to return from the mid-1930s and after the Second World War, ordinary tourists and Hollywood celebrities mingled with an increasingly visible criminal presence as mobsters such as Charles 'Lucky' Luciano and Meyer Lansky arrived. The Mafia consolidated its control over Havana after the US Senate Crime Commission under Estes Kefauver began investigating organized crime and the mob moved many of its activities to Cuba where it enjoyed close relations with the Batista regime. Tourists continued to arrive in Cuba even after the guerrilla struggle began although their numbers dried up as the rebel successes mounted. After the triumph of the Revolution, the government reluctantly took over the management of the hotels and casinos at the behest of their workers, but the notoriety of the revolutionary state and the US blockade combined to end mass tourism to Cuba until it was revived with the re-entry of the dollar in the 1990s.

Cultural encounters

Despite its invasion of their nation's political and economic sovereignty, to many Cubans the United States represented modernity. One of the main products of this fascination was the material and cultural consumption of brand names, tastes and fashions as Cubans indebted themselves in order to buy into the American way of life. For Louis A. Pérez: 'The infusion of vast quantities of capital goods and technology from the United States also meant that the North American presence provided the structure around which daily life ... organized.'[42] The interface of this cultural invasion with the evolution of ideas about Cuban identity had a number of manifestations and was certainly not a one-way process.

Intellectuals

Intellectuals had traditionally been neutralized by the Cuban state, either co-opted by government sinecures or silenced by imprisonment and exile. Disenchanted with the dire state of party politics, *bonchismo* and corruption in the New Republic, many became obsessed with the pursuit of art for art's sake, creating work that had no social or political content. Martí had attempted to combine political activism with artistic endeavours, but his early death robbed Cuba of the chance of having an intellectual as its first president and the US military government (1898–1902) 'quickly adopted a policy of divide-and-rule intended to ensure that no successor to Martí emerged'.[43] It also took direct charge of Cuban elementary education and appointed an intellectual, Enrique José Varona, to supervise the reform of secondary and higher education (only a small minority of students were involved in the latter). Varona opposed Spanish scholasticism and endorsed US views on education as vocational and scientific. Cuban teachers were sent to the US to be trained and thus imbibed American values which they then transmitted to their pupils.

Intellectuals were divided in their views about the US connection, with some embracing its dynamism and others attacking its imperialistic intentions. An important voice amongst the latter category was that of Emilio Roig de Leuchsenring (1899–1964) whose work on anti-imperialism contributed greatly to the creation of popular nationalism. His *Cuba no debe su independencia a los Estados Unidos* (*Cuba Does Not Owe its Independence to the United States*, published in 1949) was said to have been in Guevara's rucksack when he was fighting in the Sierra Maestra. In the 1920s, political opposition to Machado coalesced with growing student militancy within the context of the university reform movement. The communist activist, Juan Antonio Mella, argued that rather than being armchair revolutionaries, intellectuals must go out on the streets and spearhead national resistance to the corrosive impact of neo-colonial penetration. In so doing, they would be following Martí's example. Following Mella's assassination in 1929, Machado attacked the universities as seedbeds of communism. Very few intellectuals responded to Mella's call. An exception was the poet and lawyer Rubén Martínez Villena; under his leadership (1928–29), the communists took control of the largest labour confederation from the anarchists and strengthened their support amongst the sugar workers.

The brief 1933 revolutionary government led by Grau San Martín – a university professor of physiology – was composed of professionals, intellectuals and students. Its espousal of populist reforms and commitment to abrogating Platt notwithstanding, it demonstrated little political acumen, failed to establish a support base amongst the popular sectors and was easily outmanoeuvred by Batista. The latter embarked upon a programme of educational reform intended to strengthen centralized control (thus military teachers went into the Cuban countryside with the aim of rural pacification) and censorship. The 1940 Constitution announced that 'culture ... constitutes a primordial interest of the state', but many intellectuals felt increasingly estranged from governments which regarded culture as a means of manipulation. After 1959, the Revolution was initially received enthusiastically by intellectuals and artists. The new government invested in cultural institutions and encouraged cultural contacts as well as making some high-profile appointments (for example, the novelist Alejo Carpentier was given a diplomatic posting in Paris but his fellow writer

Guillermo Cabrera Infante refused a similar position in Brussels and soon went into exile). Official tolerance of debate and diversity lessened as the 1960s developed and once again the relationship between Cuban intellectuals and the state became a contentious one.

Musical contacts

After 1959, the revolutionary government adopted *rumba* as a symbol of popular egalitarian art and of *cubanidad*. Before 1959, the heavily percussive music and the dance forms it inspired were historically linked to the experience of Afro-Cubans, both free and enslaved. The public *rumba* event represented an invasion by blacks of public spaces usually denied them and as a means of communicating protest and commentary about the lives they led. In the 1930s and 1940s, many American musicians visited Cuba whilst Cubans 'travelled to New York City where they listened to jazz and then took home the instrumentation and improvisation they had heard. The exchange worked both ways, as Afro-Cuban music influenced rhythm-and-blues artists and jazz musicians. . . .'[44] Thus Americans such as Herbie Mann, George Shearing and Charles Mingus influenced and were influenced by Cubans such as Carlos 'Patato' Valdés, Mongo Santamaría, Israel López, claimed as the creator of the *mambo*, and the trumpeter Mario Bauza who played with Dizzy Gillespie in Cab Calloway's orchestra before starting his own band in 1940. In 1947, Bauza premiered his Afro-Cuban Drum Suite at the Carnegie Hall with Luciano 'Chano' Pozo providing the percussion. The same venue would witness the Buena Vista Social Club's first US concert in 1997, a line-up which included Israel López's nephew, the double bassist Orlando Cachaito López. The bebop craze in the 1940s saw black and white musicians playing together, an artistic rebellion against racism as much as rhythmic innovation.[45]

As with jazz so with popular music. The first radio station opened in Havana in 1920 and RCA Victor began to bring Cuban big bands back to New Jersey to record. The PCC had its own station, Mil Diez, and many *bolero* and *filin* singers and musicians associated themselves with revolutionary politics in the 1930s and afterwards. In 1932, George Gershwin visited Cuba and worked with Ignacio Piñeiro and his Sexteto/Septeto Nacional. Piñeiro's groups did much to popularize Cuban *son* (music based upon vocal and percussive call and response which had its origins in the mountains) abroad in the 1930s. Band leaders Xavier Cugat (who enjoyed a residency at the Waldorf Astoria's Starlight Roof ballroom between 1930 and 1950) and Desi Arnaz introduced *son*, *rumba*, *mambo* and *cha-cha-chá* crazes to the US charts in the 1940s.[46] American audiences did not differentiate between Cuban *rumba* and Brazilian *samba* and rich musical traditions were reduced to novelty songs such as 'El Manisero' ('The Peanut Vendor'). Commercialized versions returned to Cuba via hotels and casinos with tourists demanding to hear what they were familiar with rather than what was authentic. In the 1950s, the *mambo* phenomenon was identified with the Cuban pianist, singer and bandleader Pérez Prado and *'el ciego maravillo'* ('the blind wonder') Arsenio Rodriguez. Many Cuban musicians travelled to the United States but very few attained stardom; fame came far easier for American imitators who adopted Cuban names and musical styles.

Baseball and boxing

Baseball was and remains hugely popular in both Cuba and the United States. African-American teams (who played in black-only leagues at home) began visiting Cuba, where the sport was not racially segregated, in the 1880s whilst white stars like Babe Ruth toured during the American off-season. Cuban teams playing in the states of the Deep South did not receive a similar welcome, finding themselves subject to Jim Crow legislation. Racially mixed Cuban teams were forced to play on the black circuit and 'even those few "white" Cubans who played in the white majors found themselves constructed largely as blacks ... many black Americans identified with all Cubans while many white Americans called all Cubans "nigger" '.[47] In Cuba, baseball was a democratic sport in which classes, races and genders, the young and the old could participate as spectators. It was also an essentially national phenomenon as compared to the colonial spectacle of bullfighting. For Pérez, baseball gave 'expression to Cuban nationality, both as a means to nationhood and as a metaphor for nation'.[48] It is reported that during the height of the war against Batista, commanders of the Rebel Army stopped operations in order to listen to the final of the 1957 World Series between the New York Yankees and the Milwaukee Braves on the radio![49] After 1959, and under the influence of a baseball mad Fidel, Cubans saw baseball as a site where they could compete with – and defeat – the United States. As with baseball players, Cuban boxers such as Kid Chocolate (Eligio Sardinas) and Kid Gavilan (Gerardo Gonzalez) travelled to the US to further their careers. Kid Gavilan, world welterweight champion in 1951, later gave Fidel Castro funds to purchase the *Granma* in Mexico although he left Cuba in 1968 after his farm was confiscated by the state. After 1959 when the revolutionary state prohibited professional boxing, Cuban amateurs would also use their encounters with US opponents as a platform to demonstrate the very different natures of the two societies.

The contested nature of citizenship

The Wars of Independence and the issue of race

Discussion of the evolution of Cuban national identity and how this has defined citizenship must take into account the way that ethnic and gender identities have impinged upon that history. Such an undertaking requires us to return to the nineteenth century. The construction of a discourse which centred upon the incapacity of Cubans for nationhood was used as an ideological justification of US domination after 1898. However, the Wars of Independence had contributed to the creation of a counter-discourse which was predicated upon Cuban sovereignty. The two discourses also had much to say about what citizenship meant, particularly with respect to the issue of ethnicity. The struggle against Spain had produced generations of Cuban patriots, many of whom were killed during the wars and many others forced into exile. The most famous exile, José Martí, argued that Cuba already existed as an idea and that the future Cuban state would only be democratic and egalitarian if it was based on an inclusive citizenship and, moreover, one which was untainted by racial animosity. For Martí, 'the black Cuban does not aspire to freedom ... political justice, and independence as a black man, but as a Cuban'.[50] There should be no races in Cuba, only Cubans. The publication of the Montecristo Manifesto in March 1895 – written by Martí and the black Dominican and Cuban independence hero Máximo Gómez – can be seen as the precursor of Castro's *History Will Absolve Me* trial speech of 1956 in that although both were concerned with the constitutional issue of what Cuban citizenship must entail, they were also concrete calls to action for their particular generations. Interestingly, Castro made no reference to the position of Afro-Cubans in the future state and neither document discussed the role of women in a new society. Martí's rejection of the category of race as a signifier of citizenship contrasted sharply with the racial order existing in the United States. The iconography of a Cuba where race would not produce social differentiation and political exclusion was an explicit repudiation of the belief held by many Spaniards and North Americans that the slave origins of Afro-Cubans justified foreign control over Cuba's destiny.

Slavery was inextricably linked to the growth of the sugar economy. In 1846, 36 per cent of the Cuban population were slaves, half of whom worked on the sugar plantations; slaves and free people of colour outnumbered the white community, many of whom lived in fear of a re-enactment of the Haitian slave revolt. The choice, they believed, was between Cuba remaining Spanish – and, by inference, civilized – or returning to African savagery (implicit in these fears was anxiety about miscegenation).[51] Race relations continued to exert a contested and problematic influence upon the idea of *cubanidad* after the abolition of slavery. Challenging colonial discourse, activists such as Martí's close friend Juan Gualberto Gómez in his journal *La Igualdad*, campaigned for black civil rights. Despite voices of support within the independence movement, many nationalists were perturbed by the idea of an inclusive citizenship which encompassed blacks and whites on equal terms. When whites, blacks and mulattos came together in rebellion in 1868, they were participating as citizens in the struggle for independence and in so doing they were 'defying the racist and colonialist understandings of the times' but that consensus began to break down almost immediately.[52] Céspedes decreed that anyone encouraging slave rebellion would be executed and insurgent leaders waited until April 1869 before proclaiming emancipation in liberated territory.[53]

White fears notwithstanding, thousands of slaves responded by abandoning plantations and beginning a de facto process of emancipation. Conditions varied across the island. Eastern Cuba had far fewer slaves and slavery had 'ceased to be a pivotal social or economic institution and the image of ... rebellion ... appeared to have lost some of its power', whilst in western provinces such as Matanzas, large estates continued to be cultivated and there was little noticeable change in the lives of slaves.[54] Even so fears of black empowerment grew. In July 1869 the rebel legislature decreed that citizens should lend their 'services according to their aptitudes', inferring that the natural abilities of black Cubans placed them in the role of servants rather than masters. The 1870 Moret Law emancipated children born to slaves after September 1868 and all slaves over 60, but permitted slave owners to put in place coercive labour arrangements which condemned freed slaves (*libertos*) to work for eight years in conditions akin to slavery (the *patronato*). Many ex-slaves rejected white expectations that they should acknowledge their subordinate status and established free Afro-Cuban communities (*palenques*), often developing links with other workers.[55] It was clear that what had begun as an anti-colonial revolt had acquired another dimension as Afro-Cubans responded to the rebellion's calls for egalitarianism and liberty. Ada Ferrer has argued that this was the beginning of a discourse 'over what the new Cuban nation should be and over the roles different social groups would play in that nation. This was a war ... over the boundaries of Cuban nationality.'[56]

The Liberation Army of the three rebellions was multiracial and integrated, with black Cubans (*los mambises*) constituting approximately 60 per cent of the whole.[57] Racially anxious white Cubans and Spanish propagandists stressed the blackness of the rebellion and the dangers of licentiousness and depravity. General Antonio Maceo, an insightful political commentator as well as a brilliant strategist, repeatedly complained about the structural racism which existed in the rebel army. He contended that 'the state ... was itself uncivilized because it was mired in the politics of selfishness and racism' and, during a meeting with the Spanish commander Martínez Campos, portrayed himself and the *mambises* as the civilized ones.[58] He thus recognized the existence of a double racism both within and outside the nationalist movement. Maceo was himself frequently accused of wishing to set up a black dictatorship and attempts were made to remove him from his command.[59] Following his death in battle in December 1896 and the imminent defeat of the Spanish, the independence movement's preoccupation shifted from the issue of race to the construction of a new political order.

Afro-Cubans in the New Republic

Black veterans of the Liberation Army assumed they had earned the right to be treated equitably, but the dominant elites, and their US allies, acted to exclude Afro-Cubans from all spheres of power. The political class, led by the Liberal and Conservative parties, offered an 'interpretation of Cuban nationalism that denied or minimized the existence of a "race problem" '.[60] The consequence was continuing and wide-ranging discrimination. While there was no legal segregation on US lines, whites assumed leadership positions and black Cubans experienced discrimination in employment and education as well as being denied access to public spaces. These practices were justified by a crude Social Darwinism which decreed that Afro-Cubans did not succeed because of personal deficiencies such as laziness and stupidity rather than neglect by the state. However, the ideal of racial democracy as part of *cubanidad* was still sufficiently alive so as to prevent the total erasure of Afro-Cubans from public visibility. Politicians had to pay some attention to black Cuban grievances if they were to obtain their votes and this gave the community limited political leverage.[61] Middle-class Afro-Cubans had been lobbying for equal rights and equal protection under the law since the creation of the Directorio Central de las Sociedades de la Raza (the Central Directive of the Societies of Race) in 1887. Some activists endorsed a strategy which stressed both work and patience and saw education as the key to black empowerment. Gualberto Gómez and Martín Morúa Delgado, both members of the Liberal Party, argued against a separate organization for black Cubans.

However, many Afro-Cubans, frustrated by the slow and ineffectual response of the system, turned to political militancy, a trend which culminated in the foundation of the Agrupación (later Partido) Independiente de Color in 1908. The PIC called for full political equality for Afro-Cuban men (women did not figure in its arguments), arguing that the racial blindness propagated by the Cuban state was a myth. Rumours of a black conspiracy to massacre whites spread rapidly as its membership grew. It was outlawed in February 1910 by the Morúa Amendment which banned political parties composed exclusively of individuals from one race. Despite the fact that its leaders were tried and found not guilty of treason in late 1910, repression against the PIC intensified and in May 1912 it launched a nationwide armed protest. Cuban troops (some led by black commanders) massacred 5000 of them as US Marines looked on.[62]

The destruction of the PIC was a significant setback but did not end agitation for the achievement of Martí's egalitarian nation. Afro-Cuban grievances were endorsed in the 1920s by the radical labour movement and the Communist Party. A substantial part of the communist vote in the 1940 election came from the black community, although many others repudiated the connection and espoused a separatist pursuit of black capitalism (the PCC's belief that black empowerment was an intrinsic part of the class struggle is discussed in Chapter 4). Continued black pressure for equal participation in national life invoked rumours of conspiracy against the state, justified the latter's failure to address discrimination and kept 'the momentum for racial repression alive'.[63] In a climate of persecution of their public organizations, 'Afro-Cuban race politics went underground. It flourished in popular religious practices, such as *santería*. ... In the 1920s whites demonized *brujos* [male *santería* priests] ... Afro-Cuban religious practices came to be associated in people's consciousness with racial militancy.'[64] When West Africans arrived in Cuba to provide slave labour for the plantations, they brought their religious and cultural systems with them. Over time, Yoruba mythology fused with other African religions and Catholicism to create a syncretic belief system – *santería* – which revered a dual hierarchy of Yoruba divinities (the *orishas*) and Catholic saints (worship of Christian *santos* served to deceive slave masters).[65] The demonization of *brujería* and the secret all-male societies of *ñañiguismo* (which were accused of witchcraft, rape and bestiality) encouraged a lynching mentality within many sectors of Cuban society which mediated against attempts to improve the circumstances in which the majority of poor Afro-Cubans lived.[66]

By the late 1920s, Afro-Cubans were increasingly divided by class. A small elite of intellectuals and professionals discovered opportunities in public service and created their own social networks. The exclusive Club Atena, founded in 1917, offered a haven for black politicians and businessmen. Despite its elitist pretensions, it nevertheless endorsed communist campaigns against discrimination in education, housing and employment.[67] Afro-Cuban journalists, such as Gustavo Urrutia whose 'Ideales de una raza' ['Ideals of a race'] appeared in the conservative Havana paper, *El Diario de la Marina*, sought to explain the black experience to white Cubans and to convince them of the rectitude of their grievances.[68] The belief in education as the key to progress was undermined by the fact that the public school system was woefully underfunded and of poor quality whilst private education was expensive and segregated. Teaching appointments were also distributed by patronage networks to which black Cubans had little access. In the 1940s, campaigns orchestrated by the National Federation of Black Societies (later renamed the National Federation of Cuban Societies) sought to expand educational opportunities as part of its commitment to lobby for anti-discriminatory legislation. More Afro-Cubans entered secondary and higher education but their numbers were still not proportionate to their share of the population. It was evident that if education was going to be the way forward, it would be a slow and piecemeal process. The Federation had mobilized both workers and intellectuals and even though it worked within strictly legal limits, it was still branded a communist front by both Grau and Prío who sponsored attempts to infiltrate black organizations by pro-government forces. Additionally, despite all its efforts and the improvements in living standards it achieved, the black elite remained peripheral to the sites of power within the Cuban political system. It was, however, immensely privileged compared to the majority of Afro-Cuban citizens.

Poor black Cubans struggled to survive. As foreign penetration of the Cuban economy accelerated, Cuban peasants were dispossessed of their land by large agro-industrial companies. As employment opportunities decreased, they were also compelled to compete with cheap imported labour. When white immigrant labour from Spain had proven inadequate to meet the demand for labour during the sugar boom years, the sugar interests persuaded the government to permit the introduction of *braceros* (contract labour) from Haiti and Jamaica. With the collapse of the sugar market in the 1920s, public opinion turned against these recent arrivals. The Grau government of 1933–34 responded to racial fears by legislating for the repatriation of black *braceros* and implementing harsh immigration regulations. However, many migrants remained in Cuba, competing for jobs with Afro-Cubans. Sometimes used as strike breakers against the latter, there were instances of co-operation between the two groups during labour disputes. The consequence of massive rural to urban migration was that black Cubans found themselves at the bottom of the urban employment ladder and physically segregated in slum housing. The *solares* (large houses divided into small units where black workers congregated) symbolized the marginality experienced by Afro-Cubans (although their existence also confirmed the prejudiced view that blacks got the housing they deserved). There was particular prejudice concerning the employment of Afro-Cuban women who represented a tiny proportion of the labour force. Whilst the retail trade, for example, generated thousands of jobs, black female faces were rarely seen behind department store or shop counters. The Communist Federación Democrática de Mujeres Cubanas (FDMC, the Democratic Federation of Cuban Women) and the CTC campaigned against pervasive discriminatory hiring practices in transport, manufacturing and commerce. Even in sectors where Afro-Cubans represented a sizeable presence (such as the cigar industry) they performed the worst-paid jobs because 'employers applied racialized notions of efficiency and suitability'.[69]

A fascinating insight into the history of black Cubans can be gleaned from interactions between Afro-Cubans and African-Americans before the Revolution. There were many encounters between the two groups before 1959; these contacts were received and interpreted in different ways and highlighted the respective presence of both in their societies. Thus, African-Americans were torn between what W. E. B. Du Bois termed the 'double consciousness' of being both black and citizens of the United States, yearning for inclusion into a white society that mainly despised them. Many protested the latter's imperialist interventions in Cuba and other countries with significant black communities but also took vicarious pleasure in the power of 'their' country. There were many cultural encounters. An important one was the friendship between the poets, Nicolás Guillén (black Cuban) and Langston

Hughes (black American) who held common views concerning blackness and citizenship and who both incorporated the musical cadences of Africa and Cuban *son* into their images of social and revolutionary concerns. Hughes visited Cuba in 1930 and they worked together as journalists during the Spanish Civil War. However whereas Guillén, a member of the Cuban Communist Party, remains a constant figure in revolutionary iconography, Hughes – the poet of Harlem – was dependent upon white patrons throughout his life and has become an obscure figure in death. Marcus Garvey, the prophet of black nationalism, visited Cuba in 1921. Although received enthusiastically, his proposed mass exodus of African-Americans to a Free State of Africa received scant response amongst Afro-Cubans who remained committed to Martí's *Cuba libre*. This disagreement notwithstanding, Afro-Cuban activists appreciated that the random racism they undoubtedly suffered was qualitatively different from the structural racism which existed in the United States and that African-Americans might be justified in their belief in separatism.

Lisa Brock has contended that Afro-Cuban and African-American communities were marginalized by layers of racism and that their cultural expressions 'shared similar African roots and parallel counter hegemonic functions'.[70] The 'counter hegemonic' meaning of Afro-Cuban and African-American cultural forms may be explored in terms of the concept of the 'black public sphere'.[71] Here political activity is seen as a matter of everyday discourse between citizens, whilst a multiplicity of political identities demarcated by gender, class and ethnicity (thus, a plurality of publics) and the corresponding impacts these have upon access to political and economic power are recognized. Additionally recognized is the contradiction between a 'politics' which is *only* about relations between countries and the role of the state and prominent political actors and a 'politics' which is about the poor, the disadvantaged and the exploited. This latter 'politics' does not accept separate public and private spheres, particularly with respect to the gendered and racially configured division of power, and acknowledges the relationship between state and civil society as central to political analysis. The notion of a plurality of publics is particularly interesting in terms of the Cuban and American black experiences in that it points to the need for oppressed communities to express their identity through the creation of alternative public places such as the church, the barber shop, the beauty salon, the baseball pitch, the boxing ring, the *casa de la trova* (music club), the *santería* temple or, indeed, the location of exile. These spheres were both sources of sustenance where Afro-Cubans and African-Americans could feel 'at home' – important and equal – and sources of challenges to the prevailing dominant order. They could not, however, constitute an alternative power and were constantly at the mercy of a hostile environment. Afro-Cubans would have high expectations of a political movement which sought to destroy such an environment which would be the case following the 1959 Revolution.

Cuban women and the struggle for emancipation

Research into the condition of Cuban women is plagued by the scarcity of sources particularly in studies of the pre-revolutionary period when women were hardly mentioned at all. The daily experience of Cuban women depended upon class and ethnic background, with the poor and women of Afro-Cuban origin leading miserable, excluded existences whilst those from the middle and upper classes enjoyed privileged albeit constrained lifestyles. There was also during the latter part of the nineteenth century and into the twentieth century a growing group of professional women and political activists. Of the latter, some sought political office whilst others fought for independence. All women were affected by the stereotyped images of 'womanhood' produced by socialization through the educational system under the watchful eye of the Catholic Church. The Church was especially concerned to prohibit any discussion of women's sexuality. Under the Spanish Empire, there were strong prejudices against miscegenation underpinned by fears that interracial marriage would lead to the degeneration of the white race. Fears of black slaves raping white women abounded and often led to acts of violence against blameless black men. This underbelly of racism continued after Independence and was strengthened by US attitudes. Although women participated in the Wars of Independence and organized revolutionary clubs, they were regarded ambivalently by political leaders. Thus, Martí applauded women's engagement with the nationalist cause and supported their demands for educational and employment rights but continued to view them in an idealized and somewhat condescending manner. The politics of gender was not central to the rhetoric of the struggle for nationhood.

The achievement of independence in 1898 left Cuba a ravaged island. Women suffered particularly with one-third left as widows. Deprived of husbands, homes and livelihoods, Cuban women were compelled to seek work in the labour market in ever-increasing numbers. Women found employment in domestic service, as seamstresses, clerks and typists (the first typewriters were brought to Cuba in the 1880s) and telephone operators (for the US-owned Cuban

Telephone Company) and in the tobacco industry. Women became more educated although at very basic levels, with low literacy in rural areas and amongst black Cubans. Havana offered the best opportunities for women seeking work particularly during the sugar boom of the early twentieth century. Economic advancement and the greater personal freedoms it permitted led many women to join their voices to demands for changes in their political and legal status particularly after the Spanish civil code of 1889 designated women as non-adult incompetents giving men total control over their wives and daughters. A divorce law was introduced in 1918 although few women availed themselves of its possibilities. A hierarchical family order – which saw no moral problem in men having mistresses but believed that keeping women under control preserved the social order – attempted to resist the impulses of social change. Women's groups such as the Club Femenino (the Women's Club), which was founded in Havana in 1917, worked to stimulate educational and cultural activities amongst poorer women. In 1923 it coordinated the first National Women's Congress which called for equal pay for equal work and female suffrage as well as condemning the evils of prostitution, which was increasing dramatically with the boom in tourism, and the double moral standards applied to men and women. It also looked to the state to play an active role in social welfare provision.

Other activists adopted more radical socialist feminist agendas influenced by both the Russian and Mexican revolutions. At the Second Congress in 1925, Ofelia Domínguez Navarro called for legislation to make all children equal, legitimate or not. Conservative women objected to what they perceived as an attack upon the family. More and more young women were receiving university education in the 1920s. Many of these were attracted to the Communist Party whilst others worked through the Lyceum of Havana (formed in 1929) which adopted a politically neutral stance. President Machado promised but did not give women the vote during his 1924 presidential campaign, although he subsequently introduced wide-ranging legislation including female work quotas. As his rule became increasingly authoritarian, women joined the political opposition and later the mobilizations of the 1933 Revolution. In 1934 President Ramón Grau San Martín enfranchised women and his brief government implemented progressive labour reforms for women. In the superficially democratic phase of his rule in the 1940s, Batista's new constitution incorporated previous legislation concerning women as well as new sections guaranteeing the rights of illegitimate children. However, much of this legislation was ignored in practice.

After Batista's coup in 1952, women's demands for reform were eclipsed by the struggle against his dictatorship. Women played a significant part in the revolutionary war but their contribution was not always recognized. Although high-profile women activists such as Vilma Espín (later head of the Women's Federation), Haydée Santamaría (whose brother and fiancé were murdered during the attack on the Moncada barracks and was later the founder of the publishing house, Casa de las Américas) and Celia Sánchez (Fidel Castro's closest personal confidante until her death in 1980) worked in conditions of great danger in the urban underground, women's roles were still seen to be those of cooks and nurses.[72] Women's participation was minimized by their male *compañeros* and in subsequent revolutionary historiography. Undoubtedly a strong current of machismo flowed through the Revolution's veins and this would have resonance for the way in which women would be treated in the new Cuba.

Destierro – the experience of exile

Just as Americans journeyed to Cuba in the pursuit of profit and hedonism, so Cubans had travelled to the United States long before the anti-Castro emigration began in 1959. Many of these travellers went for business, education or pleasure but many others experienced *el norte* as a site of exile (*destierro*). Miami and Tampa and their satellite towns in Florida and the Union City/west New York area of New Jersey (Union City came to be known as Havana on the Hudson) were the main destinations for these diasporas. Density of population in exile gave identity and a sense of structure and resilience to these communities although, to varying degrees, they all underwent processes of assimilation and Americanization. The latter had positive and negative consequences. Cuban nationalist networks operated in a more liberal atmosphere in the United States and were able to publish their newspapers away from Spanish censorship, but exiles were also affected by the racial discourse of their host country. Thus Afro-Cubans were expected to use separate schools, churches, hospitals and leisure spaces. They also encountered racism within the Cuban community. In October 1900, the Martí–Maceo Society of Free Thinkers of Tampa was formed by black exiles after they had been expelled from the previously integrated El Club Nacional Cubano. Black and white Cubans experienced exile differently. Although Martí organized the cigar workers around the idea of a colour-free Cuba, he did not manage to reconcile the races.[73]

In the twentieth century, the communities tended to appropriate the past in order to create signifiers of unity for the present. For María Christina García: 'The community was too politically factionalized to rally around any current symbols, so instead they chose nineteenth century heroes and events to honor, which provoked no controversy and symbolized the idealism and patriotism the community hoped to emulate.'[74] The result was that streets, parks and festivals were named after Martí, Maceo and other heroes and exile life became an extension of the political battles fought out in Cuba. The fact that the communities were divided by class and ethnicity impeded unity of support for the nationalist movement. In Florida, employment was to be found primarily in the cigar trade with manufacturers and businessmen being predominantly white whilst there was a large black presence in the labour force. In the late 1880s, a wave of militant unionism with strong anarchist and socialist attachments swept the émigré communities and bitter strikes further accentuated splits within them. One of Martí's significant contributions to the vision of *cubanidad* was his insistence that respect for workers' rights had to be an integral part of a nationalist project, although he eschewed the idea of class conflict.

Many immigrant workers adopted revolutionary sentiments but there was also a sizeable sector which supported the annexation of Cuba to the United States. Some viewed North American intervention in the final War of Independence in a positive fashion. The most significant representative of this point of view was Tomás Estrada Palma, Martí's substitute as delegate to the PRC and first president of Cuba. Miami was the centre of resistance to the Batista regime, with political parties seeking the patronage of wealthy exiles and establishing their putative governments in exile there. In 1955 Fidel Castro spent five weeks travelling from one patriotic club to another in a fund-raising effort for the 26 July Movement. At one meeting, he appealed to his working-class audience in the following manner: 'You are more than exiles, you are immigrants from hunger ... the exiles are few and some of them are millionaire thieves.'[75] Certainly the racism, anti-unionism and McCarthyism which were features of life in Florida in the 1950s created a threatening environment for poor immigrants, particularly Afro-Cubans. After the Revolution, between January 1959 and October 1962, some 200,000 persons left Cuba and arrived in the United States. The political nature of *destierro* had been irrevocably transformed. I turn now to the ideological debates which underpinned Cuban political history and the route to the Revolution.

4
Generations of Protest

> ... the generation of 1930 blamed that of 1895 for failing to win true independence; and Fidel's generation, that of 1953, blamed the 1930 group for the failure to consolidate reform.[1]

It has been argued that the sense of 'having failed' to resolve national problems and the subsequent transfer of blame between generations produced a fragmented political tradition which offered few guidelines for the future. This led to disillusionment with the ineffectual promises of impotent and venal governments and frustration which often manifested itself in futile political violence. However, there are certain sustained elements of an ongoing national political project which can be detected at each stage of struggle against the status quo. Recognition of such continuity has been an enormous part of revolutionary iconography. The 1953 attacks on the Moncada and Bayamo garrisons echoed Antonio Guiteras's 1931 plan to assault Moncada and his actual attack on the San Luis barracks whilst Castro's 1956 defence speech was overtly influenced by Martí. The Sierra Maestra Manifesto of July 1957, which called on all Cuban patriots to unite behind the Rebel Army, was a conscious allusion to the challenge made by Manuel de Céspedes to the Spanish Empire in 1868. Amongst the constituent parts of an evolving counter-discourse have been the desire for freedom from Spanish and American domination; the trade union, anarchosyndicalist and communist activism of the first half of the twentieth century and calls for empowerment by Afro-Cubans and Cuban women. Underpinning all of these elements was a commitment to egalitarianism, personified by José Martí, as well as a perception that these things would be gained through struggle and personal sacrifice. Viewed in this way, the notion of 'generationalism' (that is, of each new generation

69

continuing the march forward despite setbacks and failures) could be embraced in a positive fashion. The rebels of the 1950s certainly believed that this time the Revolution would not be frustrated.

Rather than decrying the paucity of influences upon the development of Cuban nationalism, it can be argued that Cuban patriots were stimulated by an eclectic and wide-ranging ideological tradition. Cuban nationalists were inspired by other independence struggles such as the American Revolution, the wars of liberation in Latin America in the nineteenth century and the Mexican Revolution. They were also the products of a political and intellectual background which encompassed both Enlightenment values, a commitment to the power of education and a strong masonic tradition, was impressed by both liberalism and socialism and enjoyed European connections. The Cuban middle class was attracted to positivism's commitment to technological development and modernity, whilst anarchism and socialism gained ground amongst specialist trades such as tobacco and printing. Exiled Spanish and Catalan militants established a significant presence both in Cuba and in Florida where the most radical opinion was to be found. It is no wonder that it was there that Martí concentrated his organizational work. The formation of the PRC by Martí, Carlos Baliño and others in New York in 1892 represented 'the synthesis of a vibrant internationalist radicalism and a profoundly moral, socially conscious, nationalism'.[2] Martí's vision of *Cuba libre* was contingent upon his belief that the power of the *Colosio del Norte* (the Colossus of the North) was so overwhelming that any struggle against it had to be internationalist in its dimensions; this understanding would be endorsed by the revolutionary government after 1959.

José Martí

Martí is the seminal figure in the history of Cuba's nationalist struggle; his reputation has been appropriated by successive political generations and his ideas remain central to political discourse. The iconic representation of Martí in post-revolutionary culture – his designation as *el apostolo* (the apostle) – has often overshadowed the substance of his work. As was the case with Marx, his political writings were never collected in one synthesized text and are open to being interpreted by or filtered through diverse perspectives, becoming the 'Martí' that each critic or group wishes him to be. After 1898, his role as a political activist was downplayed and his status as an artist privileged in order to prevent any adverse commentary upon the deficiencies of the New

Republic. His radical memory was kept alive by Cuban workers. Fidel has been accused of creating a 'pro-Castro Martí ... the intellectual author of the narrative of the Cuban Revolution before and after 1959'.[3] In this reading, Martí offers legitimacy to Marxism-Leninism despite the fact that in life he was neither socialist nor anarchist, his politics republican, humanist, progressive but constrained by his time and place.

Born in Havana in 1853, José Martí was arrested at age 16 for mocking a military parade. Prison, exile and a peripatetic life followed. Returning to Cuba in 1878 as part of the amnesty which followed the Treaty of Zanjón, he was deported again as a consequence of his political activities and arrived in New York in 1880. There he embarked upon an intense period of writing, journalism and activism which focused upon the idea of a free Cuba. Much of his time was spent trying to unite the Cuban exile groups as well as advocating solidarity across the Americas.[4] After the departure of Calixto García to lead the *guerra chiquita*, Martí was appointed interim president of the revolutionary council in New York. The Old Guard exiles, most notably Máximo Gómez, were suspicious of a young man who was both a civilian and a poet although Martí enjoyed a warm friendship with Antonio Maceo. Martí's brilliance was that he introduced a socio-economic perspective to what had previously been seen as a purely political struggle. This endeared him to the tobacco workers, to the revolutionary clubs and to Afro-Cubans but made the more traditional leadership uneasy, although Martí developed good relations with the cigar manufacturers who appreciated his advocacy of cooperation between labour and management. Following the formation of the PRC, the organization grew rapidly with 62 affiliates by 1895 as well as support from many anarchists. On the eve of the Third War of Independence, Martí had succeeded in creating a strong political consensus. Appointed as president of the nation in waiting, he travelled to Cuba where he was killed in a skirmish on 19 May 1895. Following his death and US intervention in the war, the unity of the exile community dissolved and it appeared as if Martí's efforts had been fruitless. His successors, Tomás Estrada Palma and Enrique José Varona, editor of the movement's newspaper *Patria*, 'focused exclusively on the political question ... and made few efforts to promote Martí's socio-economic vision'.[5] As the New Republic came into being, its political leaders wished to emphasize national unity and class conciliation and attempted to ignore the issues of class and ethnic differentiation. Many workers and black Cubans were disillusioned by this shift away from

Martí's intentions and came to believe that the new Cuban state neither recognized nor represented them as citizens.

One of the major aspects of Martí's importance is the manner in which he combined being a man of letters with his role as political activist and a fighter on behalf of Cuban independence. He insisted that political freedom had to precede artistic freedom but that both were dependent upon spiritual renewal. It was important that a distinct creative sphere existed which although separate from politics could feed into it. Art was only real and authentic if it invested in the struggles of the people. However, he became pessimistic about the role of intellectuals in the fight for liberty and after 1892 set aside his intellectual pursuits in order to work as a full-time activist for *Cuba libre*. The marriage of Martí's intellectual arguments and his concrete actions would prove to be immensely influential over future generations of Cuban nationalists, not least the 26 July Movement. Martí argued that the process of national independence must always be seen within the context of American liberation and that neither would be attainable until the political and economic hegemony of the United States was challenged. As a long-term resident and observer of 'the monster', it is evident that Martí harboured very mixed feelings about it. Fascinated by its republican political tradition and the lure of its modernity, he was, nevertheless, acutely aware that its very power and dynamism rested upon the continuing subjugation of the nations of Latin and Central America and the Caribbean. Presaging the ideas of the dependency theorists, he argued that the ties of domination must be destroyed if Cuba and other countries were to be free: 'The nation that buys, commands. The nation that sells, serves. ... The first thing a nation does to gain domination over another is to separate it from other nations. ...'[6] Martí's sophisticated analysis led him to appreciate that US foreign policy processes were not monolithic and that Spanish American countries could exploit differences within the Washington establishment in order to advance their own interests.

With respect to Martí's status as the intellectual father of a self-proclaimed Marxist revolution, it is true that he never embraced socialist or Marxist views; similarly he enjoyed close links with anarchists whilst never accepting their political philosophy. His involvement with exiled Cuban workers in the US was profoundly important to him but his writings do not demonstrate a structural analysis of their relationship to the capitalist class. In *Nuestra América* (1891), he proposed an alliance between the enlightened middle class, the peasants and working class against the landowning oligarchy and US imperialism.

This was a policy position which, in the twentieth century, was reflected better in the views of populist and social democratic rather than revolutionary socialist parties. It is clear that his ideas grew more radical as he aged but they also remained utopian in many aspects. Jorge Ibarra situates Martí within a contemporary tradition which included the American agrarian populist Henry George and the dominant social democratic trend within the Second International (whose reformism was the object of the fury of 'maximalist' Marxists such as Lenin). Martí's critique of capitalism was an inherently ethical one which castigated the 'dehumanising power of monopoly capital' and contrasted 'the moral republic' [of 'Our America'] with 'the imperial republic' of the United States.[7] Employing remarkably similar imagery to that later adopted by Guevara when he spoke of the new man and socialism, Martí contended that 'the yardstick of any human civilisation is the kind of men and women it produces'. Che would certainly have agreed with his adage that 'luxury rots the soul' and that the achievement of national independence and of modernity must include the development of a 'new spirit'.[8]

Students, communists and *pistoleros*

In the early years of the New Republic, Martí was recognized as one of the architects of the struggle for independence but little interest was expressed in his political legacy until the 1920s. In that tumultuous decade, a new generation of students, intellectuals and ex-*mambi* veterans embraced his call for a Cuba freed from foreign domination and inspired by social and racial egalitarianism. The Federación Estudiantil Universitarial (FEU, the University Students' Federation) was at the forefront of such agitation. Beginning with a critique of university management and the conservative nature of the academic curriculum, students moved to a broader political platform which condemned corruption and adopted an anti-imperialist position. Subscribing to the belief that an educated elite should address the nation's problems and taking their cue from Martí himself, they also sought an alliance with Cuban workers and peasants. The creation of the Universidad Popular José Martí in August 1923 symbolized this strategy.[9] The Popular University then established the Cuban branch of the Liga Antiimperialista [the Anti-Imperialist League]. The rapid unionization of Cuban workers occurred under the influence of the Confederación Nacional de Obreros Cubana (CNOC, the Cuban National Workers Confederation) which emerged in 1925 with moderate socialists replaced by anarchosyndicalists. Carlos Baliño had organized the First Socialist Workers Party in 1905 and this had affiliated with the Second International. Tiring of the endemic factionalism of the anarchists and influenced by the Russian Revolution, he formed the Agrupación Comunista de Habana (the Havana Communist Group) in 1923 and the PCC itself in 1925. The involvement of Baliño – a member of the generation of *libertadores* and an intimate of Martí – meant that the PCC could be perceived 'not as an "international" movement but rather as an "off-spring" of the revolutionary traditions of Cuba, and of inserting itself into the real social and political processes of the country'. However, Cuban radical and nationalist circles grew to distrust the PCC, contending that it placed Moscow's strategic interests above those of the cause of *Cuba libre*.[10]

The new party was soon joined by the charismatic student leader, Juan Antonio Mella. Mella believed that it was time to liberate Martí from the pantheon of national heroes and restore him as symbol of the struggle against oppression. Originally, Mella adopted a political programme which called for a broad, multi-class anti-imperialist struggle, but he subsequently moved to a Marxist perspective which stressed the importance of building a worker–peasant alliance which would focus upon destroying capitalism and building socialism.[11] He was an inspirational figure within the Latin American left in the mid to late 1920s but his influence in Cuba dwindled after Machado forced him into exile. The PCC adopted a bureaucratic and dogmatic style with its policies closely following the various twists and turns in Moscow's foreign policy. The party finally became a full member of the Third (Communist) International (Comintern) in 1928, Mella having been expelled the year previously.[12] In the early 1930s, influential figures such as Francisco Calderío (under the pseudonym, Blas Roca, he became general secretary in 1934) and Anibal Escalante (purged by Fidel in 1962 and 1968) were rising in the party; it also attracted a number of intellectuals including the poets Ruben Martínez and Nicolás Guillén. Party membership increased under the impact of Machado's dictatorship and the advent of the Great Depression and the PCC eventually wrested control of the CNOC from the anarchists.

Student agitation had dissipated in the later 1920s but protest revived under the aegis of a reconstituted students' organization which was met by accelerating repression (for example, the arrest of its leadership in 1931). The pressure of circumstances precipitated political rifts within the opposition between nationalist and anti-capitalist groups. Many students argued that it was impossible to break completely with the United States but that the relationship could be modified in Cuba's favour under the aegis of a broad multi-class alliance. The anti-capitalist view, taken by the Ala Izquierda Estudiantil (the Student Left Wing which comprised members of the Liga and the Universidad as well as Marxists), was that the working class and, to a lesser extent, the peasants would constitute the revolutionary force. The left wing contended that there could be no accommodation with the United States, only outright repudiation of its neo-colonialism. There was also an increasingly disgruntled middle class which desired economic modernization and state reform; it found political expression in support for activist groups such as the Sociedad Revolucionaria ABC (the ABC Revolutionary Society – the 'ABC' had no meaning). Founded in 1931, this was a secret, resolutely anti-communist terrorist organization with a corporatist strategy which sought to avoid class conflict. Inclined more to the left was Joven Cuba (Young Cuba) which emerged in 1934 under the leadership of Antonio Guiteras. Guiteras, who was assassinated in 1935, elaborated an anti-imperialist philosophy which valued action rather than words. Highly influential in his own time and over subsequent generations, his romantic vision was of a revolutionary elite acting on behalf of the masses. All these groups looked to Martí to legitimize their identities and strategies but their effectiveness was diminished by the intense rivalry and divisiveness which characterized Cuban politics at this time.

The PCC, the labour movement and the fight against racial discrimination

I wish here to return to consideration of working-class politics and the PCC's relations with organized labour and the political establishment. Mella had argued that the communists must champion the rights of Afro-Cuban workers. In 1925, he called for black Cubans to take justice into their own hands, arguing that racial fraternity was not possible without equality. He stated that 'Justice is to be conquered; otherwise slavery is deserved.'[13] Following the fall of Machado, the communist-controlled CNOC was particularly successful in mobilizing immigrant Jamaican and Haitian labourers on the sugar plantations and subsequently the Sindicato Nacional de Obreras de la Industria Azucarera (the National Union of Sugar Industry Workers) was founded in 1932. The CNOC's influence grew as that of other labour confederations waned. Their image had been tarnished by their association with the dictatorship and advocacy of the repatriation of foreign, principally black, workers.

By the early 1930s, both the PCC and the CNOC had committed themselves to placing Afro-Cuban empowerment at the top of their political agenda and promoted the rise of black militants through their own ranks. Thus, by 1934, Blas Roca (a mulatto) was the party's general secretary and the Afro-Cuban Lázaro Peña led the CNOC. In adopting the Comintern policy of national self-determination for the world's black peoples, the PCC argued for the creation of a black independent state in Oriente province (the *faja negra* or black belt). Separatism was not a strategy which appealed to most Afro-Cubans as Marcus Garvey had found in 1921. The communists' espousal of black separatism contradicted their claim to be the political heirs of the colour-blind vision of *cubanidad* associated with Martí and Maceo. It could be argued that by claiming that race had been transcended in the struggle for Cuban independence and that Afro-Cubans who identified with their race were themselves racist, Martí had undermined the very real demands of blacks for equality. As I have shown, the idea that the race question had been resolved with the establishment of the Republic worked against Afro-Cuban efforts to end social, political, economic and cultural discrimination. Clearly the PCC's proactive policies were important in the latter respect but it was apparent that most workers, including Afro-Cubans, favoured a nationalist vision. The party abandoned its separatist strategy in 1935 when, in the spirit of the Popular Front, it called for class unity.

Under Blas Roca's leadership, the party was regarded as one of Comintern's best hopes of revolution in the Americas. It also became strongly identified with Browderism (named after Earl Browder, general secretary of the American Communist Party). Browderism was later castigated as a tendency which promoted class collaboration and the self-destruction of communist parties. In fact, it merely represented Comintern's position at the end of the 1930s, and its advice to the PCC was to construct political alliances with other 'progressive' parties against the forces of the right. Legalized in 1937 as the Unión Revolucionaria Comunista (URC, the Revolutionary Communist Union), the party initially sought alliance with Grau San Martín but this move was forestalled by Chibás's profound anti-communism. The communists then came to the extraordinary view that Batista might be seen as a bulwark against reaction. In May 1938, Batista permitted the publication of the party newspaper *Noticias de Hoy* and in July, the Central Committee decided to pursue an understanding. It also claimed, retrospectively, that it had never belonged to Comintern.

The communists' reputation was severely compromised by the party's relationship with Batista which endured for six years. Regarded as its biggest historical mistake, it estranged other radical elements and undermined its labour support. Initially, the unholy alliance did appear to have borne some fruit when the six communist delegates elected to the constitutional convention of 1940 succeeded in pushing the relationship between citizenship and racial discrimination to the forefront of discussion but their party was tarnished by its electoral support for Batista's presidential candidacy. The weight of coalition politics resulted in the constitutional commitment to racial equality being fudged in a series of compromises. In December 1945, the renamed Partido Socialista Popular (PSP, the Popular Socialist Party) joined the governing coalition under Grau with the slogan 'Economic progress, social security, victory and popular peace' which confirmed its withdrawal from revolutionary politics.[14] It continued to compete with the Auténticos for control over the labour movement, finally losing the CTC to the latter in 1947. The communist presence close to the heart of government (albeit in a relationship of which the contrours were determined by the wily Batista) provoked the opposition of the Cuban bourgeoisie and aroused Washington's ire. After his 1952 coup, Batista outlawed the PSP and initiated a McCarthyite purge of communists and labour leaders. Militants including Lázaro Peña were accused of complicity in the attack on the Moncada barracks and were prosecuted whilst Blas Roca went underground. This was despite the fact that the 26 July Movement distrusted the communists' political integrity (the Batista pact was crucial in this estimation) and relations between the two organizations were fraught.

Revolutionary war in the 1950s

The beginning of the war against Batista was not an auspicious one. The ill-fated attack on the Moncada barracks was not intended to be a direct assault on power but rather an attempt to rally anti-Batista forces and stimulate mass rebellion. In fact, it ended in the imprisonment and then exile of the main leaders. The *Granma* expedition which landed in November 1956 could have ended as disastrously as previous adventures (Fidel had been involved in the abortive 1947 expeditionary force which aimed to liberate the Dominican Republic) and, indeed, almost did. The 26 July Movement had no definite political programme but rather a number of influential forebears such as Guiteras and Chibás. In many ways, it resembled other youthful, radical movements of the 1950s such as the Peruvian Apra Rebelde.[15]

However, there were other factors which contributed to the emergence of a genuine revolutionary struggle after Moncada. One was that Batista's 1952 coup dashed hopes that the Cuban political system could be democratized. He was able to seize power because of his control over the army and because opposition to him was weak and fragmented with rival groups preoccupied with infighting rather than articulating coherent programmes of action. Older politicians were tainted by their complicity in the venality of previous governments whilst many younger activists were mired in the violent but aimless politics of the university campus or street gangs. What Castro and the 26 July Movement realized was that a direct military challenge to the increasingly isolated government had to be mounted but that such a challenge had to receive popular endorsement to make it legitimate. In his famous trial speech, later entitled *History Will Absolve Me*, Fidel asserted that 'the only remedy against force without authority is to oppose it with force'.[16]

The Moncada rebels were very conscious of the weight of Cuban history. In proclaiming themselves 'the Centennial Generation' (in homage to the centenary of Martí's birth), their manifesto – which would have been issued had the Santiago de Cuba operation been successful – identified itself as inheriting his democratic and anti-imperialist vision as well as aiming to complete the programme of the 1933 Revolution. *History* enunciated the need for the structural reform of the Cuban economy, including the nationalization of public utilities and a programme of social welfare, the end of corruption and restoration of the rule of law. Agricultural diversification, industrialization and the extension of trade relations would attack sugar dependency. There was a strong commitment to raising the living standards of ordinary Cubans. Both documents were radical but in no shape or form socialist. Sheldon Liss has suggested that during the time in the *sierra* (the mountains), Castro toned down his political ideas in order to win the support of the Cuban middle classes and assuage foreign opinion. Shortly after coming to power, Fidel admitted that publicly proclaiming its commitment to Marxism would have isolated the 26 July Movement at a time when anti-communist sentiment was strong, when many people were politically confused and the PSP was a peripheral organization. However, he contended that although he did not himself yet belong to the party, he was already a 'passionate communist' during the war.[17] This may have been a justification after the fact but it does seem likely that his political ideas underwent a transformation as the military struggle developed and political circumstances changed. The long-standing debate on when Fidel actually became a Marxist (and whether this conversion was an instrumental one in order to attract Soviet support) seems superfluous to this author. More significant is the socialist content of the programme implemented after 1 January 1959 (well before the Soviet relationship was cemented), a socialism which being intrinsically Cuban in nature would soon exasperate Moscow and which would set Cuba on a collision course with its propertied classes, US corporate interests and Washington itself.

In the post-1959 period, revolutionary histories stressed the heroic nature of the seizure of power and the iconic figure of the guerrillas (*los barbudos* – the bearded ones) in the mountains. The role of urban insurgents was underplayed. The mythic status ascribed the guerrilla helped to legitimize the new government and to cement its relationship with the Cuban people. It thus acted as a foundational myth which was particularly important at times of crisis. The actual relationship between *sierra* and *llano* (mountains and the plain) was more complex. The *llano* represented many different groups and did not have the cohesive unity of the guerrillas and its leaders had strategic disagreements with those in the *sierra*, believing that the war should have been brought west much earlier. As he drew closer to the communists, Fidel admitted that the pre-eminence given the rural struggle 'tended to play down the role of those who fought in the cities, the role of those who fought in the clandestine movement, and the extraordinary heroism of young persons who died fighting under very difficult conditions'.[18] The urban underground which operated in extremely dangerous circumstances (Che called the cities 'the graveyard') and endured a very high death rate was essential to the success of the Revolution in that it prevented Batista from concentrating upon destroying the rebels in the Sierra Maestra. Recent historians have stressed the important role of Frank País and others from the *llano* who made most of the strategic decisions in the first 18 months of the two-year insurrection and who negotiated the 26 July Movement's tense relations with the middle-class opposition which provided much of its financial and logistical support. Such a reading inevitably shifts attention away from the traditional view which sees Castro's political savvy as the key to securing victory. In truth, *sierra* and *llano* were indispensable to each other.

The uprising began in the west, announced by strikes by industrial workers, on plantations and in the universities. When Fidel and the others were released from the Isle of Pines, they began preparations for the 'necessary war' conceived by Martí in 1892. Castro organized the military operation whilst José Antonio Echeverria assumed responsibility for the Directorio Revolucionario Estudiantil (DRE, the Student Revolutionary Directorate). The latter was involved in sabotage, agitation and propaganda activities as well as creating supply networks for the guerrillas. Following the *Granma*'s landing in the east and the guerrillas' campaign in the Sierra Maestra, popular support for them grew and was cemented by the creation of liberated territories where the guerrillas attended to the medical and educational needs of the peasants. This convergence of *sierra* radicalism and popular approbation was central to the success of the revolutionary war. Once the Rebel Army had Batista's troops on the defensive, the intention was that the DRE would initiate armed urban insurrection sparked by a general strike. In 1957, Frank País created the Movimiento Resistencia Civica in order to train workers, peasants, professionals and business people in the use of the strike as a weapon of struggle. The rebel movement was undoubtedly weakened when he was killed in a skirmish in Santiago de Cuba on 30 July 1957. One consequence was the failure of the general strike of April 1958. After this, the MRC virtually disappeared (except in the province of Matanzas where workers formed armed detachments) to be replaced by the *celulas revolucionarias de base* (base revolutionary cells) in all other provinces. The national leadership of the 26 July Movement became increasingly centralized under Castro's leadership before the final victorious entry into Havana in the first days of January 1959.[19]

In August 1958, Fidel had sent Che and Camilo Cienfuegos from the Sierra Maestra towards the central region (effectively cutting the island in two; Che's capture of Santa Clara at the end of December prepared the ground for the final march on the capital). Aside from his military orders, Che was also charged with coordinating with other revolutionary organizations active in Las Villas and the Sierra de Escambray. These included the 26 July Movement and the DRE but also the PSP and the Second National Front of the Escambray. Che's radical position on land reform drew him close to the communists whilst Fidel tended to agree with moderates like Humberto Sorí Morin (later minister of agriculture and subsequently executed for conspiracy) who rejected any collective forms of ownership. Che developed a strong friendship with Carlos Rafael Rodríguez (the PSP leader who had been sent to the *sierra* in February 1958 following the party's belated endorsement of the armed struggle). It might be argued that this early intimacy contrasted sharply with his growing disillusionment with the communists in the later 1960s. However, his ideological sympathies with the PSP did not prevent him criticizing them in terms of tactical mistakes nor in refuting their attempts to take control of the revolutionary process.

Che and Fidel

Ernesto Guevara

> Che Guevara gave himself away ... through his eyes. I remember that clean, morning-fresh look; the look of people who believe ... someone who abandons a revolution which he and a handful of crazy people had already made, to throw himself into beginning another one. He lived not for triumph, but for struggle – the ever necessary struggle for human dignity.[20]

A great deal has been written about Che Guevara and I do not intend to replicate the various admirable biographies which supply the history of his life. Here I wish to make just a few comments about him and his contribution to the Cuban Revolution. The first point is that although Che committed himself to the guerrilla struggle against Batista and was indefatigable in his efforts to help build the foundations of socialism in the 1960s, he was always essentially an outsider who regarded his time in Cuba as temporary. Proud to accept Cuban citizenship (and then to return it once he decided he must finally leave the island), he was also true to his Argentinean roots and to his commitment to helping liberation struggles elsewhere in the Americas. Embarking upon what would be his final journey to Bolivia, he was convinced that this next stage would stimulate a continental revolution, one which would have reverberations elsewhere in the world. In his pursuit of the 'two, three, many Vietnams' that he talked about in his message to the Tricontinental Conference of January 1966, Che was highly aware of the differences between himself and Fidel. He acknowledged this in his final letter to Castro in which he wrote: 'Other nations are calling for the aid of my modest efforts. I can do what you are unable to do because of your responsibility as Cuban leader. ...'[21] Writers critical of Castro have asserted that Che was forced to leave because Fidel regarded him as a rival whilst others have blamed the Cuban government for not coming to Che's aid as his Bolivian insurgency collapsed.[22] It is difficult to judge whether there was a rift between the two men but, on the whole, I find it unlikely although there were clearly disagreements. Thus, Fidel felt Che should not have been so *publicly* critical of the Soviet Union; Castro was capable of being very critical of Soviet policy but usually tended to do it in a more private and circumspect manner.[23] It is now impossible to unravel their relationship with one long dead and the other remaining silent. My reading is that there was intense mutual admiration felt by them which was able to rise above specific issues and arguments. It is apposite, however, to speculate what role Che could have played had he stayed in Cuba particularly as the Soviet friendship deepened and 'given that the whole thrust of policy from 1975 was increasingly contrary to Guevara's ideas, prescriptions and image'.[24]

As with Castro, Che experienced a process of personal radicalization during the revolutionary war and in the years after 1959. He committed himself to a programme of rigorous political education at the same time as occupying his various governmental posts and assuming a high profile in Cuban foreign policy.[25] He was always at pains to take the position which he believed truthful to his world view rather than a more accommodating one. Hence, the growing rift between him and Moscow despite the early warmth and good relations he had enjoyed with top officials. He was not inclined to accept unquestioning allegiance to dogmatic doctrine nor to believe that the Soviet Union was better able to decide what was best for Latin America. He profoundly disagreed with its position on the nature of revolutionary struggle and particularly its objections to guerrilla struggle.[26]

Che's contribution in his writings to the strategy and tactics of the Latin American revolution may be less significant than the influence of his dedication, integrity and humanity upon contemporaries and successive generations fighting for social justice. For Castañeda, Guevara 'will endure as a symbol, not of revolution or guerrilla warfare, but of the extreme difficulty, if not the actual impossibility, of indifference'.[27] The official Cuban view would take issue with this interpretation, citing the intrinsic importance of Che's political philosophy. I am not sure that you can differentiate between the two. Wright makes the point that the ideas encapsulated in *Guerrilla Warfare* did not offer original insights into the nature of the rural insurgency as developed by Mao or Vo Nguyen Giap in China and Vietnam. Indeed, those *focos* (literally centres or points of action) which most closely appeared to follow his precepts were those – the Peruvian insurgency of 1965 and his own in Bolivia – which failed most miserably. After Che's death, the most tenacious insurgent movements of the 1970s such as the Tupamaros in Uruguay and also the Fuerzas Armadas de Liberación Nacional and the Ejército Revolucionario del Pueblo of Argentina focused upon urban struggle and were more influenced by ideas expressed by Carlos Marighela or Abraham Guillén than by those associated with Che, although one can argue that much of what was represented as Che's approach was the bastardized version put forward by Regis Debray.[28] Others, such as the Frente Farabundo Marti de Liberación Nacional of El Salvador and the Colombian Fuerzas Armadas Revolucionarias Colombianas combined both urban and rural strategies in terms of what they felt was appropriate to local conditions. This Che would certainly have approved of.[29]

To recognize the significance of Che as 'the heroic guerrilla' is not to disparage his life. The Cuban government has always been critical of the marketing of Che as global icon and the appropriation of his image by popular culture and much of this disapproval is valid. However, it has not been above such use of the image itself. This was particularly apparent when Guevara's name became so central to political discourse in the darkest moments of crisis in the late 1980s and 1990s. A cynical view would be that the political leadership was using Che to repackage the Revolution and make it attractive again to Cuban people, particularly the young. There may have been an element of this within official thinking but to see that as the whole picture would be to ignore the undeniable fact that many Cubans still feel respect and affection for the Argentinean who came to join them in their struggle and who still represents the best of what the Revolution was about.

Fidel Castro

> We have to say that we made this revolution on our own ... we defended it ourselves, we saved it ourselves, and we will continue to defend and save it as many times as necessary.[30]

There are many images of Fidel: anachronistic caudillo; charismatic leader; someone who was prepared to take risks in order to protect Cuba's interests but was not prepared to be deferential to either the US or the Soviet Union; someone who lacks personal ambition but is fiercely ambitious for Cuba and someone who is constantly involved in dialogues with the Cuban people but is unwilling to relax political control. It is known that Castro has little love of delegation ('His interference in the most minute economic decisions at all levels of government is a major explanation for the disorganization, wild experimentation, and eventual collapse of the Cuban economy in the late 1960s'[31]). It is also true that his personal domination over politics since 1959 has led to charges of paternalism and has certainly inhibited the development of authentic popular power. His demonization by émigrés and US governments has certainly rendered the prospects for negotiation and the normalization of relations less likely. Castro has always been identified as privileging action over ideas (he and Che agreed that it was more important to get on with the revolution rather than wait for the perfect objective conditions, so beloved by orthodox communists, to appear) which has led the ideology of the Revolution to be branded as *Fidelismo* rather than socialism. Although the leaders of the Rebel Army moved ever closer to the communists in the early 1960s, culminating in unification in 1965, he resisted its claims of hegemony: 'Castro stressed that the Communists did not recruit him; rather, he recruited himself. ...'[32] Castro and the Cuban leadership were perfectly at ease using the terminology of Marxism but they were not prepared to submit to any ideological control. Fidel's political style was based upon 'using established Marxist precepts where applicable and feasible and innovating where orthodox Marxist ideas did not suit Cuba's needs'.[33] Over time, he would however identify himself and Cuba increasingly with that very orthodoxy and particularly the central role of the Communist Party.

Manuel Piñeiro contends that Fidel and Che complemented each other in that 'Fidel had the strategic task of uniting all the revolutionary forces and of educating our people about the revolution and its measures. ... Meanwhile ... Che spent more time conceptualizing the strategy and tactics that had led our movement ... to victory.'[34] For Jorge Castañeda, Che lacked Fidel's immense political astuteness; whilst Castro has been able to make flexible decisions as political circumstances have changed, Guevara was unyielding and uncompromising. The fundamental distinction was that Che '... was *not* the commander-in-chief. Real responsibility resided with Fidel ... for whom Che was a sort of left flank or critical conscience.'[35] The inference here is that with Che gone, who would question Fidel's judgement and if he had stayed, would the trajectory of the Revolution have been wholly different? Fidel stressed that unity was essential to revolutionary struggle as divisions aided imperialism. Revolutionaries did not have to be Marxist and should unite on the basis of existing conditions rather than putting off action until perfect circumstances existed. The Second Declaration of Havana of February 1962 called upon all sections of Latin American society except large landowners and those sectors of the bourgeoisie tied to foreign interests (the *comprador* class) to form a united front to fight for national independence and social justice. In March 1965, he called upon Moscow and Peking to end their ideological differences and work to unite the world communist movement. As discussed below, his views became more radical as the Soviet Union responded poorly to Cuba's endorsement of revolutionary struggle in Latin and Central America and then grew more moderate as that revolutionary tide ebbed.

Che, on the other hand, always contended that the national bourgeoisie as a class in Latin America was not capable of sustaining a struggle against imperialism because it was entirely dependent upon it. He emphasized the need for popular support for guerrilla struggle and the paramount role of the workers and peasants in any revolutionary process. National revolutionary struggles would be defeated if they remained isolated from each other because of the repressive capacity of US imperialism. This was the nub of his Message to the Tricontinental. Prefacing his remarks with a quotation from Martí: 'It is the hour of the furnace, and the light is all that can be seen' and ending them with the following sentiment: 'Wherever death may surprise us, let it be welcome if our battle cry has reached even one receptive ear, if another hand reaches out to take up arms, and other men come forward to join in our funeral dirge with the rattling of machine guns and with new cries of battle and victory.'[36] This was clearly not a man who would be willing to accept the Soviet strategy of broad political alliances, electoral activity and reform as espoused by Latin American communist parties.

Cuba and the Latin American revolution

After the Revolution, Manuel Piñeiro was appointed to the Dirección General de Inteligencia (General Office of Intelligence) in the Ministry of the Interior where he directed counter-insurgency work against the Miami émigrés and the CIA itself. He was also responsible for Liberación, the part of the ministry which conducted relations with communist parties, their dissidents and guerrilla movements in Latin and Central America. In its support for revolutionary movements, Liberación operated as a latter-day Comintern, continuing the tradition of fraternal intervention – or interference depending upon your viewpoint – into the internal affairs of left-wing parties which had begun when the Third International established its Latin American Secretariat in 1924. In its dealings with the young communist parties of the Third World, Comintern assumed that the Soviet revolutionary path would provide the template for all future revolutions. This extra-Latin American perspective provided a great political opportunity to reformist movements such as APRA which stressed the *American* nature of the problem and its solution. The domination of Soviet interests prevented parties from developing policies appropriate to national conditions and rigidly defined their parameters of action. It forced the Latin American communist parties to follow the increasingly tortuous twists and turns of Comintern policy (which itself reflected the power struggles waged in the Soviet Union in the 1920s).[37] Thus, the Cuban communists first adopted the so-called 'Third Period' tactic of class against class which maintained that there was no difference between fascist and reformist parties before jettisoning this for the Popular Front strategy of 1935 which was used to justify their dubious flirtations with Grau and Batista.

At the time of the Cuban Revolution, Soviet hegemony over the world communist movement was being challenged by Maoism and Trotskyism and the Latin and Central American communist parties were experiencing splits and schisms as they disputed competing strategies and political loyalties. Cuba would provide more ammunition for these ideological battles as well as inspiring a new generation of revolutionaries, known collectively as the New Left.[38] The Cubans viewed the work of Liberación, both in terms of its inputs into internal party debates and the practical and logistical support it provided insurgent groups, as their moral duty, an obligation which they had inherited from Bolívar, Martí and all the others who had struggled for Latin American independence. As well as Liberación's clandestine networks, support for armed revolution became state policy and the Cuban capital acted as a magnet for political activists and exiles. Cuban leaders also travelled extensively in the Eastern bloc and to Third World states. Perhaps the most famous trip was that made by Castro to New York in order to address the UN General Assembly in September 1960. Charged with extortionate rates by the Sheraton Hotel (whose management feared the fatigue-clad Cubans would bring chaos to its pristine corridors), the Cuban delegation found refuge in the Hotel Theresa in the heart of Harlem. Here, in a public relations coup which must have mortified the White House, Fidel held court to the leaders of the African-American community, most notably Malcolm X, as well as world statesmen such as Khrushchev and Nehru.[39]

Che developed close links with the Nicaraguan militants Carlos Fonseca and Tomás Borge who were highly critical of the gradualist strategy of the communist Partido Socialista Nicaragüense (PSN, the Nicaraguan Socialist Party) and who would soon form the FSLN and, intent on eventually leading a guerrilla insurgency in Argentina, he also promoted the formation of an armed column led by Jorge Ricardo

Masetti.[40] He was also deeply involved in the launching of the Movimiento 13 de Noviembre (the Revolutionary Movement of November 13th) in Guatemala in 1962 by the ex-army officers turned guerrillas, Turcio Lima and Yon Sosa. Disinclined to respect either ideological niceties or Soviet sensibilities, Che's aim was always to seek out those revolutionaries who were committed to the armed road and who appeared most likely to stimulate popular support. This attitude would lead to tension in his relations with the Cuban leadership and provoke animosity in Moscow.

Cuba's early American revolutionary strategy was ultimately damaging to the fortunes of its sister left-wing parties and guerrilla movements in that its very success propagated the belief that all future insurgencies would triumph if they followed the Cuban way. It cannot be denied that there was a certain arrogance in the Cuban attitude which led them to believe that 'they knew more about revolution, guerrilla warfare, international relations, and political alliances than the neophytes on the ground in Guatemala, Colombia, or El Salvador'.[41] However, the Cubans cannot be held responsible for the mistakes made by their imitators. A case in point is the Peruvian insurgency of 1965. The guerrillas of the Movimiento de Izquierda Revolucionaria (MIR, Movement of the Revolutionary Left) and the Ejército de Liberación Nacional (ELN, National Liberation Army) were amongst the first to take the *fidelista* road. For Béjar, Cuba 'had placed the problems of the revolution on the order of the day ... [and] achieved respect for the emerging heresies of the new left'.[42] The ELN's Ayacucho front survived the longest – four months! Despite Guevara's warning that 'every country and every party must seek forms of struggle which their historical experience suggests', the application of his ideas easily descended into militaristic distortions and an underestimation of the importance of political organization and mass support.[43] This was particularly true of the vulgar interpretation made of them by the French journalist, Régis Debray, whose *Revolution in the Revolution* (published in 1967) transformed *foquismo* into a full-blown revolutionary theory, elevating the Cuban experience into a rigid model and misunderstanding the subtleties of Guevara's approach. In his earlier *Castroism: the Long March*, Debray had argued that the *foco* facilitated a mass overthrow of an authoritarian regime, but by the time of writing the later book he had abandoned the centrality of mass struggle. This was in sharp contrast to Che's position in *Guerrilla Warfare* where he clearly states that guerrillas must never forget the political mandate entrusted to them by the people.[44]

Debray contended that even if a *foco* could not precipitate a revolutionary situation on its own, it could provoke a military coup which itself might trigger a popular rebellion (a highly perilous strategy given the repressive capacity of Latin American militaries). The Peruvian insurgencies pre-empted many of Debray's ideas, providing a handbook of how *not* to wage a revolutionary war. The MIR and the ELN publicly announced the armed struggle at a time of popular demobilization and when the reformist Alliance for Progress policies of the government of Fernando Belaúnde Terry seemed to offer much. They took up arms believing that victory was theirs for the taking, that the subjective conditions of organization and consciousness could be either forced or ignored and that mass involvement could be replaced by the armed actions of ill-prepared elites. The sorry experience – leaders killed or imprisoned, peasant communities devastated, political parties repressed – convinced the Peruvian communists (the most significant presence on the left), that armed struggle was futile and led them to endorse a strategy of change from above in the form of the military Revolution of the Armed Forces which took power following the coup of 1968.

This was an age of revolutionary optimism. Salvador Allende, president of the Chilean UP government and proponent of the idea that it was possible to introduce socialism through constitutional means, nevertheless believed that 'the Cuban Revolution is a national revolution, but it is also a revolution of the whole of Latin America. It has shown the way for the liberation of all our peoples.'[45] This was true at one level but also led to guerrillas attempting to replicate that revolution. In many ways, Che was also guilty of viewing 'the Revolution' in uniform, undifferentiated terms. Thus, he criticized those people 'who affirmed that the form and paths of the Cuban Revolution are a unique product and that the historic transition of the peoples in the other countries of America will be different'.[46] The only exceptional features about the Cuban experience which Che was willing to concede were the significance of Fidel's role; the fact that the US was taken by surprise by the Revolution; the fact that the national bourgeoisie had 'up to a certain point' showed itself 'favourable to the revolution' and that the rural population was more class conscious. The overriding determinants of revolution were 'the permanent roots of all social phenomena in America' which were underdevelopment and 'the hunger of the people'.[47]

Whilst the collective roots of oppression and social injustice in Latin America are still easily identifiable, this was too simplistic an analysis to take into account the many different types of struggle taking place in the 1960s, the levels of organization and political maturity of left-wing parties and the repressive capacity of incumbent governments and their military establishments. Over time, and as political and military defeats accumulated, voices on the left were heard questioning the centrality of the Cuban model to revolutionary practice and Havana's continuing interference in the private lives of individual parties. The clash between the Partido Comunista de Venezuela (PCV, the Venezuelan Communist Party) and Douglas Bravo demonstrates the downside of Cuba's *liberación* strategy. The PCV had resisted the coup which installed Acción Democrática (AD, Democratic Action) in government in 1945, but both parties eventually joined together in order to oppose the Pérez Jiménez dictatorship (1948–58). The PCV, adopting a policy of collaboration with what it termed the 'national bourgeoisie', supported Romulo Betancourt's coalition government between 1958 and 1959 but this estranged many of its militants (particularly after he imprisoned the party's leadership). After the PCV launched a disastrous insurrection in 1962, dissidents left the party with Bravo and his colleagues creating the Fuerzas Armadas de Liberación Nacional (FALN, the Armed Forces of National Liberation) with Cuban backing. Cuba supported Bravo in a vitriolic argument with the PCV leaders which drew in other *latino* parties and Moscow.

Despite Fidel's repeated calls for unity on the left, the influence of Guevara's revolutionary internationalism, the intensity of internal divisions within Latin American communist parties and the successive waves of insurgencies inspired by Cuba throughout the 1960s placed heavy strains upon Havana's relationship with Moscow. It was evident that although Cuba had aligned itself with the world communist movement, it determinedly maintained its own views on the nature of revolutionary change. Relations between Havana, Moscow and the orthodox communist parties were extremely complex and in constant flux until the late 1960s. Thus in November 1964 at the Conference of Latin American Communist Parties, held in Havana, it was announced that Cuba would only enter into relations with those parties which acknowledged ongoing guerrilla struggles; furthermore, Cuba promised to promote splits in those parties which still pursued the electoral road. The 1965 US invasion of the Dominican Republic increased Moscow's anxiety about Cuba's strategy and it joined the Latin American communists in calling for an end to armed actions and the pursuit of broad-based alliances with non-Marxist and centrist parties.

At the Tricontinental in 1966, Castro's blistering attack on the PCV provoked a three-way split between the pro-Moscow, pro-Chinese and *fidelista* factions of that party. Tension rose even higher at the OLAS Conference in August 1967 with the Cubans excluding pro-Chinese and Trotskyist parties as well as the Venezuelan and Mexican communists, whilst the Argentine, Brazilian and Ecuadorian parties refused to attend. The OLAS represented the high point of the *fidelista* armed road and the nadir of Cuban relations with other communist parties. The radicalism of Cuba's position was reflected in its Declaration which stated that armed struggle was the fundamental road to national liberation. In his closing speech, Fidel referred to an international 'mafia' of right-wing communist leaderships which sought to undermine Cuba. The fallout from the OLAS was considerable, as new revolutionary communist parties such as César Montes's Fuerzas Armadas Revolucionarios (FAR, the Revolutionary Armed Forces) and Marighela's Acción para Liberación Nacional (ALN, Action for National Liberation) launched armed struggles. However, after the OLAS, the balance of power shifted rightwards in the wake of Che's death, the failure of the rural insurgencies and the military backlash which began with the 1964 coup in Brazil followed by those in Peru, in Chile and Uruguay (1973) and Argentina in 1976. The revolutionary momentum of the New Left had been halted, and Cuba's promotion of revolution was sidelined in order to address reasons of state. I turn now to consider the development of the Revolution's domestic programme during the 1960s.

Revolutionary triumph – the building of *Cuba libre*

During the first decade of the Revolution, Cuba attempted to remove sugar dependency by promoting domestic manufacturing and industrial diversification. By the end of the decade, that dependency was as strong as ever as a result of failed domestic policies and Cuba's relationship with the Soviet bloc. The revolutionary state's economic development policy was underpinned by ethical considerations derived from Martí, for as Fidel observed, 'What would remain of the dignity and honor of every man and woman in this country [without socialism]? ... the first thing Martí talked about was the dignity of human beings.'[48] The commitment to securing a decent life for all Cubans had loomed large in *History* and also reflected the impulses behind Liberation Theology and the *dependencia* (dependency) theorists. The former represented a Catholic humanism which stressed social justice and was motivated by what it termed 'the preferential option for the poor', whilst the latter was influenced by North American Marxism (particularly the ideas of Sweezy, Huberman and Baran), the world systems theory of Theotonio Dos Santos and Samir Amin and Andre Gunder Frank's work on underdevelopment.[49] Dependency was inherently critical of the Soviet model of the construction of socialism in one country which regarded the economy as being distinct from society: 'In essence, it put forth a "socialist" distribution of wealth but did not change the relations of production in accord with the type of equality Marx ...' [Che convinced Fidel] 'that a different, more human-oriented, egalitarian social order should accompany Cuban socialism'.[50] The nature of the Cuban transition to socialism was debated intensely amongst the top leadership, within party and intellectual circles and by foreign academics and commentators. The political and economic trajectories chosen by Cuba were of immense interest to foreign observers because the Revolution had stimulated a discourse concerning Marxist strategy which nurtured the New Left's critique of already existing socialism.

The Great Debate

Many of the early important decisions about the future of the Revolution were taken during the Tarará Group meetings held in early 1959.[51] Here, the Cuban leaders agreed to set up the Rebel Army and a state security apparatus, committed their government to land reform, talked about an alliance with the PSP and reiterated their belief in world revolution. Tarará was the first stage in a Great Debate during which the political elite discussed which economic model the Revolution should adopt. The orthodox position stressed 'market mechanisms, decentralisation, indicative planning, material incentives and a concept of enterprise profitability', whilst the 'radicals' (led by Che but also including Raúl Castro, Osvaldo Dorticos and Antonio Núñez Jiménez) argued that political consciousness must motivate economic development and any retention of capitalist market mechanisms 'would simply exacerbate capitalism's inherent inequalities and perpetuate capitalist thinking'.[52] Cuba's small size and relatively well-developed communications system allowed it to introduce central planning and a budgetary system of finance 'that would allocate resources to enterprises according to social need'.[53] The modernization of the economy would go hand in hand with the emergence of a new type of human relations: 'We will not do an adequate job if we become simply producers of goods ... without becoming ... producers of men.'[54] Moral incentives would gradually replace material ones as human consciousness changed from being motivated by selfish to social interests.

Che was opposed to a decentralized market socialism (as that practised in Yugoslavia under Tito which had received a deal of critical approbation from Western left-wing commentators) because he argued it continued to imbue individuals with self-oriented interests, but his critics maintained that he was propagating economic chaos through his optimism about the possibility of changing human nature.[55] By giving priority to decisions made by individual enterprises, the overall profitability of industry and agriculture would be enhanced and Cuba would enjoy greater economic security in the short term. Che's theory of value, the hegemony of moral incentives, was predicated on a longer time perspective. He accepted that wages should be tied to qualifications and the satisfactory fulfilment of work norms. The aim was to encourage work as one's duty to society, not as what has to be done to earn a wage. In return, citizens would be provided with a very high level of service provision by the state to be paid for by the profits accrued by higher productivity. One fundamental danger here, as Ken Cole has pointed out, is that in a centralized economy, it will be the state which defines what 'the social good' is and which policy priorities are to be set. This could mean that there would be no room for popular participation at the macro-level of the decision-making process; citizens would be the recipients not the progenitors of policy.[56]

Building the new Cuba

After 1959, the new government targeted those grievous social problems which had plagued Cuban society for generations. Its main focus was upon health and education and its target constituency were the mass of the Cuban people who had been long neglected in these areas of provision. The government had other major concerns, principally the imposition of state control over agriculture, industry and business and the safeguarding of political independence. These motivations coalesced around the theme of national sovereignty. The Revolution was guided by a desire to make things happen rather than to concentrate upon institution-building and the formalization of government practice. It was led by a group of passionate women and men who had recently been guerrilla fighters but who were now in the business of government and economic management of which most had no experience. They certainly did not have a comprehensive development strategy, although they attempted to remedy this by initiating a process of wide-ranging policy discussions which, perversely, may have contributed to the incoherence of policy making. The state socialism which emerged in the 1960s was egalitarian and dynamic but disorganized; it has been termed 'the Moncada Barracks approach to getting things done'.[57] Government was conducted with an ad hoc managerial style, a great deal of experimentation and enthusiasm and improvised organization which led to as many problems as policy successes. It has been contended that this resulted in 'commandism and bureaucratic centralism' in both the economic and political spheres which focused upon individual personalities rather than popular control.[58]

As the 1960s progressed, a slow process of political institutionalization began with the creation of a new official party, the Organizaciones Revolucionarias Integradas (ORI, the Integrated Revolutionary Organizations) which was founded by the merger of the 26 July Movement, the PSP and the Directorio Revolucionario. There was considerable tension between the communists and veterans of the guerrilla struggle which came to boiling point in early 1962. The veteran communist Anibal Escalante had been given the task of transforming the ORI into the Partido Unificado de la Revolución Socialista (PURS, the Unified Party of the Socialist Revolution) but was then accused of assigning the communists too much power and attempting to undermine the 26 July at the grass roots. The ORI was suspended and half of its members were expelled. The Partido Comunista Cubano was created in 1965. Great stress was laid upon popular participation which was intense at this time but it was 'largely confined to the implementation of the policies made by Fidel and his lieutenants'.[59] As a result of the historical absence of legitimacy and accountability at the heart of the Cuban state during the Republic, ordinary Cubans had not been used to being involved in politics. When this lack of tradition was combined with the absence of a coherent system of government following the Revolution, it was perhaps understandable that undue attention was placed upon the top leadership and particularly upon Fidel who was already a commanding presence and the symbol of resistance to US aggression. Thomas Wright argues that the management style of the 1960s reflected Fidel's personality. Thus 'his impatience for economic development, especially evident in the failed crash industrialization program, was a dysfunctional approach to economic management' but his 'maximalist approach' was vital in other areas such as the 'speed of agrarian reform, the boldness of the literacy campaign, and the brashness of the nationalization of U. S. investments ...'.[60]

Conciencia comunista

Underpinning all revolutionary initiatives in the 1960s was the belief that Cubans were creating a 'new society through transforming the common man into a revolutionary man'. The Cuban leadership intended to accomplish this by transforming human and social relations under the aegis of *conciencia comunista* (communist consciousness). This new man would be 'devoid of egoism' [and would put] 'service to society above service to self ...'.[61] The creation of *conciencia* would be effected by a combination of revolutionary education and activism, and its aim was to eliminate the politics of difference and inequality between rich and poor, between black, mulatto and white, between male and female, between the rural and urban sectors and between intellectuals, workers and peasants. It was, in sum, the culmination of Martí's political philosophy. In practical terms, *conciencia* would be created through voluntary labour in literacy and basic health campaigns, in the sugar harvests and in building projects and infrastructural development in the cities and villages as well by participation in the newly created mass organizations and neighbourhood committees. With people from different social backgrounds working together for the common good, class, gender and ethnic distinction would break down and a nation of united Cubans would emerge.

Education and health

Education was deemed vital to the growth of the new revolutionary Cuba. It was seen as both a political tool which would forge loyalty to the Revolution and as a social instrument which would facilitate the growth of *conciencia*. Thus, in experiencing the difficulties of rural life, the urban students who volunteered to take part in the 1961 literacy campaign were expected to jettison any feelings of superiority, whilst children who were sent to *las escuelas en el campo* (boarding schools in the countryside) applied themselves both to academic subjects and farming projects. After 1959 there was a massive surge in the building of primary schools and the training of new teachers (which provided a great opportunity for the employment of young women) as well as significant investment in secondary education, polytechnic and vocational schools, and universities. The state-controlled Federación Mujeres Cubanas (FMC, the Cuban Women's Federation) targeted housewives and by 1984 more than 300,000 had completed sixth-grade education whilst former prostitutes were retrained as seamstresses.[62] The accomplishments of the programme were impressive and laid the foundations for regarding Cuba's educational system as a beacon within the Third World and, indeed, one which had much which could be fruitfully emulated by the rich nations. However, the quality of education was often marred by narrow and ideologically constrained curricula, the attribution of stereotypical roles and expectations to boys and girls, and an underlying tendency to avoid contentious issues and fail to develop critical thinking. A health revolution was launched in 1960 with a massive programme of building and training (the latter was essential as nearly half of the island's doctors left Cuba in the first few years after the Revolution). All medical school graduates had to undertake one year's rural practice as a means of repaying the government for their education; some regarded this as an imposition and a motive for emigration. The state's strategy emphasized preventative medicine using the mechanisms of educational campaigns, inoculation programmes and outreach projects such as those aimed at reducing infant and maternal mortality.

Economic performance

The success of the revolutionary government's development strategy depended upon Cuba's ability to create sustained economic growth which would be predicated upon diversification in production and trade and the creation of a broader domestic market for consumer goods. Owing to the extent of US ownership in the Cuban economy, the new government 'was unable to initiate any meaningful reforms without incurring the opposition of the [Cuban] bourgeoisie and U.S. capital, backed by the U. S. government'.[63] It attempted to break the stranglehold by taking ever more radical measures which, inevitably, increasingly angered Washington which responded with escalating aggression. The radical programme of nationalization saw the state take control of most of the industrial sector and about 40 per cent of the best arable land, as well as banks, railroads, telecommunications, utilities, airlines, ports, major retail outlets, hotels and export/import businesses. The seminal transformation was that of agrarian reform because it affected those sectors of the population most excluded and neglected under previous regimes. Previous patterns of ownership had been predominantly based on large sugar plantations and cattle ranches. Brundenius notes that of the 2.5 million hectares of land owned by the sugar *centrales* in 1959, only 1.3 million were actually cultivated. The rest were left in reserve or used for cattle. Twenty-two *latifundistas* owned 70 per cent of the sugar land and 20 per cent of the total acreage of farmland.[64]

The Agrarian Reform laws of May 1959 and October 1963 placed agriculture at 'the centre of the political stage' and gave a major strategic role to the newly founded Instituto Nacional de Reforma Agraria (INRA, the National Institute of Agrarian Reform).[65] The *latifundios* were converted into large-scale state farms. There was little pressure for redistribution into smaller properties; landless rural workers sought higher wages and better living conditions rather than more radical organizational forms such as cooperatives. Smaller plots of land were distributed to those peasants, sharecroppers and squatters who had worked them before 1959. This process was overseen by the Asociación Nacional de Agricultores Pequeños (ANAP, the National Association of Small Farmers) which was set up in January 1961. The government would later buy out many of these smallholders and tried to persuade the rest that they should form producer cooperatives. There were strict controls over the latter, with peasants forbidden to sell their land except to the state; they were also compelled to sell a fixed quota of agricultural produce to it at fixed prices. The state was determined to maintain central control over land in order to safeguard the food supply and to prevent income differentials which diverse forms of management would undoubtedly have created. The initial process of conversion into state farms was slow owing to the lack of skilled personnel and resources, but the pace was accelerated in the light of food shortages and the opposition of some farmers particularly in the Escambray mountains.[66]

Cuba enjoyed relative economic buoyancy between 1959 and 1961 which facilitated the state's redistributive policies and supported an increase in domestic consumption. This masked the disorganized management which characterized the new economy as political leaders made decisions without consulting the Junta Central de Planificación (JUCEPLAN, the Central Planning Council) which was established in early 1960. A decline in sugar production and, thus, of export revenues in 1963 as well as growing evidence of low productivity and idle capacity produced a serious crisis which threatened the government's health and education budgets, necessitated food rationing (which affected the middle and working classes in the towns far more severely than the rural population) and, more fundamentally, suggested that there were inherent obstacles which would inhibit the accumulation of capital needed for industrial take-off.

This was the context in which the Great Debate over moral and material incentives and centralization versus decentralization was joined. The state first adopted Guevara's preferred strategy: a centralized economy in which non-monetary and moral initiatives played the primary role. This was a system based upon a narrow range of wage levels, free health and education, the rationing of basic goods at subsidized prices, the distribution of basic goods such as electrical appliances on the basis of collective decisions made by workers' assemblies and the promotion of *conciencia comunista* through voluntary work brigades and 'socialist emulation'. Revolutionary zeal was at its most intense in May 1966 when Fidel announced that Cuba would undertake the parallel building of socialism and communism. For orthodox communists, this replicated the Trotskyist heresy of permanent revolution but Fidel demurred, arguing that 'aspects of communism could be constructed in Cuba without an advanced standard of living because social relations are more significant than wealth'.[67] The ideological push of the mid to late 1960s involved many elements including taking private plots away from state farm workers; encouraging private farmers to join the state sector and form Mutual Aid Brigades (collective harvesting, credit and service cooperatives); the nationalization of all remaining small businesses in 1968; wage increases for the poorest paid workers in an effort to equalize wages and the guarantee of full employment. The government prohibited strikes and outlawed independent trade union organization. It also conducted an anti-bureaucracy campaign which saw the abolition of the Ministry of Finance in late 1965, a reduction in the powers of JUCEPLAN and the National Bank and the appointment of political cadres to technical posts.

It was becoming apparent, however, that these ideologically driven measures were at odds with the economic needs of the country and that it was not yet practicable to curtail the role of the market and money in favour of moral incentives. As the levels of absenteeism and low productivity appeared to indicate, Che's example had 'failed to stimulate a sufficient number of people to work primarily to develop society'.[68] The radical strategy had also deepened dependency upon sugar. The Cuban government had, in effect, abandoned its attempt to introduce industrial and agricultural diversification and reverted to the promotion of outward-oriented economic growth based upon sugar. Small farmers resisted the imposition of a state monopoly over rural production in order to free their labour for sugar and there were bloody clashes between the Cuban army and farmers in Matanzas. The culmination of this ideological push – what Ken Cole has termed the period of 'socialist evangelism' – was to be the 10 million tonne sugar harvest of 1970.[69] Its failure led to a reformulation of national economic policy. At the end of the 1960s, Cuban revolutionary optimism had experienced both domestic and international setbacks. The death of Che and the failure of the 1970 harvest appeared to presage a transition to a new and unknown era. Many observers, who had hoped that the Cuban Revolution could create a new type of state socialism which would repudiate the Soviet experience, began to have doubts. For Jorge Castañeda, Cuba in the 1960s had been 'freer, more democratic, disorderly, tropical, and spontaneous, as well as being intellectually more diverse and politically more liberal. With time, the resemblance between the models would grow, and Cuba would come to look more like the Soviet Union.'[70]

5
The Revolution Matures

The Revolutionary Offensive of the 1960s came to an abrupt close with the failure of the 1970 sugar harvest. Fidel acknowledged responsibility and offered to resign. This was, of course, refused.[1] As the heroic period of the Revolution ended, the Cuban political system and Cuban society became more institutionalized and, in many ways, more resistant to innovation and debate. In adopting a state socialist model in the 1960s, the Cubans were able to make great advances in the war against poverty and in the promotion of egalitarianism, but these successes were tempered by an inability to ensure a move away from dependency and to avoid the centralization of decision-making.

Social and economic policy

After 1959, the Cuban Revolution committed itself to what would be an enduring obligation to provide mass education and to expand cultural opportunities, to create an inclusive health service, to offer full employment and to shift resources and production to the previously neglected rural sector. The latter policy would contribute to the deterioration of the urban environment, particularly in Havana. Before 1959, the capital had been highly privileged with 75 per cent of national industry (excluding sugar) and 90 per cent of foreign trade.[2] In the cities, the government forced the sale of urban land, prohibited land speculation and abolished mortgages and loans. Unfortunately, housing programmes failed to keep pace with demand or to maintain existing housing stock and infrastructure. The result was physical decline and, over time, rampant illegal building and the creation of slums particularly in Havana. There was a continuing expansion of medical provision with low-cost health campaigns and the establishment of a system of polyclinics which stretched to the most remote points of the island. In the 1980s, a campaign for a doctor 'on every block' was directed at both urban and rural areas.

Health and education continued to be regarded as basic human rights and as the underpinning of socialist democracy but the cost of their provision imposed a huge burden. The Cuban government adopted a command economy strategy as it attempted to control the surplus that emanated from industrial and agricultural production in order to pay for the welfare state. The negative consequences were that production became highly inefficient, top-heavy in management terms, bureaucratic and overmanned. The poor quality of manufactured goods became a constant feature of Cuban life. Nevertheless, Cardoso and Helwege argue that Cuba still managed to avoid the structural poverty endemic in other Latin American and Third World states and 'succeeded in achieving substantial economic growth with distributional equity'.[3] However, this growth was constrained by the dependent relationship shaped by Cuba's links with the Eastern bloc. The demise of the latter at the end of the 1980s would cast the Cuban economy adrift and challenge its ability to maintain the high levels of service provision the Cuban population had come to expect. There were serious consequences including economic restructuring and the emergence of a changed social–political climate which I consider later in the chapter.

There was a vigorous economic recuperation following the disappointment of 1970. It was aided by better organization and allocation of capital, the postponement of Cuba's debt to the Soviet Union and the promise of new Soviet credit which underpinned accelerated industrialization. Cuba also received more investment in the form of joint ventures with Western European and US businesses.[4] Temporarily high sugar prices led to more imports from European and Japanese trading partners but these relationships developed slowly and were hampered by political disputes. Thus France traded in computing equipment and petrochemicals although resisting Cuban pressure for longer-term credits; Franco-Cuban trade fell sharply in the late 1970s when the French government responded to Cuba's suspected support for the terrorist Carlos by expelling Cubans from France. The United Kingdom sold fertilizers, machine spare parts and harbour dredgers as well as negotiating the Anglo-Cuban Economic and Industrial Cooperation Agreement in 1975. British companies judged Cuba to be highly efficient in its business dealings. There was a sharp deterioration in trade with both countries as a result of Cuba's activities in Africa.

Ideological differences did not, however, prevent the consolidation of trade with Spain both before and after Franco's death. Much to Washington's displeasure, European governments were cautiously defying the blockade and they clearly resented the US ban on the re-export of US manufactured goods to Cuba.[5] When sugar prices remained high and Cuba enjoyed growing trade and hard currency, the impact of the blockade upon Cuban economic performance was tempered. The US business sector increasingly resented the opportunities given their European and Japanese competitors and began to argue that the blockade was detrimental to American interests. The consequence was that the US was inclined to greater flexibility in its application of the legislation. Thus Gerald Ford withdrew the prohibition on foreign subsidiaries of US companies exporting to Cuba and the Carter administration, although it made no legal modifications, certainly applied the blockade less vigorously.

Although its immediate economic prospects looked good, Cuba was storing up problems for the future as its dependency deepened and its debt mounted. These problems were inextricably linked with the country's role in the world sugar trade and the preferential relationship it enjoyed with Moscow.[6] The latter had agreed to buy Cuban sugar at prearranged prices. This put Cuba at an advantage when world prices dropped as they did between 1966 and 1969 and the Soviets paid at least two or three times over the odds but clearly disadvantaged it when world rates rose. The counter-argument was that Soviet preference ensured Cuba a secure market and released its economy from the impact of fluctuations on the world stage, allowing it to implement long-term planning objectives. The pace of Soviet support accelerated in the early 1970s so that by the end of 1974, those enterprises and plant built or modernized by the Soviet Union comprised 10 per cent of Cuba's gross industrial profit.[7] Cuba's trading relationship with Soviet bloc countries was formalized when it joined the CAME. Moscow raised the prearranged price of sugar and continued with its long-term, low interest financing of Cuban development but the problem was that Cuba was defined as an exporter of sugar. Its fellow CAME members were not interested in buying more than a limited range of Cuban manufactured goods. Thus, the attempt to introduce import substitution industrialization continued to be stymied.

From the mid-1970s, there was a conscious attempt to effect the institutionalization of economic planning in line with a similar trend in the political system. Modest market reforms were introduced, notably the *Sistema de Dirección y Planificación de la Economía* (SDPE, the

System of Direction and Planning of the Economy) which was set up with the intention of improving efficiency through the decentralization of decision-making by granting managers more independence and by setting up workers' assemblies. There was recognition of the importance of profit incentives as well as increased tolerance of private economic activity in agriculture and the service sector and, from the early 1980s, in retail and housing. Moral incentives and voluntary work were replaced by an increasing emphasis upon individual self-interest. In 1980, a new pay scale reduced earnings spread among manual workers and increased the earning potential of administrative and service personnel, managers and technicians. Susan Eckstein has argued that these trends effectively reversed the egalitarian emphasis of the early revolutionary years.[8] Certainly, the existence of greater managerial autonomy within the central planning structure facilitated the emergence of a new class of privileged entrepreneurs who enjoyed foreign travel and whose access to hard currency enabled them to purchase expensive consumer goods. Improvements in economic performance were, however, overshadowed by a massive drop in world sugar prices in the late 1970s. Despite continued attempts at diversification, sugar remained central to Cuban prospects. A gendered interpretation can be placed upon these trends. In the early 1970s, the government increased the supply of consumer goods as well as facilitating women's participation in the labour force and offering them a support structure in terms of expanded day care facilities, free school lunches and maternity leave rights. However, women's employment was the first priority to be discarded when falling sugar prices halted growth. It must be remembered that this 'growth' was, in many ways, a spurious one in that it was based upon an 'expanding trade deficit [which] had to be covered with huge Soviet credits, while income inequality, bureaucratism, and corruption increased'.[9]

In the early 1980s, Cuba's trade deficit grew as the price of its imports from the Soviet bloc rose faster than the price of Cuban exports. The nature of the trading relationship oscillated between years when Moscow supported Cuba through price subsidies and other years when it focused upon supplying Cuba with low-interest loans. The Cuban government naturally preferred the former as it relieved its indebtedness. It has been argued that both approaches consolidated dependency but that this in itself did 'not prevent Cuba from pursuing its own programs' but did curtail 'the scope of Cuba's possible divergence from Soviet policies'.[10] Thus, it was not the case that Cuba had no choice but to slavishly copy the Soviet model, but rather that the options open to it were severely circumscribed and that any action or policy deemed too independent or radical would be prevented. There were frequent tensions between Cuba and its Eastern bloc trading partners. Growth in the capital goods, electronics, chemicals and computing sectors was undermined by spiralling debt and plummeting world sugar prices. The price of sugar was determined by a number of factors, many of which were beyond Cuba's control such as the EEC's agricultural policy which allowed for the subsidization of the production and export of sugar. Additionally, the worldwide increase in interest rates after 1978 hurt all debtor states. Cuba, which has been more prudent in the management of its debt than other Latin American countries, applied for rescheduling in 1982. It has always promised to repay its debts under appropriate terms; this is an attitude quite distinct from its advice to its fellow creditor states which has been to refuse to pay.

Cuba's production of consumer goods was disappointing in terms of quality and quantity; this had a negative impact both upon the economy's export capacity and its ability to satisfy the domestic market. Cubans were being offered a poor selection of often shoddy goods and, as the macroeconomic system deteriorated, they were also being asked to contend with rationing. Nutritional levels had increased in the 1970s but began to decline again in the late 1980s; however, whilst the quality, availability and variety of food declined, Cubans maintained minimal nutritional standards. Cuban life expectancy continued to reflect North American and West European rather than Latin American levels. Excellent health standards had also created another problem for the government in that the ageing of the population meant an ever-rising demand for pensions which it could ill afford. However, the commitment to a pension for all remained fundamental.[11] Popular dissatisfaction with difficult daily conditions resulted in a growing incidence of pilfering from state factories and the hoarding of agricultural produce, a burgeoning black market and low productivity and high absenteeism. The government responded with a series of regulatory laws which failed to prevent these trends and certainly did not contribute to restoring public confidence. Discontent was accentuated by Cuba's 1979 agreement to allow visits back to the island from relatives now living in the United States. Their tales of prosperity highlighted the differences in lifestyle in the two societies and must have contributed to the pressure for emigration which culminated in the Mariel exodus of 1980 as well as creating the climate in which a 'retreat' to the market could be considered.

Foreign policy

Cuba, Latin America and the Caribbean

Before discussing the economic changes of the late 1980s, I turn first to Cuba's relations with other Third World states in the 1970s. Its commitment to reconstructing North–South relations elided with its need to be seen to be acting independently of Moscow as well as repudiating Washington's efforts to frustrate its international ambitions. The latter involved US interventions in the bilateral relations that Cuba enjoyed with other states, particularly those of Latin and Central America and the Caribbean. Although OAS sanctions against Cuba were lifted in 1975, Havana maintained a wary attitude towards an organization which it considered as an instrument bent upon implementing Washington's hostile intentions. However, it vigorously pursued diplomatic and trading relations with individual neighbours in the 1970s. This strategy was facilitated by its downgrading of the promotion of revolutionary movements in the region and its acceptance of more conventional state-to-state relations. Jorge Domínguez has summarized the shift in emphasis thus: 'Regimes, even if they are right-wing and authoritarian need not be opposed if their policies toward Cuba advance important Cuban goals.'[12] Thus, Havana maintained diplomatic relations and improved its commercial ties with Argentina even after the 1976 coup and the military junta's decimation of left-wing parties and trade unions. This low-key approach continued into the 1980s as Cuban policy emphasized the importance of building links with the black eastern Caribbean, but was increasingly overshadowed by its endorsement of radical governments in Grenada and Nicaragua and its support for mass insurgencies against US-backed regimes in Guatemala and El Salvador.

Cuba and the Non-Aligned Movement

When Castro addressed the Fourth Non-Aligned Summit Meeting in Algiers in 1973, he called upon the organization to adopt a more explicitly anti-imperialist stance but his demand for a more politicized NAM was not a view shared by all participants. The movement frequently failed to reach a consensus concerning ongoing conflicts and Cuba became involved in difficult and divisive decisions. Thus, when radical Arabs castigated Anwar Sadat for acquiescing to the US-brokered Camp David Peace Accords with Israel and called for Egypt's expulsion from the NAM, Havana agreed in theory but realized that this would incur the anger of many black African states and, therefore, did not support the move. Cuba continued to advocate the creation of new regional groupings which would strengthen NAM solidarity and hinder further US penetration as well as advising the OPEC nations to recycle their oil revenues into development projects. It matched its rhetoric with extensive aid programmes and the despatch of increasing numbers of Cubans to Third World countries.

The Cuban presence in Angola after 1975 stimulated the launching of ambitious educational and health programmes in the impoverished and war-torn state. Cuba's internationalism emphasized the importance of human capital rather than financial aid but, nevertheless, the doctors, agronomists, engineers and military advisers who spent years away from the island did represent a significant drain upon sorely needed domestic resources. Cuba's contention that non-aligned should mean anti-imperialist was dealt a body blow by the Soviet invasion of Afghanistan in late 1979. The Cuban government's public defence of the act (despite its private misgivings) seriously impaired its reputation amongst non-aligned states as well as costing it a seat on the UN Security Council. However, its earlier incursions into Africa did not incur similar condemnation; indeed both the NAM and the OAS applauded Havana's involvement in Angola. In hindsight, one can argue that no matter the internationalist motives behind its military expeditions, its African adventures resulted in it being caught up in superpower configurations which it was not in a position to control. Although its Angolan and other African policies can be seen as Cuba's assertion of its right to determine its own initiatives, these policies also hardened US resolve against the Revolution.

Cuba in Africa

Cuba had enthusiastically pursued good relations with black Africa since the 1960s and continued to be involved with a number of countries and liberation movements within them. Thus, it became immersed in the highly complex set of relations between the Eritreans (who were demanding independence), the Somalis (who claimed the Ethiopian-controlled territory of Ogaden) and Haile Selassie's pro-American monarchy. Although it distanced itself from both rebel groups after the overthrow of the emperor in 1974 and the establishment of Mengistu's 'socialist' government in early 1977, Cuba remained entangled in the Horn of Africa. The Somalis (now patronized by Washington) invaded the Ogaden in July 1977 whilst a civil war waged between the various Ethiopian factions. Confrontation became inevitable when Siad Barre expelled all Cuban and Soviet personnel from Somalia. With Soviet military assistance, Ethiopian and Cuban troops forced the Somalis back to the border. Although Cuba refused to crush the Eritrean rebels, it did not attach sufficient value to its alliance with them that it would reject an understanding with Moscow's protégé, Mengistu.

The most significant of Havana's foreign policy initiatives in Africa was, undoubtedly, in Angola where Cuban troops began to arrive in autumn 1975. The diversity of support for the factions competing for post-independence control revealed the serpentine nature of international power relations at the time. Thus, Holden Roberto's highly corrupt FNLA was sponsored by the United States (he had been on the CIA's payroll since the early 1960s), Zaire and China; Cuba and the Soviet Union (the latter somewhat less than wholeheartedly because it disliked Neto's independence of spirit) backed the MPLA and Jonas Savimbi's UNITA received South Africa's patronage as well as being groomed by the CIA as an anti-communist alternative to the MPLA.[13] None of the groups developed an effective fighting force but the MPLA was the best organized and the Cubans respected Agostinho Neto.

In January 1975, the three movements signed the Alvor Agreement which committed them to joint negotiations to create a transitional government once independence was granted in November 1975. Civil war broke out almost immediately under the Portuguese army's passive gaze. The US National Security Council authorized $300,000 in covert aid to Roberto who used it to buy arms and attack the MPLA. By July 1975, the latter's forces, backed by Soviet military aid and Cuban advisers, had expelled all FNLA and UNITA troops from the environs of the Angolan capital, Luanda, and were in positions of strength elsewhere in the country. In October, a massive South African invasion moved through Namibia and up the coast in an attempt to take Luanda. It was supported by a pincer movement from the north by Zairian troops and white mercenaries paid by the FNLA and UNITA. Initially repulsed, the MPLA and Cuban troops launched Operation Carlota and achieved a number of significant military victories over the South Africans, succeeding in turning the tide by November. Fighting continued on several fronts in different parts of the country until Vorster decided to begin withdrawing South African troops in January 1976. Without their powerful ally, the forces of the FNLA and UNITA crumbled. The US's ability to help them was prevented by the Clark Amendment passed in the Senate in December 1975 which forbade the use of US troops and any further covert assistance (although Washington had never wished to get involved in the conflict on the ground). MPLA and

Cuban soldiers advanced towards the Namibian border but then slowed down in order to avoid a major confrontation with South Africa. By March 1976, the MPLA was in control and in May of that year, Cuban troops began to return home.[14]

Despite the fact that the UN Security Council condemned South Africa's aggressive incursion into Angola, the Ford administration uttered no public criticism but instead castigated Cuba for its adventurism. The absence of a coherent Washington strategy in Africa was demonstrated by the fact that it eschewed diplomacy (it never tried to make Alvor work) in exchange for covert operations and the payrolling of foreign mercenaries. Both the US and South Africa were taken by surprise by Cuba's involvement and by its military ability (Gleisejes has described Angola as 'South Africa's Bay of Pigs'[15]). Both saw the chance of an MPLA victory as extending the influence of the Soviet bloc and leading to the destabilization of the whole of Southern Africa whereas, in fact, Pretoria's policies towards its neighbours were at the core of the crisis. Cuba's decision to send troops to Angola was a *response* to the South African invasion of that country and not, as Washington maintained, the act which *provoked* it. Cuba did not consult Moscow before deciding to move into Angola and, indeed, Brezhnev was against participation, fearing that it would offend other African states although he was clearly pleased by the success of the mission. Cuba identified with poor, non-white Third World countries and felt it could make a contribution to the anti-colonial struggle in Angola. Its natural propensity to support Latin American revolutionaries was, of course, circumscribed by the proximity of the US.

Havana and Washington

Terrorism and diplomacy

Despite its high profile in international politics, Cuba's position in the world continued to be shaped by US efforts to undermine its sovereignty and Washington's policies were disproportionately influenced by the Cuban-American émigré community. The latter grew rapidly, reaching a total of more than 650,000 by 1977.[16] With the 'freedom flights' finally ending in 1973, commercial flights between Miami and Havana resumed in April 1978 after a 16-year hiatus. Cubans were given temporary visas whilst waiting to complete processing procedures. Hardliners continued to adopt intransigent attitudes and still dominated the public profile of the communities, but in 1975 a *Miami*

Herald poll 'revealed that at least 49.5% of Cuban émigrés were at least willing to visit the island ...'.[17] Many more émigrés were now prepared to acknowledge that they would not be returning to Cuba on the backs of an invasion force, and there was a small although growing body of opinion which urged the opening of discussions with the Castro government. Thus, the Brigada Antonio Maceo began organizing trips to Cuba in 1977 whilst the Comité de los 75, led by the Miami banker Bernardo Bener, arrived in Havana in November 1978 in response to Fidel's call for dialogue. However, many who favoured discourse kept quiet for fear of reprisals. The trend towards normality would be interrupted in 1980 with the Mariel boatlift and the arrival of Ronald Reagan in the Oval Office in 1981.

President Lyndon Baines Johnson evinced only a fitful interest in Latin America preoccupied as his administration was with Vietnam, although he was responsible for dispensing more Alliance for Progress funds than his predecessor. Business leaders and bankers such as David Rockefeller (who ran the Business Advisory Group and the Council for Latin America which had Standard Oil and IT&T on its board) saw huge opportunities for investment in the mainland although Cuba did not figure in their calculations. There was a slight thaw in Cuban-American relations in the early 1970s under the auspices of Nixon's strategy of détente; this was expressed in measures such as the 1973 anti-hijacking agreement which obliged each country to either prosecute suspects or return them to the other side. However, as the US continued to harbour anti-Castro terrorist groups such as Alpha 66, the treaty was frequently broken. The end of the Vietnam War saw many CIA operatives joining such groups. Emigrés attacked fishing boats and installations on the island and in October 1976 were responsible for the blowing up of a Cubana airline off Barbados, killing 73 people. Castro blamed the Coordinadora de Organizaciones Revolucionario Unido (CORU, the Coordinating Body of United Revolutionary Organizations) which was led by Orlando Bosch.[18] Further evidence of a willingness to negotiate was demonstrated in 1975 when the United States voted with the majority of OAS states to end multilateral sanctions, although the White House indicated that it had no intention of raising the blockade (foreign subsidiaries of US companies had already been permitted to trade with Cuba under certain conditions). When Assistant Secretary of State William D. Rogers affirmed Washington's desire to move forward so long as Cuba met it halfway, reconciliation or rather a mutual recognition of difference appeared possible. A secret series of meetings between important officials were held in New York.

However, whilst it became apparent that Cuba was willing to engage in detailed discussions on specific issues, the Americans were disinclined to offer anything more than general statements of intent. As has always been the case, the American strategy was to place the onus upon Cuba to be seen to be the one to compromise.

Cuba's military involvement in Angola stalled intra-governmental contacts and the Ford administration made its withdrawal a condition of their resumption. Serious discussions resumed late in 1978 in accord with Jimmy Carter's commitment to normalization. However, his government relayed mixed signals in terms of the nature of its Cuba policy. Whilst Secretary of State Vance argued that improving relations was a priority, National Security Adviser Zbigniew Brzezinski remained hawkish and the president himself was inconsistent, a fault which became the hallmark of his foreign policy. The first government-to-government negotiations since 1961 delivered positive results including agreements on fishing rights and a provisional maritime boundary in the Straits and, most importantly, the opening in 1977 of US and Cuban Interests Sections in the Swiss embassy in Havana and the Czech embassy in Washington respectively. These operated as de facto embassies without either country having to formally recognize the other. US diplomats were given access to 'political prisoners' and arranged visas for those released by the Cuban government. The existence of the Sections facilitated cultural and other exchanges as well as providing communication links between Havana and Washington. Wayne S. Smith (who became chief of mission in Havana in 1979) reported a conversation with Fidel Castro in summer 1978 in which the Cuban leader admitted that there were things he would have done differently with respect to the way the relationship with the US developed in the 1960s and that he was keen to pursue a dialogue. However, he was frustrated by the different signals coming out of Washington. It was true that whilst Cuban experts in the State Department and the Interests Section itself endorsed negotiation, there was no consensus on the breadth of the agenda for discussion and the blockade was generally regarded as off-limits. This was an issue that Cuba constantly identified as crucial.[19] The National Security Council, on the other hand, appeared set on an aggressive, static policy which did not involve dialogue, indeed a strategy which was aimed at preventing dialogue.

The fragility of the negotiating process was demonstrated by further events in Africa. In March 1977, after Katanganese troops who had been trained in Angola, invaded Zaire's Shaba (formerly Katanga) province, Zaire received troops from Belgium, France, Egypt, the Sudan and Morocco whilst President Agostinho Neto of Angola asked for Cuban assistance. A further invasion of Shaba took place in May 1978. Brzezinski claimed that the CIA had reported huge Cuban reinforcements and launched a savage attack upon Havana, blaming it for the escalation of the conflict. The Cubans argued that they had actually sent Washington information which could have been used to protect the pro-Western Mobutu regime in an effort to restore stability in the area. Brzezinski's statement had been pure invention (Wayne Smith remarks 'I thought the NSC's position ... to be outright rubbish'[20]). When the Senate Foreign Relations Committee found the evidence behind Cuban culpability to be circumstantial rather than conclusive, Jimmy Carter then accused Castro of not doing enough to stop the invasion which was tantamount to calling the Cuban leader a liar.

It was quite clear that Cuba was determined to protect the new Angolan government from South African encroachment. Thus, if the US wished to pursue a peace policy, it should have protected Angolan sovereignty and talked directly and calmly to Cuba. Cyrus Vance was retrospectively highly critical of the policy of the administration in which he played an important role: 'I believed the reason the Angolans kept the Cubans in Angola was because they feared further incursions by South Africa and South African support of UNITA. I felt the solution lay in removing these Angolan concerns that, in African opinion, legitimised the Soviet and Cuban presence.'[21] Erisman has contended that Cuban–US relations from 1975 to the election of Ronald Reagan in November 1980 alternated between 'normalization and strident antagonism'. Whilst Havana insisted that the two countries seek rapprochement through discussion of bilateral issues (such as immigration), Washington raised the stakes by playing 'linkage politics, demanding that the Cubans make changes in other policy areas [loosening ties with the USSR or withdrawing their troops from Africa] as the price'. The inference here was that Washington had veto power over Cuban policy (this attitude has continued to the present day). Thus Kissinger and then Brzezinski seized upon the example of Cuban involvement in Angola to resurrect the surrogate thesis. If Havana had no independent foreign policy, then 'normalization would have to occur within a larger East–West framework'.[22] This absolved the US from the responsibility of developing an intelligent Cuba policy, one which would recognize that the island posed no threat to the superpower's regional hegemony and that both states should be able to live in peace.

Cuba and Reaganism

The backyard

The election of a right-wing US president in November 1980 would have serious repercussions for Cuba in both the foreign and domestic policy spheres. Reagan, who viewed international politics through Manichean eyes, believed that all issues were dominated by the East–West confrontation and that the outcome of each world event would impinge upon the outcome of that fundamental conflict. Thus the Soviet Union and all its perceived allies (including insurgent movements in Central America championing social justice for indigenous peoples and an end to military repression and political authoritarianism) needed to be contained at all times. For Reagan, Central America was 'rapidly becoming a Communist lake in what should be an American pond'.[23] In this climate, it was apparent that Cuba would receive no offers of friendship from Reagan and his secretary of state, Alexander Haig, although Havana continued to offer feelers including the reduction of arms transfers to the FMLN in El Salvador and the suspension of military aid to the Sandinistas in November 1981.[24] Immediately after their 1979 Revolution, Fidel had advised the latter that they should not offend Washington by introducing radical legislation (that is, they should not follow the Cuban road. This was also the Soviet viewpoint). Anyone familiar with the trajectory of FSLN rule between 1979 and 1990 will be aware of the moderate nature of its actions. Nevertheless, this was not enough to save it from the ire of the United States. For Fidel, the content of the Nicaraguan government's programmes was incidental 'because Washington wanted a war to teach the lesson that nobody can conduct a progressive fight for independence and social justice in the area'.[25]

Another friend of Cuba was also subject to US aggression in the early 1980s. Cuba had developed strong links with Grenada through a number of development projects including the construction of a new international airport which the Reagan government used as a pretext for its invasion of the island on 25 October 1983. The White House argued that the airport would be the landing strip for the arrival of communist revolution in the Caribbean. This action reflected the rationale underpinning Reagan's Caribbean Basin Initiative which resulted in Dominica, Antigua, St Kitts-Nevis, Barbados, St Lucia, St Vincent, the Grenadines and Grenada all having military bases which served US strategic concerns whilst Washington gave generous economic aid to conservative ruling elites. With the electoral defeat of the FSLN in

1990, the capture of Manuel Noriega in Panama and the El Salvador peace settlement, US interest in the region waned and some degree of normality returned to it.

Despite such a hostile environment, Cuba managed to participate in a number of positive diplomatic initiatives in the region in the 1980s, including supporting the Grupo Contadora of Mexico, Panama, Venezuela and Colombia in their efforts to achieve a Central American peace settlement.[26] Fidel also assumed a high profile in the debate over Third World indebtedness, declaring that the debt was both economically impossible to pay and politically and morally indefensible. It had left Latin and Central America 'worse off ... than we were in the period prior to the struggles of Bolívar, San Martín, O'Higgins, Juárez, Morelos and Sucre'.[27] Economic integration and the creation of alternative trading networks were essential to prevent further aggrandizement by the North. Cuba's commercial links with Latin American countries rose sharply in the latter part of the decade and these paved the way for greater political closeness. By 1989, Havana had diplomatic and economic relations with all countries except Chile (these were restored by President Patricio Aylwin in 1991), Colombia (angered by Cuban support for its guerrillas) and Paraguay. Latin American states were increasingly willing to rebuff Washington's attempts to keep Cuba isolated; in November 1987, eight presidents agreed that Cuba should be readmitted to the OAS and in 1989, Costa Rican President Oscar Arias was attacked by the White House for suggesting that Cuba should play a leading role in the Central American peace discussions.

At the same time as Cuba appeared to be being brought in from the cold, *latino* reaction to its domestic policies remained ambivalent. This was particularly so on the part of the Latin American left.[28] Many regarded Cuba as a political dinosaur which was part of the problem of already existing socialism and which had little to do with the contemporary left's engagement with democracy and citizenship rights. Some applauded the disintegration of the Soviet bloc and expected the Castro government's imminent demise. Others were more even in their judgement. Cuauhtémoc Cárdenas, leader of the Mexican Partido de la Revolución Democrática (PRD, Party of the Democratic Revolution) defended Cuban resistance to political democratization so long as the US threat remained, whilst Luís Ignacio Lula da Silva (then leader of the Workers Party, elected Brazilian president in 2002) agreed that Cuba continued to be vulnerable to American aggression but called upon it 'to allow arguments, open up political debate, allow opposing ideas'.[29]

Mariel and the Cuban American National Foundation

The vast majority of Cuban-Americans identified with the Republican Party; in 1980 and 1984, 90 per cent of émigrés voted for Reagan in Miami, 65 per cent in New York and 68 per cent in Chicago.[30] However, their support was fickle in that they would switch allegiance to Democratic politicians if they appeared more proactive on behalf of community interests. Intransigents within the émigré community had been frustrated by the twists and turns of a US Cuba policy which appeared to them to be based on inertia and lack of resolve. They sought to exert a greater influence over policy making but their efficacy was diminished by the large number of groups claiming to represent the authentic émigré voice and the frequent infighting which took place between them. Ultra conservative voices continued to dominate liberal and left-wing ones and they abhorred the idea of conciliation with the Castro government. The RECE offered financial support to terrorist groups such as Omega 7 and Bosch's CORU. Omega 7 was held responsible for more than 20 terrorist acts between 1975 and 1980, including the bombing of missions to the United Nations, the murder of a Cuban diplomat in 1980 and the attempted assassination of Cuba's UN ambassador, Raúl Róa Kouri.[31] The US government countenanced such illegal activities whilst some of its agencies, principally the CIA, actively encouraged them.[32] Émigré politicians and business people endorsed terrorist operations but were acutely aware that they needed to project a more respectable image if they were to be accepted as actors on the stage of domestic American politics. Their opportunity came with the Mariel boatlift.

Mariel

The boatlift crisis began on 28 March 1980 when six Cubans stole a bus and crashed into the Peruvian embassy in Havana. With Cuban guards and hostile crowds surrounding the compound, 10,000 Cubans had occupied the embassy by 6 April whilst Cuban émigrés in the United States pressed the government to come to the aid of those inside the embassy. Having blocked international aid and after failed discussions with possible destinations such as Peru, Cuba opened the port of Mariel (32 kilometres west of Havana) and invited relatives to collect the *gusanos* ('worms'). The first boats of the 'Freedom Flotilla' arrived on 20 April and over the next six months an estimated 125,000 people left Cuban territory. The official Cuban version was that most of the 'boat people' were 'scum' including social deviants (that is, gays), drug addicts and criminals and this view was endorsed by much non-Hispanic (and, indeed, some Cuban-American) opinion in Miami and on the East Coast.[33] Mariel became emblematic of the complex ethnic relations which existed within the American cities where significant Cuban communities had settled. Thus, fears about an influx of new immigrants were underpinned by the knowledge that many were Afro-Cuban, of lower-class status and with poorer education. Many African-Americans complained that *marielitos* were accorded privileged treatment and established émigrés believed that they would tarnish their reputation, whilst immigrant groups, such as the sizeable Haitian community who had arrived in southern Florida to escape the dictatorship of the Duvalier regime, felt that the Cubans were treated better because they were more ideologically useful to the government.[34]

Notwithstanding their private fears, the public stance of the émigré organizations, which was echoed by Washington's pronouncements, was that the Mariel boat people were fleeing tyranny and embracing democracy. The Carter administration's initial pragmatic response was to attempt to restrict the exodus but it backed down for fear of alienating Cuban-Americans. It then pledged to accept all arrivals but later backtracked, arguing that all boats should be sent back and their occupants and future emigrants screened by the Cuban authorities. Cuba refused to consider this eventuality, declaring that it violated its sovereignty. It is not surprising that Carter's mixed signals resulted in a solid majority of Cuban-Americans voting against him in November 1980. The boat people experienced dangerous conditions during their sea voyages and there was considerable loss of life. The US Coastguard tried to discourage the flotillas but was also involved in many rescues. On arrival, the illegal immigrants were entangled in a web of bureaucracy with many *marielitos* being placed in overcrowded and unsanitary holding camps during the long wait for their visas to be dealt with. On more than one occasion their frustration erupted into violence such as on 6 May when a state of emergency was declared in Florida in an attempt to maintain public order. The American Civil Liberties Union would later initiate legal proceedings against the US government for human rights abuses in the camps and in prisons. The behaviour of both sides during the Mariel crisis has been criticized.

Wayne S. Smith castigates the US for its previous failure to resolve the issue of the proposed emigration of political prisoners from Cuba. Protracted negotiations had failed to reach a conclusion mainly due to the ambivalence of the relevant US agencies; the eventual release of some prisoners was regarded as the outcome of the burgeoning dialogue between Castro and liberal émigrés. Washington had failed to respond to persistent Cuban complaints about the hijacking of vessels and was responsible for not policing the activities of émigré terrorist groups. As head of the US Interests Section, Smith had anticipated the possibility of a massive sea exodus as Cuban sugar production declined, world prices plummeted and food rationing intensified. However, and not for the first time, his political bosses failed to take notice of warnings from the ground. Smith is equally critical of Castro's position as being too precipitate and for underestimating the depth of feeling amongst those willing to make such a dangerous journey in order to leave Cuba. The Cuban government had initially accepted Costa Rica's offer to take refugees via an airlift but reneged upon this accord for fear of the adverse publicity it would generate. Although he makes some concession with respect to Castro's personal circumstances at the time of Mariel (his long-term partner, the revolutionary veteran Celia Sánchez, had died of cancer in January 1980), he nevertheless believes that the daily violent, vigilante-style scenes at the Peruvian embassy and later around the Interests Section (to which about 400 Cubans moved in early May) were a 'blot on Cuba's history' and undoubtedly damaged Cuba's image abroad (particularly amongst those who supported ending the blockade and a normalization of relations).[35] The last of the refugees had left Cuban soil by late September but the political ramifications of Mariel would continue to reverberate within the US and set the scene for a hardening of its relations with Cuba in the 1980s and 1990s.[36]

The Cuban American National Foundation

The main architect of America's Cuba policy since the 1980s has been the CANF which emerged in 1981 and which was promoted by CIA director, William Casey, as an agency for gathering support for Reagan's commitment to a more masculine, abrasive foreign policy. It enjoyed strong links with the National Endowment for Democracy which offered support to like-minded groups in the Third World, such as the Nicaraguan Contra, as correctives to pro-Soviet and pro-Cuban tendencies. CANF leaders Mas Canosa, Raúl Masvidal and Carlos Salmán collaborated closely with conservative Cuban-American academics such as those at the Center for International and Strategic Studies at Georgetown University in Washington, DC. Reagan's ideological initiative coincided fortuitously with the Cuban-American right's decision to reinvent itself, concentrating on becoming a lobby within US domestic politics rather than focusing all its efforts upon planning for a return to a post-Castro Cuba (although this remained the ultimate objective). The pretext for the creation of CANF was the November 1980 'antibilingual' referendum which rejected the parity of English and Spanish as official languages in Miami. The émigrés decided that they must organize in order to bring out the Cuban-American vote and increase the number of its elected representatives. The trend towards political respectability necessitated a decline in the promotion of terrorism although not its disappearance as émigré groups courted political parties and intellectuals. In an interview with *The Miami Herald* in April 1986, Mas Canosa said: 'We had to take the fight out of Calle Ocho ... and into the center of power. ... We had to stop the commando raids and concentrate on influencing public opinion and governments.'[37]

The CANF happily embraced those ideological perspectives propagated by the leading New Right think tank, the Santa Fe Committee. Its 1980 policy document announced that as the era of détente was dead, the US should reassert its rights under the Monroe Doctrine and take back 'the backyard' from encroaching Soviet influence. In 1981, *National Security Directive no. 17* outlined the new Cuba policy which aimed 'to develop public pressure against Cuba, bringing to light human and political rights issues and using the Cuban exile community to transmit this message ...'.[38] Mas Canosa, the putative Cuban president-in-waiting, had been a self-proclaimed professional counter-revolutionary since the 1960s although he had never actually seen active duty. A highly successful businessman, albeit with a tarnished reputation (one of his nicknames was Señor Mas y Mas – Mr More and More), he directed CANF's multiple activities which included lobbying, research and education as well as bestowing huge financial resources upon political candidates from both the Democratic and Republican parties at local, state and national levels. In such a manner CANF was able to exercise significant political influence upon presidents Reagan, Bush Senior, Clinton (whose receipt of a $400,000 gift played a decisive role in his response to the 1992 Torricelli Act) and Bush Junior. CANF's legal and philanthropic activities masked abuses of its power such as using its huge funds to suppress dissident voices within the émigré community as well as promoting the defection of Cuban athletes, particularly the baseball players, with huge cash inducements. The Foundation was also associated with sinister campaigns of harassment and bombings. In 1990, it created the Commission of Information which kept records on its political enemies and liaised with both the FBI and the police.

The US government's Project Democracy envisaged a two-track approach towards the Castro government. The first track, embodied in the National Endowment for Democracy (NED), was granted a federal budget by Congress and managed legitimate activities such as domestic NGOs and think tanks as well as financing foreign organizations identified with the promotion of democracy. A major coup for the project and for the émigrés was Congress's approval of funding to Radio Martí and TV Martí in 1990. Foiling Cuban attempts to block them, the stations' broadcasts represented a major publicity victory for anti-Castro forces. The remit of the NED did not allow it to hand over funds for political lobbying but it did just this in terms of large donations to the CANF. The second track was an illegal one which did not enter the realm of public knowledge until the end of 1986 when the Iran–Contra scandal broke and it was revealed that funds had been diverted to Oliver North's nefarious activities which included drug dealing and gunrunning. In the 1990s, the CANF remained the dominant Cuban-American lobby although its hegemony was challenged by other groups: some predicted the speedy collapse of the Castro regime and felt it was being too cautious; some anticipated a much slower transition in which international pressure would play a significant role and a third tendency pinned its hopes upon the growth of opposition groups within Cuba itself.[39]

Cuba and the US enter the 1990s

The blockade remained the most intractable problem between Cuba and the United States as the decade of the 1980s ended. During those years, a number of secret talks between representatives of the two governments had floundered as Washington refused to place the issue on the table. American intransigence contrasted with the evident willingness on the part of other states to improve trading and diplomatic relations. Cuba's growing, albeit still modest, links with Latin and Central America and the countries of the Caribbean have been mentioned previously in this chapter. Western Europe, Canada and Japan also continued to pursue trading and political contacts as well as beginning to create joint ventures with the Cuban state (particularly as the latter turned its attention to tourism), although they were bullied by the Reagan administration into excluding some imports, such as Cuban nickel, from their markets. The patience of its allies would be severely tested by the offensive mounted by a Democratic president, William Jefferson Clinton, in the early to mid-1990s which had the aim of strengthening the blockade and prohibiting third-party trade with Cuba. Another pressing issue for successive American administrations was their persistent attempts to mobilize international condemnation of Cuba's human rights record. Indeed, Cuban concessions in this area were regarded as central to any future bilateral relations. The Cuban government released over 5000 political prisoners between 1978 and 1986 often at the behest of celebrity mediators such as Jesse Jackson and Senator Edward Kennedy. The US lobbied to have Cuba officially investigated by the UN Commission on Human Rights and a UN team eventually visited Cuba in 1988 but, whilst its report criticized the government for the denial of basic liberties, it found no grounds to state that either secret executions or disappearances were taking place. It also disputed Washington's claims that 15,000 remained behind bars.[40]

In a speech of May 1989, President George Bush signalled his intention to continue Reagan's belligerent approach towards Cuba: 'Until Fidel Castro shows a desire to change the behavior of Cuba and its policies, we will maintain our current policy towards Cuba.'[41] The Bush agenda for normalization of relations stipulated the introduction of a multiparty system, the holding of US-approved elections, the release of all political prisoners, a reduction in the size of the Cuban armed forces and an end to Cuban involvement in the affairs of other countries. US policy in the 1970s and 1980s was both short-sighted and ill-conceived and was permeated by an 'intransigent anti-Cubanism'.[42] This mindset persisted into the 1990s and I discuss this in Chapter 7, but I must now turn to the period of domestic crisis which Cuba entered in 1986.

Rectification – invoking the spirit of the 1960s

When Fidel Castro announced the Rectification Campaign in 1986, it was an acknowledgement of the precarious state of the Cuban economy and the pressing need for urgent reform to counteract bureaucratic tendencies, inefficiency and the loss of popular confidence in the government. There had been recognition of such difficulties on many occasions prior to 1986, but these had been offset by a generally vigorous economy and problems had been explained as temporary, reflecting the need for adjustments to the SDPE and for limited experiments with more market-oriented economic activity. However, Rectification was different because of its much larger scale and the fact that it was taking place in more difficult circumstances, both domestically and internationally. Opening up the economy to domestic private enterprise and to foreign capital would inevitably have political repercussions which might go further than the government intended. In a bid to save the Revolution, the Cuban government might have initiated processes which would undermine and eventually destroy it.

Underpinning a plethora of economic and management problems was the low price of sugar on the world market and Cuba's inability to meet its debt obligations to capitalist bankers. The Cuban debt at this time was generally estimated to be between $6 and $7 million which was a small figure compared to that owed by other Latin American states but serious given Cuba's unique position (the impact of the blockade and its dependency upon a Soviet camp which was itself experiencing economic and political difficulties).[43] The National Bank unilaterally suspended all its interest and principal debt payments in July 1986. Cuba could no longer afford to pay for its previous level of imports because it lacked sufficient capital. This crisis occurred at the very time that the Soviet Union and its new leader, Mikhail Gorbachev, were sending unmistakable signals that they were no longer able or indeed wished to continue to treat Cuba as a privileged trading partner and that Cuba might have to go it alone. The Cuban response was a strategy of austerity and self-sufficiency, but it was a strategy which was couched in the ideological clothing of a return to the heroic period of the 1960s. Particular stress was placed upon the reinvigoration of revolutionary enthusiasm and the invocation of Guevara's ideas about moral incentives. One Cuban commentator argued that Rectification should not be seen as an admission of defeat but as a 'revitalization of the Cuban road to socialism. ... It strengthens a style of work rooted in the daily commitment of the masses ... a democratic impulse that had diminished in the face of bureaucratisation. ...'[44]

Corruption in high places

The Cuban leadership admitted to failures of political judgement in allowing this 'bureaucratisation' to develop and also accepted the existence of corruption at the highest levels of state. The government portrayed the 1987 trial of General Arnaldo Ochoa and other high-ranking officials as evidence that it was willing to punish those within the revolutionary leadership who had been found guilty of wrongdoing. Ochoa, a *sierra* veteran and close friend of Castro, had been widely praised for his military command in Angola. He was accused of corruption and drug trafficking, his criminal activities being undertaken under the aegis of CIMEX, the government agency which handled tourism and other foreign business, and the Departamento de Moneda Convertible (the Department of Convertible Currency). Ochoa and four others were executed whilst Division General José Abrantes, the minister of the interior, was charged with the abuse of power and operating on the black market and imprisoned for 20 years. Other top military officers and civilians (including the heads of the Customs Service and Immigration) were either imprisoned or fired.[45] There was speculation that Ochoa and the others had been targeted as a result of profound disagreements concerning the political and economic trajectory of the Cuban future and that the crisis was instigated by a power struggle between the party and the army with the former giving the latter a warning that it was not autonomous. The scandal represented 'a turning point for a profound institutional, political and moral improvement'.[46]

Although the Ochoa affair was profoundly shocking and revealed that the top leadership was not immune from criticism, the elitist structure of decision-making within the Cuban state remained intact and no systematic explanation was offered as to why such high-level criminality could have occurred. In this context, Rectification could be seen as a government manoeuvre to pre-empt criticism concerning corruption and inefficiency and neutralize the potential for large-scale discontent rather than as a conscious attempt to return to the roots of the Revolution. It is more likely that the government's motives were a mixture of both. However, a strategy which aimed to reanimate the spirit of egalitarianism but which, at the same time, wished to involve Cuba more fully in capitalist market relations appeared ambivalent and would be a difficult one to pursue.

Economic reforms

What then were the specific problems besetting Cuba and what was to be done about them? In a series of policy speeches, Fidel admitted a catalogue of errors which included the poor distribution of food and services; the failure to regulate private markets which then bred corruption; the payment of high wages which bore no relation to the amount of work done or the quality of goods made and the payment of pay and overtime bonuses and other material incentives which compounded inequalities between workers as well as a growth in absenteeism, pilfering and small and large instances of corruption.[47] It was essential that the government rectify these problems by ensuring that rewards suited the nature of the work done and that state enterprises introduced new management techniques which eschewed hierarchical relations in favour of creative decision-making. The Ochoa case was presented as an example of the fact that those managers and functionaries engaged in foreign exchange operations had enriched themselves through illicit profiteering by means of the creation of dummy corporations. State-sector managers were criticized for enjoying too many privileges and for inept administration and many lost their jobs, being replaced by younger professionals.[48]

In 1984, Castro attacked the technocrats of JUCEPLAN for failing to control the financial demands of individual ministries which, it was implied, had created their own cultures and priorities which were not in tune with national needs; many of the agency's powers were assumed by a new political formation, the Grupo Estatal Central (Central State Group). This initiative entailed greater 'centralization of control of the macroeconomy' but, paradoxically, 'decentralization of day-to-day economic activity at the micro level' as individual units were encouraged to make decisions without waiting for directives from above.[49] The first of these experiments, the Revolutionary Armed Forces Initiative (which was launched at the military's Che Guevara Industrial Complex in 1987) was hailed as a triumph. A further step towards decentralization took place in 1988 when a system of 'continuous planning' was introduced, with managers and workers taking the initiative in the formulation of policy. This scheme, which had been taken up by some 900 enterprises by 1990, might have had a positive impact upon Cuba's mercantile production if the Soviet crisis had not intervened.

Feeding the nation

The government also turned its attention to the problem of the availability and distribution of foodstuffs and consumer goods, introducing wide-ranging adjustment policies in order to respond to shortages and closing farmers' markets which were said to generate inequalities in the consumption of basic foods' and to create 'too many millionaires'.[50] The state-run agricultural markets (the *agromercados*) began to offer greater variety and better quality food than was available in the *acopios* or subsidized shops where rationed goods were sold. However, government supply networks remained inadequate and the farmers' markets would reopen in the 1990s. The 1989 *Plan Alimentario* (Food Plan) aimed to reduce Cuban dependency upon imported food and to achieve as much self-sufficiency in feeding the nation as was possible.[51] All available land in the towns and cities was turned over to production whilst in the countryside, large state farms were broken up into smaller Unidades Básicas de Producción Cooperativa (UBPCs, Basic Units of Cooperative Production). The units represented the deepest structural reform of the period. Whilst the state retained legal ownership of the land, the cooperative owned the rest of the means of production and the product. The UBPCs adopted new farming methods which were shaped by local experience and knowledge and which employed crop rotation and organic techniques. The hope was that this approach would eventually see a shift from sugar dependency to crop diversification and popular ownership of the farming sector. One commentator hailed these innovations as the way forward for the Cuban economy because of their combination of 'social ownership of the fundamental means of production' with 'the incorporation of other forms of ownership of the nonfundamental means of production when they guarantee higher levels of efficiency and employment'.[52] Continuing experiments in agri-business and the application of biotechnology are discussed in Chapter 7 below. The government tried to reduce the political significance of rationing by exhorting workers to increase their productivity in order to have more money to spare. It also invoked the spirit of self-sacrifice of the early days of the Revolution by re-emphasizing the role of voluntary labour (for example, in the use of building micro brigades); of course, voluntary labour could be used to mask rising unemployment rates, a fact which was embarrassing to a government which had sworn to maintain full employment.

Constructing a better relationship between state and society

At the Third PCC Congress held in 1986, Fidel called for proactive measures to be taken to address the growing gap between party and people and to resolve the issues of gender and racial discrimination and the alienation of Cuban youth. He argued that popular participation must be deepened in order to energize all other aspects of Rectification: 'people are not born corrupt, they get corrupted. ... We realized that our system failed to prevent ... corruption because it did not provide for sufficient popular control.'[53] Ken Cole has argued that Rectification and the following Special Period were directed at restructuring the Cuban economy in response to changes within the international political economy, but were also intended to address domestic problems and particularly the fact that 'the chaotic incentive system and the somewhat arbitrary distribution of national income in the 1970s and 1980s had begun to erode the national consensus, and demobilize popular support'.[54] Particularly worrying to a political system which had always stressed a collective approach to resolving issues was the increasing tendency for individuals to depend upon their families, friends and informal social networks rather than look to the state to provide solutions. Aware that it must be seen as responding to a climate of insecurity and dissatisfaction, the government responded by loosening various social controls. Thus, there was a relative relaxation of press censorship and political leaders, academics and intellectuals entered into a public although restricted debate about the perceived shortcomings of recent years.

Rectification was always going to be a risky business because it created as many tensions as it sought to resolve. In attempting to combine *guevarista* ideals with market criteria, it was viewed as a corrective process and as a rerouting of social development which might experience setbacks but which would, over time, restore Cuban productivity and popular confidence. However, it was also viewed within the context of continuing Soviet support. The implosion of the Eastern bloc governments and of the Soviet Union itself following the abortive coup against Gorbachev in August 1991 removed this support and brought Rectification to an end after only a few years. It was replaced by the crisis management of the Special Period as the Revolution struggled to survive.

The Special Period

> In the 1990s, Cuba ... had to face: the collapse of the Soviet Bloc and the CAME; a tightened US economic blockade; ... the economic and social crisis facing less developed countries in 'the debt trap'; ... and the need to integrate the Cuban economy within the world market.[55]

The disintegration of the CAME was a devastating blow for Cuba; although the terms of trade had forced Cuba to maintain its sugar dependency and had been inimical to long-term economic diversification, nevertheless the trading bloc had accounted for the bulk of Cuban trade. In the late 1980s, there had been mounting criticism within the Soviet and East European press concerning the huge cost of subsidizing the Cuban economy at a time when their own were failing. The deteriorating relationship was made public when Fidel was conspicuously absent from Chernenko's funeral and later made disparaging remarks about *perestroika* and Gorbachev's flirtation with market forces and the West. In foreign policy terms, Fidel was furious, for example, that Gorbachev had been willing to discuss reconfiguring Cuba's role in Central America with the United States without involving Cuba itself. By 1991, Soviet troops had left Cuba.

Flirting with the market

Despite Fidel's vehement condemnation of the market mechanism (usually couched in invocations of the spirit of Che; for instance, his 1987 pronouncement that Che would have been appalled 'if he had been told that money was becoming man's main concern'[56]), others appeared more willing to think the unthinkable. Before the fall of the Soviet Union, some political leaders opined that economic liberalism was inevitable and would need to be combined with greater political openness. Thus, Armando Hart, the minister of culture, 'began to re-introduce ideas from Lenin and Engels into the public discourse as a way of recalling the utility of market mechanisms in socialist countries'.[57] Others warned that political liberalization could lead to the weakening, and even the demise, of the present leadership. Within the Cuban army, there was considerable tension between military professionals and party apparatchiks, between generations, between those who had served in Angola and those who had not. Articles in the academic and party press echoed what was evidently an intense and fractious debate. With the fall of Gorbachev and the creation of the Russian Federation under Boris Yeltsin, however, this intellectual debate was overshadowed by political reality. In December 1990, the Soviet government and Havana had announced a new trading arrangement which replaced the five-year deals with one lasting only a year. All trade – except that of sugar – would now be priced in hard currency at world market prices whilst the sugar price would be pegged higher than current world prices but considerably lower than it had been previously. The incoming Russian government did not initially honour many promises with respect to future levels of trade and this contributed to a huge fall in Cuban imports of grain, foodstuffs and oil with its attendant effect upon domestic consumption. However, later in the 1990s, the trading relationship (with raw sugar from Cuba and chemicals and machinery from Russia) prospered again as a large delegation of politicians and businessmen visited Cuba and the Russian government condemned Helms–Burton. When President Vladimir Putin came to Havana in December 2000, he publicly regretted the earlier abrupt rupture of relations.

The Special Period saw the acceptance of market trade in agriculture and the export sector, a growth in the acceptance of joint ventures with foreign firms and governments and the pursuit of foreign exchange which resulted in the partial dollarization of the Cuban economy. Castro was keen to stress that this did not imply that Cuba was going down the neo-liberal road already trodden by the rest of Latin America. Rather than embracing a free market model which compounds wealth differentials and increases social inequality, the Cuban economy was relinking into the world system but under strict state control. The long-term prospects for traditional exports such as sugar and tobacco might be limited (in that they needed huge inputs of resources merely to sustain current levels of profitability), but their short-term earning capacity would help pay for the import of capital and consumer goods. In order to shape the economic future, Cuba needed to develop new industries such as tourism and pharmaceuticals and to ensure that all sectors, both traditional and modern, benefited from the absorption of greater technology and knowledge in order to improve efficiency.[58] Unlike other Third World states caught in the poisonous embrace of neo-liberalism, Cuba did not sell off state property, resources, schools or pension funds to private foreign investors although it did sell half-interests in existing facilities as well as entering into joint ventures for new ones and wooed private capital with generous inducements. Nor did Cuba introduce the shock treatment policies including currency devaluations, drastic cuts in state expenditure and services and price hikes which have been endemic in Latin America. Rather Cuba attempted to maintain the social achievements of the Revolution whilst engaging with an international financial environment which has no interest in the survival of a socialist society.

The social consequences

Many commentators were confident that, over time, the centrally planned Cuban economy would be overwhelmed by the incursion of foreign capital which would operate as a Trojan horse and eventually force political change. The creation of a dual peso/dollar economy would have important social repercussions in terms of dividing Cubans between those who had access to dollars (through working in the growing tourist sector or receiving remittances from relatives living abroad) and those who did not. The possession of dollars would give individuals privileged positions within Cuban society in terms of their consumption capacities and the extraordinarily low levels of salary paid in the state sector. It would also create a new class of black marketeers with no feelings of loyalty to the incumbent government. Market reform undoubtedly stimulated production, but private producers manipulated it to their own advantage by, for example, selling only their poorest quality goods to the state at the same time as it was supplying them with credit, seed and other resources. Profits were to be made by selling produce in private farmers' markets rather than concentrating activity in the cooperatives.

Resisting the trend towards the market opening were those groups – including government bureaucrats, professionals, the military and politicians – who had a vested interest in the status quo (some within these groups also sought personal advantage in playing the market game; many did not). In the middle were the majority of Cubans who enjoyed the privileges of neither the dollar nor political influence and for whom daily life was becoming intensely difficult as food scarcities and rationing were extended, the deterioration of basic services and infrastructure continued and unemployment rose. Energy conservation led to many factories being closed as well as the imposition of controls on domestic electricity provision. The physical environment of the island was transformed as buses and cars were replaced by bicycles and oxen-driven carts substituted for tractors. The early to mid-1990s witnessed an increasingly palpable sense of disenchantment amongst the young who desired the symbols of Western consumerism and amongst Afro-Cubans who did not have access to dollars. Illegal departures from the island increased in the early 1990s and when Castro threatened another mass emigration, Clinton talked of a naval blockade although émigré leaders tried to persuade the community not to encourage another Mariel. Nevertheless, history did repeat itself in August 1994 when the *balseros* (raft) crisis began and the two governments were compelled to once again enter into negotiations about immigration controls.

Cuba faces the future

Clearly the early 1990s were a difficult and often desperate period in post-revolutionary history. Despite strong misgivings by many in the top leadership, including Fidel himself, the collapse of the economic relationship with the Soviet Union left the government little choice but to engage with market economics. Castro publicly refused to give in to pessimism about the future as he frequently maintained that Cuba was not concerned with just surviving but was repositioning itself in order to continue with socialist development. It was true that the Soviet Union had provided a solid bulwark but now: 'We are our own bulwark, together with all the people throughout the world who ... admire our people's heroism and determinism.'[59] The Revolution was compelled to make concessions to prevailing global trends but it was not going to sacrifice what had been accomplished since 1959. Despite these defiant pronouncements, it was evident that there were many important things at stake, including the principle of egalitarianism which had underpinned revolutionary discourse since 1959 and which provided one of the lines of continuity with Martí's vision of social justice as intrinsic to Cuban citizenship. Jean Stubbs contended that as Cuba undertook its own form of economic restructuring by introducing more 'cost-effective, less technified basic-needs approaches in its "special period", new pressures will be on the rural household, social welfare and social equity will again be at stake'.[60]

Whilst acknowledging the parlous state of the economy, one should not forget the advances which had been achieved and which the state was adamant would remain. Thus at the height of the crisis in 1992, 'Cuba's health statistics rivalled those of the developed world. Infant mortality had dropped to 10.2 per 1,000 births ... [there was a] 98.8 percent survival rate of Cuban children during the first five years of life. Maternal mortality was at 3.2 per 10,000 births. Overall life expectancy in Cuba had reached 77.22 years.'[61] Fidel had promised that no school, hospital or nursery would be closed and no one left destitute. In reality, schools and hospitals suffered from shortages in medicines and materials although as the 1990s advanced, the budgetary allocation to the social services actually increased as Cuba continued to address social needs despite limited resources.

Whilst it struggled to maintain domestic calm, Cuba's precarious hold upon survival became ever more fragile as the United States sought to tighten the blockade with new legislation, principally the 1992 Torricelli Cuban Democracy Act (which Clinton declared would 'put the hammer to Fidel Castro') and the 1996 Helms–Burton legislation.[62] European governments and Canada complained about these laws, arguing that they violated international norms and usurped countries' legitimate rights to trade with one another. The tide of international opinion was clearly turning against the United States. In 1992, the UN General Assembly vote on the blockade was 88 against to 4 for it; by 1997, it was 143 against to 3 (the US, Israel and Uzbekistan; the latter two both traded with Cuba).[63] The fact that no government collaborated wholeheartedly with US policy did not deter Washington. The objective behind its robust initiatives was crystal clear. It was to destroy what Senator Robert Dole called 'the last communist domino' by imposing increasingly intolerable economic circumstances upon the Cuban people who would respond by overthrowing Castro and his supporters.[64] The fallout from this legislation and particularly the reaction in Cuba and elsewhere to Helms–Burton as well as the political repercussions of Cuba's opening to the market are discussed in Chapter 7. In the next chapter, I consider the evolution of the relationship between the Cuban state and civil society which accompanied the political and economic processes addressed in this chapter.

6
The Cuban State and the Cuban People

In the decades since 1959, whilst Cuba experimented with different forms of economic management and established its role within world affairs, it was also developing a network of political relationships between state and people. Despite the egalitarian instincts of its social philosophy, distinct hierarchies and relationships determined by professional status, economic activity and political identity as well as by gender, ethnicity and sexuality exist in Cuban society. The purpose of this chapter is to offer a commentary on the development of the internal political and social dynamics of the Revolution. I consider how its political evolution has shaped the socialist democracy which the state subscribes to, relations within the political elite and the operation of *poder popular* (popular power). The state has both instigated and attempted to contain critical discourses and has sometimes responded in an authoritarian and intolerant manner to attempts to debate fundamental issues. It has also had to operate in an international environment where the dominant world power is dedicated to its destruction. In these circumstances, the development of a siege mentality within official circles may not be surprising but it has had unfortunate consequences for the quality of intellectual and cultural life and an adverse impact upon the strengthening of socialist *conciencia*.

The nature of political rule

After 1959, the urgent demands of social and economic reconstruction produced what William Leogrande has described 'as a kind of "guerrilla administration" structured much as the war had been waged: unorganised, chaotic, with little formal control'.[1] As Cuba faced external threats and internal rebellions, it was vital to respond rapidly to events, to be able to trust colleagues and to stretch existing skills and resources as far as possible. The debates of the early to mid-1960s indicated that there was little consensus on future state-building and great ambivalence in the relationship between the 26 July Movement and the PSP. The two maintained separate identities demonstrated by the retention of two newspapers, *Revolución* and *Noticias de Hoy*, until 1965 when they fused into *Granma*. It would take a number of years and two purges before unity would be complete. It made political sense to delay instutionalization until these contradictions were resolved.

Leogrande's point about 'little formal control' is, however, misleading. There was, in fact, huge control being exercised, but it came not from the state per se or from the political movements but from a small group of leaders and principally Fidel Castro himself. Here a major feature of post-revolutionary Cuba emerged, one which has continued to both assist and hinder the country's development. Fidel's political experiences before 1959 had imbued him with a profound distrust of Cuban constitutional history and its sorry litany of illegitimacy, inefficacy and corruption. This led him to contend that there was no urgency in either framing a new constitution or in creating elaborate governmental structures. The immediate tasks were to defend Cuba against US aggression and to implement those social programmes which would begin to fulfil the revolutionary commitment to egalitarianism. Fidel believed he could best establish order in Cuba 'through a benevolent authoritarian system, which he felt would subsequently give way to a more democratic state'.[2] This was not to say that the Cuban people's voices would go unheard. One of the fundamental tenets of Cuban socialism in the 1960s was the centrality of activism, the idea that a revolution that would endure could not be the act of a few individuals or of a political movement but of a whole people. A revolution was not a single event but a continuous process which needed to be constantly revitalized by popular participation. This process was made manifest by the staging of mass demonstrations and their re-enactments of the intimate links between Cuban society and its political leaders. The Cuban concept of direct democracy – which was embedded in a long radical tradition linking Rousseau, socialists and anarchists and the Paris Commune of 1871 – incorporated both consultation and approbation, the creation of 'a situation in which all the people are the lawmakers!' There is, however, a fine line of distinction to be drawn between autonomous and controlled participation.[3]

In the formative, largely unstructured early period, people's opinions and needs would be expressed through the mass organizations such as the CTC, the FMC and the ANAP, the Comités de Defensa de la Revolución (the CDRs, the Committees for the Defence of the Revolution), the short-lived People's Courts and the Fuerzas Armadas Revolucionarias (FAR, the Revolutionary Armed Forces) and the Milicias Nacionales Revolucionarias (MNRs, the National Revolutionary Militias which were created in October 1959). Other representative organizations included those of the university and secondary school students and the Unión de Jovenes Comunistas and the Unión de Pioneros de Cuba (the Unions of Young Communists and Pioneers respectively) as well as the Communist Party itself. The overwhelming majority of the population belonged to at least one of these and some had multiple memberships. It was felt that the Cuban people would benefit from being consulted at the formative stages of discussion about policies and by participating in their *implementation*. However, strategic decisions concerning the type of policy to be adopted were to be decided by the political leadership. Participation was not systematic and the people were not hegemonic. Returning to Fidel's role, it could also be said that his paternalism and his need to be intimately involved in all facets of policy making helped create an official culture which was haphazardly but often intensely bureaucratic (as anyone who has ever tried to get either in or out of the island through Cuban immigration will testify) and which inhibited popular empowerment. It can be argued that Cuba had to maintain its vigilance against persistent external aggression but was centralized control the best way to maintain legitimacy? Would not the Revolution have benefited from cultivating a culture of debate and constructive critical support underpinned by popular participation rather than trying to shape and determine public opinion?

Popular participation in politics

The 1960s witnessed an intense politicization of social relations through the structural transformations initiated by the state. Agrarian Reform fundamentally changed social and productive networks in the country-side as well as radically altering the relationship between the rural and urban sectors. The revolutionary messages of egalitarianism and citizen-ship rights were inculcated in schools and universities and broadcast by the media which facilitated 'political orientation and ideological educa-tion' and were further underpinned by participation in the literacy cam-paigns, work brigades (*contingentes*) and mass organizations.[4] *Poder popular* was regarded as both instrumental in that it constituted the building blocks of the new socialist Cuba and normative in that it aimed to consolidate the Revolution's value system. In September 1960, the General Assembly of the Cuban People endorsed the restoration of the 1940 Constitution as well as introducing modifications to it with the enunciation of the First and Second Declarations of Havana. It also established the first concrete expression of *poder popular*. The CDRs represented a collective defence mechanism at the neighbourhood level, the people mobilized against enemies both within and outside Cuba. The *comités* were given responsibility for the protection of public order and safety and the distribution of rationed goods and services as well as acting as liaison between management and workers, for example in the organization of *contingentes*. Following the purge of Escalante's micro-faction in 1962, they were reorganized and their leadership cadres subjected to a process of professional training. Party membership was not a condition for *comité* membership. There were ample opportunities for the emergence of illegal exchange networks in the distribution of jobs and resources involving friends and relatives. It should, however, be stressed that such exchanges took place in very trying economic circumstances as the blockade made itself felt.

A critical feature of the CDRs was their ubiquity and their capacity to act as policing agents as well as trying to impose conformity of thought and behaviour upon neighbourhoods. Another initiative was the Juntas de Coordinación, Ejecución e Inspección (JUCEI, the Councils for Coordination, Implementation and Inspection) which operated between 1961 and 1965 and which aimed to regulate the relationship between central agencies and the mass organizations in an effort to create coherent social and economic policy. They were replaced by *poder local* (local power) whereby delegates listened to voters' complaints, answered questions and reported on the activities of local government. Delegates were unpaid volunteers who attempted to mediate between communities and agencies in terms of social service provision and economic enterprises. However, *poder local* lacked power and resources and was also beset by those centralizing tendencies which were becoming apparent in all areas of public life. Other forms of representative mass organization were also falling foul of this concentration of power; it was clear that the state needed to revitalize its links with Cuban society.

Poder popular

The failure of the 1970 harvest convinced the political leadership of the need for a reappraisal of economic policy and the importance of addressing increasing administrative inefficiency, a fragmented political structure and the fragility of local democracy. There are conflicting views on whether the outcome was greater centralization or a reinvigoration of local democracy under the auspices of *poder popular*. For Carollee Bengelsdorf, the result was 'the verticalization of political power, the isolation of decision-makers at the center and the people beyond the structured periphery'.[5] Whilst admitting that the political system required further democratization of its power structures, a contrasting opinion was put forward by Juan Antonio Blanco: 'We consider our party democracy to be supported by a structure of power that is equally democratic as and much more desirable and satisfactory than a "market democracy" in which the political–legal system is based on a polarized structure of economic and financial power.'[6] *Poder popular* was seen as the key to this vision of socialist democracy as well as ensuring more efficient management of the productive sectors by taking account of local inputs, needs and problems. It operated at the municipal, provincial and national levels with each level being represented by delegates to respective assemblies.

Although the procedures for nominating delegates were supposed to be guided by the party, in reality there was a considerable degree of popular involvement in the process. In order to facilitate the operation of *poder popular* and to create linkages between the grass roots and national agencies, Cuba was divided into 58 regions and 407 municipalities (the *comités* and the trade unions were used as coordinating networks for the new mechanism and were reinvigorated as a result). The first experiment took place in Matanzas province in 1974 when direct, competitive elections were held for municipal assembly delegates whilst those serving in the provincial and national assemblies were elected by the lower municipal ones. Thus there was less popular participation and control the higher one went up the structure. Delegates were not allowed to campaign, although voters had access to information about their backgrounds and activities in public service. They were obliged to meet periodically with electors and were subject to immediate recall. However, their efficacy was impeded by the fact that they were volunteers and often did not have the time or knowledge to find their way through the bureaucracy; the consequence was that they could lose their credibility and their constituents' trust. The Matanzas model became the prototype for the national scheme.

The Communist Party and people's power

The formal institutionalization of the Revolution began at the First Congress of the Communist Party of Cuba, which took place in

December 1975, and was consolidated by the promulgation of a new Constitution in the following year. All Cubans were given the right to work free of exploitation and peasants were granted access to land. Adults and children were given access to free health, education, culture and leisure. Universal accident and sickness insurance, maternity leave and job protection, equal pay for equal work, racial equality and the right to join trade unions were guaranteed. A Family Code was introduced at the same time. The Constitution granted the PCC unconditional power over state institutions, the mass organizations and the organs of popular democracy. The party was accorded this dominant status because of its exceptional role during the revolutionary struggle and in line with Martí's belief in a single revolutionary party. Although power was concentrated in the party with Fidel at its head, attempts were made to depersonalize and decentralize decision-making outside of the leadership circle.

The new Constitution created five major governmental bodies: the National Assembly (the supreme organ of state power), the State Council, the Council of Ministers, the People's Supreme Court and the Comptroller's Office. The Council of Ministers provided the administrative and bureaucratic elements of government whilst *poder popular* was accorded a legislative and legitimizing role. This arrangement was officially presented as 'the institutionalised participation of the masses in state administration in general rather than just in the election of their representatives'.[7] Despite the rhetoric, this has never been an equal relationship. Although Castro maintained that 'the party doesn't administer the state', in practice local government officials looked to 'the local PCC committee as a strong source for help in resolving local problems, increasing local autonomy, and cutting through bureaucratic bottlenecks'.[8] Although it appears that there has been little party manipulation with respect to the election of delegates and although relations between party and assemblies have generally been positive and codependent, it is, nevertheless, a politically skewed relationship with the party having the potential to assume a paternalistic role. In contrast to capitalist political institutions, all productive and service organizations were supposed to be managed by and answerable to the assemblies, but in practice the central government retained control over all national economic activities as well as defence, foreign policy, trade and monetary policies. It also set norms and regulations for wages, production standards, health and sanitation. The cumulative effect was that the executive arm dominated the legislative element of the state, reducing the National Assembly to a largely deliberative body. Castro's location at the apex of power was manifest in a number of ways. As president of the State Council, he presided over the Council of Ministers; he had the power to intervene in any aspect of state policy no matter how minute and he was given the right to monitor the performance of *poder popular*. This enormous concentration of power has been inhibiting to the exercise of people's power and poses the perennially interesting question of what will happen when Fidel is no more.

Problems of participation and control

The parallel processes of experimentation and institution-building in the 1970s aimed to create 'a constantly mandated system of national and local governance, widening the scope of participation in the allocation and use of goods and services'.[9] The rights and obligations of Cubans were identified as being realized within a complex participatory framework which pervaded daily life and was responsible for complicating individual and family dynamics. Added to these commitments was the frustration caused by the inadequacies of that daily existence. Thus, the SDPE's programme of decentralization was only realized in part and ordinary Cubans' participation in decision-making through workers' councils and assemblies was often more formal than real. Given that one of the roles of these councils was to allocate scarce resources, it is not surprising that this caused dissatisfaction. Similarly, participation in the mass organizations and voluntary associations such as school councils, youth clubs, cultural and recreational groups could lead to feelings of overload. The responsibility of being active and conscious citizens was overwhelming for many Cubans. The problem with such intense participation, Hernández and Dilla have argued, is that it has not always been connected to the exercise of real power: '[t]o participate is not simply to have access to multiple areas of discussion but to contribute to decision making in these areas. Participation in discussion and execution is relatively high; in political decisions and their control it is considerably less.' Although admitting that this situation was far from ideal, they explained it by arguing that in Cuba 'centralization of a number of important aspects of policy-making seems to be a necessity'. Presumably by this, they were alluding to the needs of national security but it seems a weak defence.[10] Martínez Heredia maintains that participation has been flawed because 'the tendency has been to wait for guidance from above'.[11]

Another source of dissatisfaction was that party members enjoyed certain material privileges although they 'did not enjoy the same institutionalised prerogatives that their Eastern European comrades did, if for no other reason than fewer opportunities'.[12] This does not detract from the ethos of incorruptibility which has generally permeated public life (in marked contrast with political elites in other Third World countries). More dangerous than the existence of opportunities for personal enrichment was the entrenched position of the governing elite which made it difficult for new generations of political leaders to emerge. For Liss, 'Castro stresses that professionals should help prepare and scrutinize governmental programs but leave the decisions to the leadership. In other words, he has not encouraged middle-level professionals to question the leadership's decisions.'[13] This practice began to change from the mid-1980s as greater use was made of small teams of troubleshooters and experts and more emphasis was placed upon the professional training of party officials. The Old Guard's monopoly was being challenged but it was a slow and piecemeal process and Fidel's own role was not questioned.

The need for political renewal

The decision to embark upon Rectification and the Special Period was motivated not just by serious concerns about Cuba's economic survival but also by recognition of the need for political renewal and a revival in popular participation. The much vaunted return to the spirit of the heroic 1960s was epitomized by the re-emergence of *contingentes* which were particularly active in the construction sector where they initiated building projects and then saw them through to their completion. This was in marked contrast with the practice under the SDPE when such projects were often abandoned through poor management and bottlenecks in supplies. *Poder popular* was perceived as a strong weapon in the war against excessive bureaucracy and as a means of democratizing the state apparatus, as well as encouraging both greater productivity and stronger ties between state and citizens. Activism must replace inertia in line with Che's belief that the problem was 'a lack of revolutionary consciousness or, at any rate, an acquiescence in things that are wrong'.[14] Critics have contended that the Cuban government was using this utopian appeal to mask the reality of a situation where there had been no diminution of the concentration of power at the centre, no opposition parties allowed and where, according to Michael Lowy, 'the masses do not yet have the power of *decision* between alternative economic or political policies'.[15]

The Revolution's justification of the absence of oppositional or critical presences within the political system has always been the threat of subversion. However, real as that fear has been, it has led the Cuban leadership to ignore the intrinsic value of the opinions of groups within civil society. The latter 'operated with a modicum of administrative and cultural autonomy – least during periods of political and economic crisis, and most during periods of major policy transition'.[16] The state adopted a policy of intermittent policing and censorship interspersed with periods of tolerance. Dissidents were harassed and arrested whilst cultural and intellectual debates were subject to arbitrary intervention which sometimes had distinctly Stalinist overtones. This was an incoherent and inherently counterproductive approach. It appeared that the state was not willing to trust the intelligence and critical judgement of the Cuban people. A clear distinction should have been made between the views of groups who wished to undermine the Revolution and those wishing to enter into dialogue about how it could be improved. Lowy's argument, which seems sensible to this author, is that 'the free organization of all political parties that respect revolutionary legality would not be a concession to the bourgeoisie, but rather the condition for the existence of ... a real confrontation of points of view and the possibility of a real decision by workers on matters essential to the country's economic, social, and political life'.[17] If the Revolution was strong enough then it should welcome, not suppress, debate. This tolerance should not, of course, be extended to major opponents of the Cuban system who have endorsed counter-revolutionary activity and have held extremely recidivist views on how Cuba should be governed.

Political reform

The government's admission that fundamental political changes were necessary was made public at the Third Congress of the PCC held in 1986. Fidel stated that the political elite needed to be democratized and called for the increased representation of Afro-Cubans, women and young people at the highest levels of decision-making. The Central Committee which emerged during the Fourth Congress held in October 1991 was certainly more representative of ordinary citizens, the under-fifties and the provinces whilst by 1993, the profile of the provincial and national assemblies reflected the same trend. However, membership was still skewed to a lighter skinned, male and older constituency. The 1991 Congress was also the first to be open to religious believers. The progressive retirement and demotion of old revolutionary veterans were accompanied, in January 1995, by a major Cabinet reshuffle which oversaw the intake of younger, more reform-minded politicians. A major shock had been administered to the Cuban leadership in December 1992 when one-third of the electorate abstained or delivered spoilt ballot papers during municipal elections. There was intense speculation as to whether this was an anti-government protest or merely the result of privation and frustration. Fidel certainly took it very seriously and campaigned vigorously for the second round of provincial and National Assembly elections held in February 1993. The result was an 88.5 per cent vote in favour of the government's policies. Whether this 'yes' vote should be seen as one of substance or merely routine is a matter of debate. What was clear was that the state had decided to implement structural reforms which affected all levels of government. These included provision for the direct election of half of all National Assembly delegates from February 1993 (the other half were still appointed following recommendations from the mass organizations).

The National Assembly continues to review, modify and approve legislation but still does not initiate it. Debates are designed to pursue consensus rather than stimulate real argument, and proceedings are still dominated by leading politicians and pre-eminently by Castro himself. Meeting every two years, the bulk of its work is done in permanent commissions and plenary sessions. It is clear that the role of the Assembly needs to be strengthened so that it really is the central organ of power. At the municipal level, elections remain non-competitive with the ostensible aim being that this prevents political infighting and allows for the participation of ordinary citizens. However, the fact that these are contests between personalities rather than about different policy alternatives tends to preclude criticism of government policy. Municipal delegates have continued to be subject to work overload and burnout with the result that important matters are often resolved by the assembly leadership. In 1999, the National Assembly Vice-President Ernesto Suarez criticized delegates for failing to reach their potential but this is hardly surprising given their circumstances.

Another 1992 innovation was that the municipal assembly executive council was replaced by an administrative council with responsibilities for coordinating its work between sessions; its activities were to be monitored by the *consejos populares* (popular councils). These were originally set up in 1988 and are composed of local elected officials, local representatives of the mass organizations and local enterprise managers. Their remit has expanded into administrative decisions regarding the coordination of productive activities; control of scarce foodstuffs and the promotion of food self-sufficiency through crops grown on vacant city lots (*huertos*); the regulation of the burgeoning private sector (including *paladares* (small private restaurants), the agricultural markets and the self-employed); the maintenance of price controls and health standards and efforts to curb crime. Increasingly supported by religious organizations and foreign NGOs, the *consejos* have evinced a great capacity for both cutting through red tape and for strengthening *poder popular*. Kapcia believes that they have 'restored some vital legitimacy to the ethos of participation, and are very likely to become a core of the evolving political system'.[18] Another innovation has been the *parlamentos obreros* (workers' parliaments) which monitor economic policies and have contributed to some restoration of the credibility of the trade unions. Similarly, the role of the *comités* has begun to change from surveillance to the collection and dissemination of information on basic issues. These are all positive changes, but much more needs to be done before popular control is firmly entrenched at the heart of the Cuban political system.

Cuban civil society

Since the late 1980s, Cuban society has undergone huge changes, one of which has been 'the decline in the state's previously unchallenged capacity to control the distribution of resources, social and political discourse and ideological production'.[19] However, long before the Revolution entered its most difficult times, it had had to contend with a number of interest groups within society, some of whom had high expectations of it (women and Afro-Cubans) and others (such as homosexual and religious communities) who feared its reactions to them. I now consider the post-revolutionary experience of these and other constituencies (such as intellectuals and sportspeople) in terms of their involvement in social and political discourse and their relationship to the Cuban state.

Cuban women – empowerment or second-class citizenship?

In August 1960, the new revolutionary state created the FMC to act as the official representative body of Cuban women. The FMC, with Vilma Espín at its head, took the orthodox Marxist view that women's emancipation would be achieved with the transformation of the relations of production and by ensuring that women entered the labour market. Its aim of promoting women's empowerment was always situated within the context of securing female loyalty to the Revolution by encouraging women to study Cuban history and political ideology and to participate in voluntary labour brigades and other mass organizations. In its depiction of femininity, it also reproduced stereotypes concerning women's nature and abilities. Tens of thousands of women and girls took part in the 1961 literacy campaign in a historically unprecedented public demonstration of female activism. However, the revolutionary state's conservative moral stance compelled Fidel to promise parents and husbands that daughters and wives would remain virtuous and be more closely supervised than their male colleagues. Whilst the government publicly and appropriately committed itself to eradicating prostitution and was highly effective in its efforts, its approach towards these women was significant. Retrained as hairdressers, typists and dressmakers, ex-prostitutes received lessons in how to dress properly (presumably demurely) and how to do their hair! The Ana Betancourt Schools for Peasant Women brought tens of thousands of women from the countryside to Havana's National Hotel for training in the practical skills of homemaking and childcare as well as lessons in health and nutrition. In 1961, the FMC oversaw the introduction of a network of day care centres (*círculos infantiles*). However, a serious shortfall in their provision meant that by 1980, only 8 per cent of children under six were attending a centre, with working mothers relying instead upon relatives and informal networks.[20] Another campaign was the Militant Mothers for Education programme which was introduced in 1970; mothers mounted patrols against vandalism, kept schools clean and pursued truants. By 1985 there were 1.7 million militant mothers organized in 12,000 brigades.[21]

Health, education and work

After 1959, Cuban women benefited from the expansion and democratization of the health service as well as being significant participants in its creation. There was an enormous growth in the numbers of female voluntary health workers, doctors and nurses. As medicine was regarded as a highly prestigious occupation, women's status rose accordingly. However, there have been areas of women's experience which the health service has been reluctant to engage with. Thus the government resisted the legalization of abortion until 1980, with the result that the number of illegal operations spiralled with concomitant health risks for the women involved. With considerable ignorance about contraception, there was also a high rate in teenage pregnancies. The authorities did not accept the existence of either domestic violence or rape until the 1990s and women who contracted sexually transmitted diseases were more stigmatized than men with similar conditions. This double standard became increasingly pertinent as prostitution grew with the boom in tourism in the 1990s.

The education sector grew rapidly after 1959 and women took full advantage of the opportunities offered them to train as teachers as well as pursuing academic careers. However, as the state of the economy deteriorated in the late 1980s, women graduates were increasingly frustrated by the lack of suitable jobs. By the early 1990s, women constituted nearly 40 per cent of the labour force but had to balance paid work with family responsibilities and participation in the mass organizations.[22] Whilst the 1975 Family Code insisted upon equality within the home and the sharing of housework and childcare, many men resented being asked to perform intrinsically 'feminine' tasks and women continued to bear the brunt of these activities. Many women resisted joining the workforce or left it because of the strains placed on them. The scarcity of consumer goods and periods of rationing similarly undermined the incentive to work for many women. Working women had to contend with male hierarchies in the workplace and resistance to women being employed in other than what was regarded as 'women's work'. Thus women would typically be employed in the service sector rather than in construction or biotechnology, although these stereotypes have faded over time.

The government was proactive in introducing regulations aimed at assisting women. The new maternity law of January 1974 gave them generous paid leave and expanded day-care facilities and they were later awarded improved pension rights. However, the state only tended to regard women's employment as a priority when the economy required it (during the expansionist 1970s, for example) but was willing to place it lower on its agenda in times of economic difficulty. By 1980, Fidel was warning that further increases in female employment might not be possible. As managers complained that employing women was counterproductive (because of the protective legislation and childcare obligations), the CTC often failed to effectively safeguard the rights of its female members until it was pressed to do so by the FMC. Amidst intensifying economic difficulties, younger women particularly felt aggrieved about the lack of good job prospects and an equitable working environment. During the Special Period, many women workers were forced to move from the waged economy to the voluntary sector (with many involved in organic food production) and to the domestic environment where the scarcity of resources and basic foodstuffs was felt most intensely.

The problem with state control

Cuban women experienced wide-ranging improvements in their living conditions and expectations. Qualitative changes occurred in individual lives despite the socio-economic problems inherited by the

Revolution and the hostile environment in which it existed. The organization of Cuban women and the representation of their interests were remarkable at a time when women's movements throughout Latin America remained weak. However, the considerable progress made came at the price of the loss of women's independence vis-à-vis the state. Bunck has contrasted the Cuban experience with that of women in the United States where feminism became a strong political force in the 1960s and 1970s (although one which provoked an even stronger backlash). In Cuba, emancipation 'originated from official objectives rather than from the aspirations of women outside of government' and Susan Kaufman Purcell has agreed, stating that 'the impetus for the modernization of Cuban women comes from above. ... Cuban women are to be made equal by governmental direction and means.'[23] With a mainly male government and in a culture still infused by machismo and the lingering legacy of the iconography of 'the heroic revolutionary', the formulation of women's rights and needs, their role within society and the nature of their relations with men and their own sexuality were very much the product of a masculine sensibility.[24] Tomás Gutiérrez Alea's 1985 film, *Hasta Cierto Punto* (*Up to a Certain Point*), highlighted the machismo which continued to prevail among the members of Cuba's artistic and intellectual elite. Focusing upon the contradiction between the revolutionary commitment to female emancipation and the persistence of macho attitudes among those who could be expected to know better, the film argues that ideological correctness often does not translate into real life and that an intellectual or a politician may harbour just as much chauvinism as a factory worker.

The FMC played an important part in contributing to the official construction of femininity as the same time as it obstructed the development of an autonomous feminist discourse. As no organizational form existed which could offer alternative ideas, the state was in a position to decide 'what was and was not necessary and appropriate concerning women's rights and needs'.[25] Over the decades, the FMC became one of the largest women's organizations in Latin America, but its commitment to women has been a fractured one in that it has generally placed the interests of the state first. Like other government organizations, it is organized at the national, provincial, regional, municipal and neighbourhood levels but policy is determined at the top. Very few women have achieved positions of seniority in the party, *poder popular*, the government bureaucracy or the mass organizations and, as is the case in other areas of policy initiative, the promotion of women-friendly policies has been dependent upon Fidel's somewhat inconsistent endorsement. Thus at the FMC's 1990 Congress, he stated that 'irrelevant women's issues' such as job opportunities and equal pay would be 'postponed because of other issues of pressing national concern'.[26] However, shortly afterwards he acknowledged the minority status of women within the PCC and the new 1992 Constitution stated unequivocally that women and men now had equal rights in 'the economic, political, cultural and social realm and in the family'.[27]

The failure to eliminate patriarchy

As in other revolutionary states, the existence of a double standard of morality can be detected in Cuban life and in the policies promoted by the government. Whilst men have historically been seen as needing to seek sexual satisfaction outside the family environment, women were expected to keep families together and were regarded as promiscuous if they imitated male behaviour. The socialist state defined the family as vital to socio-economic development and much of its legislative programme has changed power relations within it through the increase in female education, employment and reproductive rights (although it must be said that many women resist entering the labour force because of the strain of ensuring the family's survival in times of economic privation). Families have also been subject to pressures due to overcrowded housing, the demands of work brigades, involvement in mass organizations and foreign service. The 1976 Family Code introduced no-fault divorce which over time produced a complex web of family relationships and living arrangements, including a high incidence of youthful marriages, teenage delinquency and single women-headed households. Such networks were able to offer support during difficult times when state provision of goods and services deteriorated. Clearly there are serious social issues which deserve attention but there are positive outcomes. The state's commitment to health and education and other aspects of development have contributed immensely to the well-being of Cuban society, but it has been less successful in changing attitudes concerning gender relations. It underestimated how long it would take to transform stereotypical behaviour and it also failed to resolve how women could balance the demands of domestic work and childcare alongside paid employment. Work outside the home is not empowering unless women receive fair remuneration and parity of treatment and are not expected to assume sole responsibility for home duties.

Afro-Cubans and the Revolution

In two speeches given in March 1959, Fidel identified racism as the worst prejudice Cubans suffered from and called for a public debate to plan for its elimination. The new government espoused Martí's conception of a colour-blind Cuba. This view was encapsulated by Che's remarks after receiving an honorary doctorate at Las Villas. When asked what the role of the university should be in revolutionary Cuba, he responded '... it should paint itself black, it should paint itself mulatto, not only its students but also its professors'.[28] As suggested previously, the danger with this approach was that everyday racism would be masked by official proclamations that it had been eradicated. Additionally, the government's emphasis upon changing behaviour through moral invocations assumed that Afro-Cubans would wait patiently for this new sensibility to emerge. In his highly critical work on the post-revolutionary experience of Afro-Cubans, Carlos Moore contended that the Revolution made inroads into tackling racism in the educational, employment and leisure spheres of life but was far less successful in dealing with it in political and cultural terms. He also drew attention to the government's attacks upon the black middle class which included closing the *Sociedades de color* as part of its 'determination to destroy all autonomous bases for dissent or protest ...'.[29]

There was considerable opposition to the concept of racial integration from both the Cuban middle and working classes, and official attempts to integrate public spaces such as beaches and parks met with resistance. Fearful of damaging national unity at a time of great international tension, the government adopted a more conciliatory approach which targeted education and the growth of socialist consciousness. Initially progress was rapid as the state intervened to lift the racial barriers in employment (although it refrained from forcing employers to hire black workers) and desegregating access to health, education and housing (thus, the largely black shanty town and slum inhabitants were relocated to new estates on the outskirts of major cities such as the vast suburb of Alamar, east of Havana). The participation of Afro-Cubans in the *milicias*, *contigentes* and *comités* was encouraged and they were regarded as one of the government's most loyal constituencies. Cuba's racial revolution and also the prominence of Afro-Cubans around the Cuban leader, particularly Juan Almeida Bosque, head of the Cuban army, were hailed by the black press in the United States, and African-American activists, including the maverick Congressman Adam Clayton Powell, journeyed to Havana. However, the NAACP and other civil rights groups drew back following Fidel's

1961 'Soy Marxista Leninista' speech, terrified that they would be tarred with the brush of communism. Advocates of Black Power felt no such reservations. Robert Williams, the dissident NAACP activist who proposed armed resistance to white supremacy, visited Cuba twice before seeking refuge there in autumn 1961 after an armed showdown with the Klu Klux Klan.[30]

The early advances in the empowerment of both black Cubans and Cuban women were impressive but did not justify the Second Declaration of Havana's 1962 claim that the state had eliminated discrimination. Both Moore and Alejandro de la Fuente have argued that what happened subsequently was an official silence on racism until the late 1980s. Whilst recognizing the deficiencies of policies against gender and racial discrimination, it remains true that the government's redistributive policies did much to remedy those socio-economic and political inequalities associated with them. By the early 1980s, Cuban blacks and mulattos (who, according to the 1981 census, constituted roughly one-third of the total population) generally enjoyed similar access to social goods and services, and cultural taboos such as that against interracial marriages had started to disappear. However, Afro-Cubans still tended to cluster in poor tenement housing and were profoundly underrepresented in positions of political and economic power. The black press operated under strict state control and discriminatory practices were perpetuated in diverse social relations. The ambivalent nature of the Revolution's perspective upon racism became increasingly evident as the Special Period eroded the state's capacity to deliver social services and income differentials grew. Afro-Cubans did not receive remittances from abroad (because of the predominantly white nature of the diaspora although this changed after 1980) and so had scant access to dollars, were not employed by foreign firms involved in joint partnership deals with the state and were largely absent from the tourist sector. The latter exclusion was posited upon the assumption that visitors did not wish to see black faces which is highly ironic given that the iconography of Cuba presented to the potential visitor is suffused with tropes of its African roots.

Being gay in Cuba

During the last half of the nineteenth century as modern Cuban society began to emerge, homosexuality was regarded as a threat to both nationalist aspirations and to the centrality of the family in national life. An important element of 'Cuba's traditional sexual culture was the perception that in sex there must be an active and a passive partner, and the active role of power and domination was reserved for males'.[31] This perception shaped the very aggressive views towards homosexuality exhibited in the early decades of the Revolution. Male homosexuals who chose the 'feminine' role in a relationship were not real men and therefore invited ridicule and opprobrium. In addition, being a homosexual was equated with being counter-revolutionary. The heroes of the Sierra Maestra were resolutely macho as was the language of the Revolution. Fidel had told Lee Lockwood in 1965 that 'we would never come to believe that a homosexual could embody the conditions and requirements of conduct that would enable us to consider him a true Revolutionary ...'.[32] It is not surprising that given its belief in its ability to transform human nature that the new state should seek to regulate sexuality. The worst excesses of persecution in the mid-1960s saw gay men sent to highly regimented work camps, known as the Unidades de Ayuda a la Producción (Production Support Units), whose motto was 'Work Will Make You Men'. All of the camps were situated in Camagüey province which needed cheap labour, and other groups including the religious and young delinquents were sent to them until their closure in 1968.

Harassment continued through the 1970s and 1980s (for example, homosexuals were banned from teaching and there were periodic purges in the arts and in universities) but was gradually mediated by acts of legalization (far sooner, it must be said, than in many states of the North) and a strategy which stressed regulation rather than incarceration. Homosexuality was decriminalized in 1979 although until the 1987 revision of the Penal Code, no public displays of what was termed 'antisocial conduct' were allowed. The Cuban government reacted vigorously to the Aids threat, but it designated victims as members of high-risk groups such as homosexuals and those Cubans who slept with tourists, thus implying that their fate had been caused by their lifestyle. Its decision to quarantine HIV-positive patients to special sanatoriums generated foreign criticism, although there was considerable public support for the decision demonstrating deep-seated prejudice against gays. The regime within these special units has improved in recent years and Cuba's holistic approach to the treatment of Aids has been widely praised.

Émigré writers and film-makers commented upon the treatment of Cuban gays, linking it to issues of authoritarianism and human rights. Néstor Almendros's 1984 documentary, *Mauvaise Conduite* (*Improper Conduct*) on which he collaborated with the novelist and poet Reinaldo Arenas was castigated by its detractors for concealing a political attack on the Revolution within a plea for gay freedom.[33] The enormous success of the film *Fresa y Chocolate* in 1993 hopefully represented a move to greater tolerance and a willingness to debate the position of gays within Cuban society. Although its sexual politics seem dated and it did not attempt to explore the history of homosexuality in Cuba, its directors' pleas for tolerance and respect for difference had a significant impact as did *Fresa*'s discussion of censorship, the black market, freedom of artistic expression and the compulsion to conformity. Gays and lesbians enjoy greater freedoms and there is generally a more liberal approach towards private behaviour but their public presence within Cuban society remains contested.[34]

State and religion

Before 1959, the Catholic Church did not enjoy the central place it has traditionally enjoyed in Latin American societies. Closely identified with the Batista regime, it catered to a privileged social base and had little impact upon the lives of most Cubans. After the Revolution, the Catholic bishops condemned the property reforms, the execution of supporters of the old regime and the embrace of communism. The government responded by persecuting individual clergy, obstructing religious services and, for a short time in the 1960s, priests were sent to re-education camps. During May 1961, private Catholic schools were nationalized and whilst churches were allowed to remain open, foreign priests were expelled. Most Cuban priests and nuns also left, with many becoming involved in émigré conspiracies (including the participation of three priests and a pastor in the Bay of Pigs). After this initial confrontation, the official attitude towards organized religions relaxed and the churches enjoyed a breathing space. The Catholic Church gradually moved to a cautious position which was not anti-government and which was critical of the blockade, whilst the smaller Protestant denominations (except the Baptists who had strong links with the conservative US Southern Baptist Convention) entered into an increasingly cooperative relationship with the authorities. The Cuban state codified its attitude towards organized religion in Article 54 of the 1976 Constitution which, whilst guaranteeing the right to freedom of conscience, stated 'it is illegal and punishable by law to oppose one's faith or religious belief to the Revolution'.[35] There was no systematic repression but, rather, an effort to control religious activity.

The state began to move towards an accommodation with religion in the 1970s and 1980s. In 1980, the Catholic hierarchy called upon congregations not to leave Cuba during the Mariel exodus and in 1984, Fidel attended a televised church service during the Reverend Jesse Jackson's visit in a highly symbolic gesture. US and Cuban bishops visited each others' dioceses and Castro met with them and with leaders of the Protestant community.[36] In 1986, the Catholic Church was allowed to hold the first Encuentro Nacional Ecclesial Cubano (the National Meeting of the Cuban Church), during which it admitted mistakes in its past approach towards the Revolution. Membership in the Cuban churches was growing as that of the PCC declined, which might explain the decision to permit Catholics to join the party in 1991. In 1992 Fidel proclaimed Cuba a lay rather than an atheist state and in 1995, 11 Cuban bishops called for the beginning of a 'fraternal dialogue and reconciliation' with the government. By 1997, Cardinal Jaime Ortega, the archbishop of Havana, was talking of a 'new understanding'.[37]

Throughout the 1990s, Castro and the Pope pursued similar agendas such as denouncing the industrialized countries for failing to address Third World poverty and hunger and calling for a resolution of the debt, and when they met at the Vatican in 1996, John Paul II condemned Helms–Burton. When he finally visited Cuba in January 1998, many political analysts and Washington officials hoped that the Pope would inveigh against Castro's government. Whilst denouncing its human rights record, he also condemned the blockade and called upon the world to 'open itself to Cuba'.[38] His hardly veiled criticism of the US clearly delighted Fidel. The Clinton administration responded by restoring the daily charter flight from Miami to Havana and allowing Catholic relief organizations such as CARITAS to send food and medical supplies to the island.[39] The activities of the North American Pastors for Peace which included sending blockade-breaking shipments of food and medicine were acknowledged by Castro during his subsequent meetings with Methodist bishops. The Catholic Church is the only Cuban NGO with a national presence, with dozens of lay groups and a number of publications, and it has not been afraid to confront the government on economic policy and human rights. Commentators have argued that the Cuban state's dialogue with religion was a self-serving move to diffuse dissent during the period of economic crisis but it may also be seen as further evidence of its growing tolerance of civil society.

Revolutionary culture

In the 1960s, Guevara's utopian call for the creation of the New Man exercised a compelling attraction for intellectuals and artists throughout the world. The existence of the Cuban Revolution was seen as a direct challenge not just to Western capitalism and imperialism but also to the sterility and repression of creativity associated with Soviet authoritarianism. It was regarded by many as a revolution of the imagination as much as an attempt to construct a new social order. When the young LeRoi Jones (later Amiri Baraka, the African-American writer and cultural nationalist) visited Cuba in 1960, he described the trip as awakening him to the revolutionary potential of the Third World: 'The idea of a "revolution" had been foreign to me' he wrote, but seeing Fidel speak to mass crowds and travelling through the island convinced him that it was possible.[40]

Foreign intellectuals welcome the Revolution

As its economic and political isolation deepened, Cuba reached out to intellectuals as a means of communicating with the world and particularly its neighbours: 'Havana made a conscious attempt to become the cultural centre of Latin America, and thereby provided a much-needed site of exchange for writers and artists who had previously worked in considerable isolation, with little contact across national borders.'[41] Intellectuals and artists were accorded an important symbolic role in revolutionary sensibility. Thus early in 1959, Fidel met Pablo Neruda in Caracas and discussed the possibility of a press agency to cover the whole of Latin America; this would later become Prensa Latina. Alejo Carpentier was appointed vice-president of the National Council of Culture in 1959 and in 1962 head of the state publishing house. Intellectuals, academics and artists participated in congresses, symposia and study tours; many visitors found their trips enlivened by personal contact with Fidel, often in the middle of the night! Many returned home to write accounts of their exhilarating experiences. In *Listen Yankee*, C. Wright Mills used the conceit of a series of letters written by a Cuban to extol the virtues of the Revolution to an American audience; Jean Paul Sartre and Simone de Beauvoir produced volumes with a similar purpose.[42] Others organized in an effort to challenge the blockade. Thus, in spring 1960, the Fair Play for Cuba Committee counted Maya Angelou, James Baldwin, Norman Mailer and Truman Capote amongst its distinguished membership.

The high point of this flurry of activity and exchange was the Cultural Congress held in Havana in January 1968. Amongst a number of accounts is that given by Andrew Salkey, the Jamaican novelist, who attended along with other European and Third World intellectuals such as C. L. R. James, author of the seminal history of the Haitian

Revolution, *The Black Jacobins*, and the English Marxist historian Eric Hobsbawm. In his *Havana Journal*, Salkey describes intense debates concerning the relationship between intellectuals and revolutionary politics.[43] Affirmation of the revolutionary experience was expected of fellow travellers. For the Colombian writer Gabriel García Márquez (who would become a close friend of Fidel): 'The definition of a Latin American *intelectual de izquierda* became the unconditional defense of Cuba.'[44] The absence of a critical approach towards unfolding events in Cuba was common to political activists, intellectuals and academics, but over time, dissident voices were heard and solidarity with the Revolution became fragmented. Decisive political events, such as the Soviet invasion of Czechoslovakia, together with the issue of artistic freedom, were integral to this unravelling. Foreign intellectuals continued to monitor Cuban politics throughout the 1970s and 1980s, paying special attention to censorship and the condition of political prisoners through the networks of organizations such as Amnesty, PEN and Americas Watch. In the 1990s they would mount campaigns on behalf of dissident members of the Unión de Escritores e Artistas de Cuba (UNEAC, the National Union of Cuban Writers and Artists) itself as they called for a relaxation of state control. Émigré artists such as the poet Armando Valladares assumed high-profile roles in UN delegations exploring human rights in Cuba.

The dilemmas of being a Cuban intellectual

After 1959, Cuban intellectuals and members of the artistic community found themselves in a complicated position. Previously marginalized by the state, they were now called upon to participate in its educational and cultural programmes. What was not clear was what else the Revolution expected of them and whether they were able to satisfy its demands. The rapid radicalization of the revolutionary process, the polarization of class and political loyalties as emigration began and the siege mentality of the new leadership contributed to confusion amongst many intellectuals. As Kapcia has put it, the intellectual elite was not a political elite and its revolutionary commitment 'although enthusiastic and effusive, lacked coherence'. This dilemma was succinctly outlined in Gutiérrez Alea's 1968 film, *Memorias de subdesarrollo* (*Memories of Underdevelopment*).[45] It was a predicament which would lead Che to state: 'The guilt of many of our intellectuals and artists resides in their original sin; they are not authentic revolutionaries' which was not particularly helpful if you were an intellectual unsure of your footing in these new circumstances.[46]

Cultural policy was unclear in the 1960s. Whilst the newspaper *Revolución* and its supplement *Lunes de Revolución* advocated diversity of expression, the PSP argued for conformity and revolutionary leaders exhibited conservative attitudes towards morality and the representation of sexuality. An early controversy came with the release of the film short, *P.M.*, directed by Orlando Jiménez Leal and Sabá Cabera, in 1960. When the Instituto Cubano del Arte e Industria (ICAIC, the Cuban Institute of Film Art and Industry) confiscated the print, condemning its depiction of Cubans drinking in night-time Havana (one of the first revolutionary acts had been to clean up the capital's bars in an attempt to erase its lurid past), *Lunes* protested and collected a petition with the signatures of 200 prominent writers, artists and film-makers. At meetings held in the National Library, communist politicians accused *Lunes* of fostering division and undermining the Revolution as well as propagating bourgeois values which were linked to Western decadence. The National Library sessions culminated in Fidel's seminal 'Words to the Intellectuals' speech in June 1961 which included the famous dictum 'Within the Revolution, everything, against the Revolution nothing.' Fidel differentiated between those intellectuals who were committed revolutionaries, those who were unwilling to make such a commitment and those who were counter-revolutionaries. The inference was that the waverers were vulnerable to manipulation by those who wished to destroy the Revolution. The consequence of these debates was that *P.M.* was blacklisted, *Lunes* was closed and its editors (including the novelist Guillermo Cabrera Infante) subsequently went into exile. An important and dangerous precedent had been set by overreaction to an innocuous short film.

With the foundation in August 1961 of the UNEAC and the appointment of Nicolás Guillén as its director, the state began to construct the boundaries within which artistic and intellectual activity must take place. By 1969, Guillén was arguing that 'Cuban writers and artists have the same responsibilities as our soldiers with respect to the defence of the nation. ... He who does not [fulfil his duty] ... will receive the most severe revolutionary punishment. ...'[47] UNEAC presided over an increasingly polarized and vitriolic discourse concerning the rights and obligations of artists. There were several flashpoints centred around Heberto Padilla. In 1968, he won the Casa de las América's award for *Fuera del juego* (*Out of the Game*) but was then branded a counter-revolutionary and most copies of the volume were withdrawn. He also complained that Cabrera Infante's acclaimed novel *Tres Tristes Tigres* (*Three Sad Tigers*) had not yet been published in the country of its author's birth whilst mediocre works which toed the party line were. Infante responded warmly to Padilla's words, sympathizing with the problems that he was facing as a poet who had remained in Cuba. The editors of *Juventud Rebelde – El Caimán*, who had published Cabrera Infante's letter, were compelled to resign whilst Padilla and Infante were accused of having links to the Escalante microfaction and, in Padilla's case, to dissident Czech intellectuals (which inferred that he favoured both Stalinist and Velvet Revolution approaches!). Forced to recant, Padilla wrote an open letter to Cabrera Infante in which he claimed that he enjoyed total artistic freedom in Cuba. This was not the end of the affair, however, as Padilla was arrested in March 1971. Released a month later, he made a further public recantation at a UNEAC meeting. There was considerable international criticism of the Cuban government's handling of the Padilla affair and Sartre, de Beauvoir, Carlos Fuentes and Mario Vargas Llosa published an open letter in *Le Monde*. Fidel described them as 'the mafia of pseudo-leftists' in 'bourgeois salons, 10,000 miles away'.[48] The love affair between Cuba and celebrity intellectuals was clearly over.

One can argue that the fact that the Revolution was living through a very difficult period at the end of the 1960s might justify a hard line on dissidents of any category. Certainly dissident artists were open to being manipulated by émigrés and many were overtly anti-Castro. Nevertheless, the censorship of words and images, of poets, painters and film-makers is not the mark of a healthy society, let alone a revolutionary state committed to the fullest expression of human aspirations and desires. In subsequent decades, changes in official policy towards artists and intellectuals would be dependent upon shifts in the domestic and international political climate. Some leaders feared that foreign contacts and work would be subversive to Cuban values. This was despite the fact that those travelling abroad to work in development programmes, trade missions or intellectual encounters were likely to be individuals most intensely loyal to the Revolution. In 1977, Secretary for Ideology Antonio Pérez Herrero warned that because the US had failed to destroy the revolutionary government by force 'the ideological struggle [has taken on] more importance as a factor in our country's foreign relations and as an element of the greatest importance in defending our socialist society'. In commenting upon this statement, Jorge Domínguez wrote: 'The effort to prevent ideological diversionism has curtailed Cuba's cosmopolitanism.'[49]

Revolutionary sport

Sport was accorded a high position in revolutionary culture with heavy investment in both facilities and education and a massive injection of expertise from the Soviet bloc. The government exercised tight control over sports management. Thus, Alcides Sagarra, national boxing coach since 1964, was a Central Committee member for many years. Participation in sport was seen as contributing to the inculcation of revolutionary values as well as promoting Cuba's international reputation (particularly if the opponent was the US). Professional sport was banned in 1961 which meant that foreign competitions and the Olympics were the only opportunity for the best Cuban sportsmen and women to demonstrate their skills. There were noticeable successes at the Olympics (for example, Alberto Juantorena winning gold at the 400 and 800 metres at the 1976 Montreal Olympics and Javier Sotomayor receiving the high jump gold medal in Barcelona). High achievers were accorded privileges not open to ordinary Cubans, but their amateur status meant that they could not obtain the financial rewards enjoyed by their colleagues in other countries. Despite the blockade there were regular sporting connections with the US such as the Pan-American Games and, in boxing, the world championships and bilateral tournaments which began in 1977. These encounters stimulated strong emotions and, occasionally, conflict. Thus the Cuban team walked out of the 1999 Boxing World Championships held in Houston, Texas after they protested at a series of decisions against them which they claimed had been manipulated by the Americans.

Sports investment was neglected during the Special Period as priorities shifted and there were a number of defections including those of the baseball stars, Livian and Orlando Hernández, in 1995 and 1996 respectively and the boxer, Joel Casamayor, in 1996. US sports promoters have always attempted to entice Cubans to leave their country and earn huge sums in the States. In the 1970s, there was much anticipation of a contest between treble Olympic champion Teofilo Stevenson and Muhammed Ali which Don King tried to arrange. That bout never happened. When Ali arrived in Havana in 1995 with medical supplies, he was asked the probable result. His diplomatic response was 'a draw'.[50] In the 1990s, the dream ticket was Felix Savon and Mike Tyson. Savon, who won his third heavyweight gold medal at the 2000 Sydney Olympics, was asked why he had not accepted the $10 million pay cheque to face Tyson. He replied that 'the only millions that interest me are my 11 million brothers in Cuba. Money is not everything. He who abandons his fatherland has no love of anything in life.'[51]

Savon's role as an international ambassador for Cuba has been of great value to the state but his admirable embrace of amateurism is now probably anachronistic. Dollarization has seen the increasing professionalization of major sports stars and a relaxation of strict controls upon their earnings. Thus, Cuban athletes are now able to compete for large sums on the Grand Prix circuit.

Para Mi Cuba Yo Traigo Un Son – musicians and the Revolution[52]

The musical community divided in its response to the Revolution. Cuban musicians were accustomed to touring or living in the United States and many did not return after January 1959; others left in later migrations and established strong centres of musical activity in Miami and New York. Prominent among them were individuals such as Celia Cruz, Arturo Sandoval, Willie Colón and Gloria and Emilio Estefan of the Miami Sound Machine. The latter poured funds into the CANF and imbued their music with virulent anti-Castro sentiment. Other musicians embraced the Revolution in songs such as Carlos Puebla's paean to Che Guevara, '*Hasta Siempre, Comandante*', and the repertoire of groups such as Orquestra Aragón. The PCC was often sceptical of this *nueva trova*, suspecting its unconventional lyrics, and the nonconformist behaviour of its artists would often result in their access to radio and television being blocked without explanation. Rock music was famously regarded as degenerate; unbelievably, the sale of Beatles records was banned for many years in Cuba.

Official attitudes later became far more relaxed as, under the aegis of Roberto Robaina who would later become foreign secretary, the Young Communists staged concerts in an attempt to adopt a more modern and 'cool' style. Cuban jazz was promoted by a special unit set up at ICAIC directed by the classical guitarist, Leo Brower whilst in 1962, the Folklórico Nacional which is devoted to the celebration of the Afro-Cuban tradition in music and dance was founded by Lázaro Ros. Within Cuba, networks of *casas de cultura* (houses of culture to be found in towns and cities across the island) and a high incidence of televised performances created an intimacy with cultural expression which, although orchestrated by the state in order to provide 'the framing of Cuba's national image' and 'to generate foreign exchange', nevertheless attested to the high levels of literacy and sensibility amongst Cuban people.[53] Musicians have felt aggrieved by their lack of contact with other artistic communities although Coco Fusco has argued that by the end of the 1980s, the government had began to lose its appetite for strict control and was demonstrating greater sensitivity to a younger generation which 'has an unabashed interest in information about art outside Cuba. What unifies them ... is their strong opposition to any reductive or repressive definition of revolutionary culture.'[54]

In the puritan atmosphere of the immediate post-revolutionary period, the government had closed clubs and bars and, thus, reduced the number of available live music venues. It also nationalized the American-controlled recording companies which had previously monopolized the industry and imposed state control under the auspices of the Egrem label. The difficult circumstances imposed by the blockade meant that Cuban musicians faced dilapidated recording facilities. Royalties were rarely paid and musicians, even when touring abroad, only received *peso* wages and meagre living expenses. As state employees, their jobs were guaranteed but many lived in very modest circumstances. There were musical contacts between Cuba and the rest of the world particularly with West Africa (thus in the 1970s, Orchestra Baobab fused Senegalese and Cuban rhythms in a highly distinctive manner) and some thawing in the relationship with the United States (including jazz cruises in the 1970s and encounters such as that between the Cuban group Irakere, the pianist Chucho Valdés and Americans Earl Hines and Dizzy Gillespie). However, Cuban musicians experienced great antipathy if they visited émigré communities. When Orquesta Aragón played the Lincoln Centre in New York in 1978, two of its three concerts had to be cancelled following bomb attacks and there were huge demonstrations against Los Van Van in Miami in 1999. However, this resistance is crumbling as the monolithic character of these communities dissolves. As with the rest of Cuban society, the music business struggled to survive during the Special Period but in the 1990s, it enjoyed a revival as the club and dance scene revitalized in Havana and other tourist areas and as Cuban music acquired a new international audience following the spectacular success of the old musicians who reunited as The Buena Vista Social Club after 1996. Recording companies proliferated under the auspices of Cuba's first non-governmental cultural enterprise, the Pablo Milanés Foundation, and Cuban musicians, now allowed to command high fees (an important source of foreign currency for the state), once again broke into the American market.

Filming the Revolution

The history of Cuban cinema since 1959 offers a fascinating and sometimes disturbing story of great invention and boldness frequently stymied by mistaken and clumsy censorship and an unwillingness to accept that revolutionary transformations need to allow different representations of identity and perception. The state film foundation, ICAIC, was created in 1959. Before the Revolution, domestic film production had centred on routine genre and soft porn pictures but the industry was dominated by product coming out of Hollywood. Radical film-makers were subject to harassment; thus, *El Mégano* (a short about swamp charcoal makers) was seized by Batista's police and one of its directors, Julio García Espinosa, arrested. His collaborator, Tómas Gutiérrez Alea (universally known as 'Titon') would subsequently become Cuba's most celebrated director. In 1960, ICAIC founded a film archive and film journal, *Cine cubano* and by 1965, it controlled all production, distribution and exhibition rights (the same monopoly as exercised by the Hollywood studio system until deregulation in the late 1940s). It also trained directors and cinematographers and managed the import and export of films. In an act reminiscent of the Soviet agit-prop trains, it established *cine moviles* which visited isolated areas, supporting the literacy and also other campaigns. Short documentaries explained and elucidated government policies as well as offering good training for young film-makers. ICAIC had to create a production base and despite government support, it was very hard pressed in terms of resources. On his trips abroad, Che made it a point to purchase film stock, underlining the importance the Revolution ascribed to cinema. Notwithstanding its practical difficulties, output was prolific and the late 1960s saw the release of films such as Gutiérrez Alea's 1968 *Memorias* and *Lucía* (directed by Humberto Solás in 1969) which were received by critics and audiences as important statements in the vibrant movement known as Third Cinema.

The new wave of revolutionary cinema challenged the cultural domination of Hollywood which was regarded as an instrument of capitalist and imperialist ideological control. Third Cinema announced the need for a cinema of the people, a cinema which 'could be aesthetically accomplished as well as politically engaged'.[55] In Jean Luc Godard's *Wind from the East*, the Brazilian director Glauber Rocha (a leader of the Brazilian Cinema Novo of the 1960s) is pictured standing at a crossroads. Asked '... which is the way to the political film?' He responds by pointing in one direction, 'That way the Third World cinema, a dangerous cinema – divine, marvellous. ... A cinema of the oppression of imperialist consumption. . . .'[56] Notwithstanding the didacticism for which the French director's films were renowned, Rocha's statement perfectly encapsulates the hopes revolutionary film-makers shared. Cuban directors embraced the concept of what Julio García Espinosa described as 'imperfect cinema', that is a cinema which was popular, addressed social problems and aspired to make audiences 'co-creators of the work'.[57] Espinosa 'warned Third World filmmakers not to be enthralled by technically and artistically "perfect" cinema. Instead [they] should use their limited resources in innovative ways in order to confront the prettified commercial cinema of the developed countries. ...'[58] Espinosa's cinema would be one where professional stars would be replaced by workers, the art of film-making would be demystified and the passive spectator would become the spectator-creator.[59]

Despite its government's growing closeness to the Soviet camp, Cuban cinema did not adopt Soviet realism. It was open to many influences, experimenting with montage in the tradition of Eisenstein and modernism in the vein of Bergman, Resnais and the French New Wave. Directors and cinematographers used flashbacks and jump cuts, mixed fantasy and realism and employed contemporary newsreel material and straight-to-camera monologues. In addition to this rich vein of experimentation, it was also a cinema which stressed that films must be accessible to wide audiences and which recognized that although film had undeniable ideological power, it must also be human and accessible. Looking back on his career in the 1980s, Gutiérrez Alea contended: 'It's worthless to make movies that try to promote the most valuable revolutionary ideas if people won't go to see them. ... There is a dangerous tendency to cover up mediocrity, poor quality and lack of effectiveness by taking the relatively easy way out of hiding behind a slogan.'[60] It was the duty of film-makers to explore the difficulties involved in the transition to socialism and the cultural attitudes which had to be overcome during the process. This could only be done in a society where officialdom tolerated satire and ridicule: 'We maintain the revolutionary principle that reality ... can be transformed only if we have a critical attitude toward it.'[61]

The commitment of the leading Cuban film-makers to a revolutionary humanism is reflected in the significant films of the early period. Thus, Solás's *Lucía* chronicles the lives of three women named Lucía within the context of Cuban history (the sequences are called *Lucía, 1895*, *Lucía 1933* and *Lucía 196–*). Each section concerns a different class: first, the colonial aristocracy, then the middle class and finally the peasants. Lucía is the central character in each segment and thus the film merges the fight for independence with the fight against machismo: 'the female figure ... becomes the "site" in which the audience participated metaphorically in the process of national self-realisation'.[62] Kolker has called it 'a work of optimism and confidence. Its complexity is the sign of a culture aware of questions that remain unanswered and problems that stay unsolved.'[63] Another film, Alea's *Muerte de un Burócrata* (*Death of a Bureaucrat*, 1966), offers a satire on Cuban bureaucracy whilst paying affectionate homage to Fellini, Buñuel and Laurel and Hardy. Manuel Octavio Gómez's *First Charge of the Machete* (1969) recreates the First War of Independence when the machete became the weapon of choice of the *mambís* and a symbol of *Cuba libre*. Gómez shot it as a *cinema vérité* news report, complete with interviews, direct sound and hand-held cameras, with the intention of presenting history in an immediate and understandable form. For Michael Chanan, the most arresting sequence was one shot on a Havana street where an individual – whom he describes as an 'accomplice of the camera' – 'accosts passers-by and asks them their political views. A disturbance develops and Spanish soldiers arrive to quell it; Gómez's camera has travelled into the past and taken an active role in the history unfolding there.'[64]

Despite this critically acclaimed artistic explosion, it was not long before critical voices were heard bemoaning the state of Cuban cinema. Néstor Almendros, the revered cinematographer who left Cuba for exile in 1962 after a series of clashes with the authorities, had attacked Alfredo Guevara's authoritarian control over the kind of films that could be made at ICAIC.[65] The rigours of censorship fluctuated as political and economic circumstances evolved, but it was certainly the case that the nature of film production changed from the early 1970s as directors retreated from experimentation and made more formulaic genre films with conventional narrative structures and *mise-en-scène* in order to demonstrate their political loyalty. As ICAIC's budget dropped, Cuba made only 10–12 films annually, its film theatres being dependent upon Soviet and Latin American imports and pirated Hollywood movies to satisfy its audiences. This notwithstanding, Cubans remained avid movie-goers whilst Havana hosted the annual International Festival of Latin American Cinema (launched in 1979) which, over the years, would welcome 'radical' Hollywood visitors as well as establishing the International School of Film and Television.

In 1991, a heavily indebted ICAIC was absorbed into the FAR's film department. The international school floundered and censorship became harsher. The encroachment of state control was exemplified by the treatment accorded *Alicia en el pueblo de Maravillas* (*Alice in Wonderland*) made by Daniel Díaz Torres in 1991. A satire on Cuban bureaucracy and social corruption, the film is set in a clinic which aims to cure citizens who are 'different' by making them drink the bottled water it produces. The clinic's director insists that the water, which is always cloudy, will be made clear by shaking. Díaz Torres argued that *Alicia* was a mediation upon Rectification and an acknowledgement of the shortcomings of the Cuban system but denied that it harboured counter-revolutionary sentiments. Pulled from distribution, despite opening to long cinema queues, and denounced by *Granma*, the film provoked an intense debate as many intellectuals and artists criticized the government for its intolerance.[66] However, there have been recent efforts by the cinema community to resist mindless censorship. When Fidel made disparaging remarks about Gutiérrez Alea's last film, *Guantanamera*, which considered life under the Special Period, Guevara refused to withdraw it and Fidel was eventually obliged to apologize, admitting that he had not actually seen the film!

Cuban civil society: the 1990s and beyond

The difficult times Cuba lived through in the 1990s inevitably contributed to a considerable sense of detachment between state and civil society. This loss of legitimacy for the state was by no means a new phenomenon. It had been concerned for a long time, for example, with the issue of young people's disenchantment with a revolutionary myth which appeared to have no relevance to their lives. This was ironic in that in the 1960s, the Revolution was emblematic of the triumph of the New Left over the Old and Fidel had famously declared that 'Nobody under thirty can understand what the Revolution is about.'[67] By the 1970s, much concern was being expressed about the appearance of *los desvinculados* (the unconnected ones). Young people were highly critical of attendance at the compulsory *escuelas del campo* and bemoaned the lack of consumer goods. Their alienation was reflected in the fact that 41 per cent of the *marielitos* were under 27.[68] Other social sectors had also evinced growing anger with the failure of the state to make good on its promises but the dislocations of the Special Period contributed to a far deeper, and potentially more serious, disillusionment. When Fidel publicly acknowledged and made positive allusion to the existence of civil society in Latin America in his speech to the Rio Earth Summit in 1992, it was evident that the Cuban government had decided that it must shift its position and allow a more relaxed political, intellectual and artistic atmosphere in the country. Inevitably this would include at least some recognition of criticisms of the state's human rights record. As the decade progressed, it was apparent that this tentative process and an accompanying official acceptance of the value of different forms of expression would continue, although it was beset by periods when the exercise of central control was reapplied in a vigorous manner.

What is clear is that informal practices and unauthorized behaviours now coexist with the state and the PCC. Cuban civil society builds upon a variety of constituencies including the mass organizations (which have the structures to facilitate debate and the representation of interests and have periodically spoken out about specific issues although they do not generally act independently of the state) and a wide variety of NGOs (organizing around health, environmental and gender issues; for example, the Protestant Martin Luther King Center in Havana and the Center of Reflection and Dialogue in Cárdenas both sponsor community development projects). There are also trans-national links with émigré organizations and other NGOs and agencies. There are different networks within the state, bureaucracy and the PCC which articulate different interests and policy priorities and other groups (including gays, women, Afro-Cubans, youth, students, intellectuals, artists and entrepreneurs), which began calling for more autonomy in the 1990s. It should not be forgotten that the possibilities for such mobilization owe a great deal to the high levels of education and participation which have been integral to Cuban social development since the 1960s. More immediately, state policy has contributed to this movement for change by endorsing joint ventures, tourism and the self-employed sector. The policies initiated under the Special Period and consolidated in the later 1990s created the spaces within which people could mobilize in less restricted ways. They also, however, contributed to the growth of social sectors which might feel little or no relationship to the state. The question which would be of vital importance for Cuba's future would be how the state would respond to these voices for change.

7
Conclusion

The 1990s began very badly for Cuba. The collapse of the Soviet Union was an economic disaster for the island and the survival of the Revolution was called into question. In international terms, rather than pursuing new policies in the spirit of post-cold war multilateralism (the stated aim of the inaccurately termed New World Order proclaimed by President George Bush), the United States intensified its attacks upon Cuba. Charging that Cuba continued to pose a security threat to the Americas, it introduced aggressive legislation (the Torricelli–Graham Cuban Democracy Act of 1992 and also the Helms–Burton Act of 1996) which strengthened the blockade and confirmed the belief held by the right-wing Cuban lobby in the US that it was now time for the final assault upon Castro. Clinton agreed to Helms–Burton after Cuba's shooting down of two Hermanos al Rescate (Brothers to the Rescue) planes on 24 February 1996 after they illegally flew over Cuban airspace and after several earlier warnings to the US government that it would take such action.[1] The Hermanos had initially formed in order to rescue people on the seas between Cuba and the US coastline following the 1994 *balseros* crisis. The Cuban government let it be known it would not stop those wishing to leave. Thousands set off from small ports around Havana. After three decades, Washington was compelled to reverse its open door immigration policy when, on 18 August, it ordered the US Coastguard to take any survivors to Guantánamo rather than to the American mainland. They were to remain there indefinitely until they were returned to Cuba or adopted by a third country. By the end of August, approximately 17,000 *balseros* had left Cuban waters. Starting on 1 September, a series of meetings between the two governments took place in New York, Washington and Havana. Although the US persisted in its ongoing refusal to discuss ending the blockade, an agreement was reached whereby it would admit 20,000 Cubans per year whilst Cuba agreed to curb illegal immigration.[2]

Coming out of the Special Period

The question facing Cuba during the Special Period was whether the socialist character of its political and social system would be subsumed by its insertion into the world economy. The government was adamant that whilst it needed to respond to changing circumstances and probably make compromises, the essentials of its ideological commitment were not negotiable. The official view was that the need to engage with foreign capital was not an admission of defeat but rather a means of ensuring the island's survival. Carlos Lage described the strategy as 'not an opening toward capitalism, but rather a socialist opening towards a capitalist world'.[3] Despite such optimism, it was apparent that keeping control over this process would be a difficult undertaking. I now consider how the state tried to navigate the dangerous waters of the sea of entrepreneurial socialism.

Economic initiatives and social consequences

As the economic crisis began to abate, the Cuban government was engaged in a strategy of mixing public and private enterprise under the close supervision of 'a socially interventionist state'.[4] The Foreign Investment Law introduced in September 1995 offered international capital various inducements including the possibility of up to 100 per cent profit repatriation and the freedom to hire and fire workers. It also approved the establishment of free trade zones, the first of which appeared in 1997. It must be noted that these zones were not intended to resemble their counterparts in other Third World countries which have been castigated for their superexploitation of local labour forces. The Cuban government insisted upon setting minimum rates of pay and humane working conditions in order to offset the potential dangers of embarking upon such a development model.

The state's efforts to revive economic growth appeared to be bearing fruit by the mid-1990s. Cuba had agreed scores of new joint venture and foreign investment projects with firms from Argentina, Brazil, Canada, France, Israel, Great Britain, Mexico, Russia, Spain and other countries. These projects – many of which were million-dollar deals – ranged from the construction of hotels to enterprises in mining, oil exploration, telecommunications and biotechnology. In 1995, exports increased for the first time in six years whilst imports rose to 30 per cent of their 1989 level, and the expansion of land under private control (by 1998, only 34 per cent of cultivated land remained under full state control) and the growth in farmers' markets increased the availability of food and other staples such as gasoline.[5] Before the breakup of the Soviet bloc, 57 per cent of the total calories in the Cuban population's diet had come from imported food, mainly from the CAME states. Between 1989 and 1993, calorific intake was reduced by 33 per cent although special provision was made for children under seven who were guaranteed a daily quart of milk.[6] The state had insisted that even during the worst part of the Special Period, there should be a socially equitable division of social resources. Rationing had been overseen with a sense of fairness and no single social group had been targeted.

However, scarcities remained and everyday living continued to be a struggle against electricity and water cuts and the absence of consumer goods as well as the deterioration of physical infrastructure, particularly housing stock and roads. With nearly half of all factories shut down and the remainder forced to operate on much reduced levels owing to the lack of imported spares and raw materials, pervasive unemployment resulted in a shift to self-employment as the state sector fragmented. Paper shortages allowed greater state control over printed material and, thus, Cubans had more limited access to information. Newspapers and journals closed and, apart from school books, publishing dried up whilst Cuban television operated on a limited schedule although audiences still had recourse to US stations. The state's education policy also came under attack; university admissions were cut and access became highly competitive. Many young Cubans questioned the value of higher education as graduate salaries decreased and they could earn far more as guides or waiters in the tourist sector. Memories of high standards in education and health in the past became politically charged as the quality and scope of these benefits diminished albeit relatively. In the health service, signs of the emergence of a two-tier system of provision could be identified, with private clinics with first-class facilities for foreigners with dollars and public hospitals which lacked the most basic medicines. The national health budget declined from an annual $250 per adult in the late 1980s, reaching a low of $65 in 1993 and rising to $160 by the late 1990s. The situation was compounded by the ageing population and the fact that more than 50 per cent of the budget was spent on importing pharmaceuticals.[7]

Most new drugs introduced into the world market are developed by US companies and third parties are banned from exporting US drugs, scientific technology and textbooks to Cuba. This aspect of the blockade has had particularly dire consequences for women, because of the shortage of X-ray film for mammography units, and for HIV-positive people (the United States manufactures some 70 per cent of AZT and Interferon). However, with typical Cuban initiative, the government sought ways to compensate for such problems. Despite its poverty, Cuba is at the forefront of pharmaceutical and biotechnology research, pioneering work in genetic engineering and the exploration of alternative remedies such as acupuncture, homeopathy and herbal medicines. Initially, biotechnology was based on copying existing technology and products but it has become increasingly innovative. A policy of identifying and fast-tracking gifted students and devoting fiscal resources to priority areas has underpinned this process. The Carlos Finlay Institute has achieved breakthroughs such as the discovery of vaccines against hepatitis B and meningitis B and the design of foetal monitoring equipment.[8] Cuba obtained vital foreign credit by selling these items to UN agencies such as the World Health Organization as well as negotiating a deal with Glaxo SmithKline which, after many setbacks, received a licence to market the unique anti-meningitis B vaccine in the US. Washington minimized the profits Cuba could claim by insisting that part had to be paid as medicines and other goods rather than hard currency.[9]

Cuban products are competitive because of modest production costs and a willingness to sell drugs at much lower prices than multinational corporations do. The biggest obstacle to an expansion in this trade is marketing as corporations try to maintain monopoly control. As a result, Cuba tends to concentrate upon Third World markets. Self-reliance may have been a necessity in the 1990s but in battling through the Special Period, Cuba has achieved admirable levels of health care for its citizens. In 2000, the WHO's register of world health provision saw Cuba ranked thirty-ninth out of 191 countries – only two places below the United States. Despite a much smaller GDP, Cuba is still able to achieve levels comparable with those in the richest countries in the world and to offer lessons for them. British NHS doctors and officials routinely visit Cuba in order to observe its cost-effective and patient-centred strategies and have been impressed by its promotion of *consultorios* (neighbourhood practices) which ensure that no Cuban lives further than 20 minutes' walk away from health provision.[10]

Another area of policy which began as a survival strategy but which is now recognized as path breaking is what has been termed 'the greening of the Revolution'. Peter Rosset has argued that the shift from 'large-scale industrial farming toward a more human endeavour, engaged equally with traditional knowledge and modern ecological science' could be a model for other countries.[11] An organic farming programme was launched in 1991 following Raúl Castro's positive assessment of successful smallholder farming whilst on a visit to China. The Cuban army was sent to work as state farms were transformed into basic production units and cooperatives. In the cities, *organoponicos* (state-owned large urban gardens built on wasteland) and *huertos* (patio gardens) now produce 60–70 per cent of all vegetables. Volunteers and paid workers (often retired people) tend the urban gardens using natural pesticides. They are supported by the government's urban farming institute, the Granja Urbana (the Urban Farm) with the close collaboration of ANAP.[12] Cuba is involved in fair trade arrangements with other countries. Thus, Cuban cooperatives produce oranges and other fruits for juice drinks and sell them just above the current world price; included within their profit margin is a social premium which is paid to ANAP which invests it in development and welfare work. Small producers are thus able to buck the world trend towards agro-industrial production of basic foodstuffs for export and move towards establishing food sovereignty.[13] The results of this farming revolution have been spectacular, ending Havana's dependence upon food brought in from the countryside and ensuring that Cuban dietary habits have changed for the better as people eat far more fruit and vegetables. Cuba has also become increasingly involved in ecotourism, a healthy corrective to the sun and sex allure of resorts such as Varadero.

These are promising signs but it must not be forgotten that Cuba continues to face major economic problems which include its vulnerability to trade dependency and the difficulties of obtaining new sources of capital. Since its 1986 unilateral moratorium on debt servicing and the disappearance of the Soviet prop, Cuba cannot roll trading deficits into debt and credit from commercial banks has been virtually impossible to obtain. To receive new credit, it would have to pay all outstanding loans. Cuba has attempted to broker debt for equity swaps with its Latin American neighbours although these arrangements can be problematic and are subject to pressure from the US. International market prices have not been in Cuba's favour and imports particularly in food and oil increased in cost from the mid-1990s as did demand for them despite government efforts to introduce restraint. Cole makes the point that this situation is not unique to Cuba but is a fundamental dilemma for all Third World states and, furthermore, that Cuba's market transition has not suffered the same fate as the former Soviet Union and Central Europe where that change has been characterized by 'rampant poverty, family breakdown and sexual abuse, alongside rising juvenile crime, murder and suicide rates, and the reappearance of tuberculosis and diphtheria'.[14] Underpinning the problems it shares with other states are those which are specific to this small, poor island which continues to be subject to blockade. The major issue continues to be how Cuba can structure the relationship between the state and private enterprise without sacrificing social justice and national independence.

In a book which provoked considerable controversy in Cuba when it was published, Carranza Valdés and his co-authors argued that whilst the overriding concern was to retain the 'hegemony of social property', there had to be an acceptance of the coexistence of various forms of property ranging from individual through cooperative to state as well as the various types of foreign joint venture.[15] Economic diversification and promotion of tourism would contribute to growth but at too slow a rate as to earn sufficient foreign exchange. What was needed was to increase labour productivity by raising material incentives and improving the range and quality of goods and services. The consequence of rationing was that people had more money than goods to buy and this placed a brake on the expansion of the domestic market. It was also essential to end the existence of two separate currencies and the problems this created in terms of inclusion and exclusion. The *peso* and dollar economies should be merged but the operation of this new economic model must be carefully regulated by the state. One issue here is whether even the strictest of state controls could prevent the continuing dominance of the dollar.

After the Cuban government decriminalized dollar transactions in 1993, it urged families to re-establish links with relatives in the US and encouraged the latter to visit by relaxing visa regulations, although the danger was that an increased inflow of Cuban-Americans would increase discontent on the island. The state also provided for the creation of new processes of social stratification by opening special dollar shops for 'vanguard workers'. Its 1994 acceptance of self-employed economic activity initiated an informal sector boom which, it has been argued, the government proved incapable of controlling. Such ventures alongside the possibilities for enrichment for individual farmers offered by the opening of the free agricultural markets and also the opportunities for cooperative and UBPC members created new perspectives upon the nature of the relationship between state and population and once again raised the issue of the former's legitimacy. It was inevitable that painful memories of difficult times under the Special Period would stay with Cubans even after the economy began to recover. It was also clear that changes in property relations and social differentiation produced new social strata which might not subscribe to the consensus about social justice. In negotiating with them to secure their loyalty, there was a danger that the state would make too many concessions and undercut its support amongst other groups.

Another complicating factor has been the government's attitude towards criminal activity. Given that it is wholly likely that many members of neighbourhood *comités*, local assemblies and mass organizations will be involved in what the state would regard as illegal economic behaviour, it is essential that the authorities differentiate between crime and the pressing need for individual and collective survival. Government policy is often implemented in arbitrary and indiscriminate ways and this must also have an impact upon how people think about and identify with the system. The introduction of a Code of Ethics in 1996, which was intended to ensure appropriate conduct on the part of state officials, was a positive step as was the reorganization of the National as the Central Bank in late 1997. One of its major remits was to prevent illegal flows of capital and money laundering. Another important banking innovation was the creation of the Banco Popular de Ahorro (the Popular Savings Bank) which made *peso* and dollar accounts available to customers in and outside Cuba.

As the decade progressed, Cuba attempted to build upon its improving economic prospects by continuing to develop its trading, diplomatic and cultural links with Western Europe, Canada and other Third World states and by consolidating its relationship with its neighbours in the Caribbean Basin and Latin America. However, these endeavours were overshadowed by the intensification of aggressive policies against Havana which emanated from Washington.

US Cuba policy in the 1990s

New opportunities, old reactions

Cuba watchers felt some hope that relations between the two countries might improve following the inauguration of Bill Clinton in early 1993 but their optimism was short-lived. Whilst Russia under Yeltsin was quickly accepted as an ally, the United States was not willing to extend such courtesy to Cuba. The end of the cold war demonstrated that Cuba had never been an East–West problem but rather the product of Washington's desire to keep the island within its sphere of influence. It was also indicative of continued hubris: tiny Cuba was not going to 'beat' the imperial power. Clinton initially named black Cuban American Mario Baeza as Assistant Secretary of State for Inter-American Affairs. Baeza was the candidate of the anti-Castro Democratic lobby and favoured the idea of dollar diplomacy with the island. However, the CANF contended that he would be 'soft on Cuba' and forced Clinton to find him a less contentious job at Commerce. His replacement, Alexander Watson, had been ambassador to Peru and had no difficult Cuban connections. During the 1992 election campaign, Clinton declared that the blockade would remain the centrepiece of his presidency's Cuba policy and was rewarded, in 1992 and again in 1996, with strong émigré support. Mas Canosa proved himself adept at playing off candidates greedy for CANF's financial support. In March 1994, Clinton thanked Cuban-Americans for pledging $3.5 million to the Democratic Party and his policies became increasingly aggressive.[16] The administration had, in effect, been purchased by the CANF.

As president, Clinton oversaw a raft of policy initiatives relating to travel restrictions, limiting Cuba's access to hard currency, denying visas to Cuban diplomats, artists and academics, and pressing Latin and Central American and Caribbean states not to trade or have political links with Cuba. Thus, when Chile restored full diplomatic relations with Cuba in 1995, Washington threatened economic sanctions and said the act would endanger Chile's admission to the North American Free Trade Association. However, the cornerstone of his time in office were two pieces of legislation which directly strengthened the blockade. The Torricelli–Graham Act had been signed, somewhat reluctantly, by George Bush before his November 1992 election defeat. He had feared the reaction of the US's trading partners but was spurred on by candidate Clinton's enthusiastic endorsement of the legislation (an approach summed up by his statement 'I like it' at a fund raiser in Little Havana). Torricelli reinstated the ban on trade with Cuba by US corporate subsidies in third countries (a ban lifted by Gerald Ford in 1975). This ended some $768 million in annual trade, 90 per cent of which was in Cuban imports of food and medicine. The law also prohibited the use of US harbours by ships that had previously docked in Cuban ports. It gave the executive branch the option of 'calibrated responses' (that is a selective lifting of sanctions) to reward positive actions by Cuba, although it also restricted presidential initiatives by spelling out the conditions for such relaxation. This inflexibility would be further underlined by Helms–Burton.

Helms–Burton

The Cuba Liberty and Democratic Solidarity Act (widely known as the Helms–Burton Act) was formally introduced to Congress in February 1995.[17] The CANF and Bacardí-Martini (which was keen to prevent the Cuban government's own Havana Club brand threatening its market share) were deeply involved in the preparation of the bill.[18] It was approved by the House in September and the Senate in October (although the latter only accepted Titles I and II after much heated debate and pressure from the White House). A joint House–Senate Committee met to reconcile the different views on which titles should be included. A final version was approved by both Houses in March 1996. Clinton had initially threatened to veto the bill for fear of antagonizing world opinion but changed his mind after the Hermanos incident.

Helms–Burton could not be described as a sophisticated document. Its political intentions are clear and brutal. Its provisions are presented in four separate titles. Title I prohibits any financing of transactions involving property 'confiscated' since 1959 (this involves both US citizens and residents); it also codifies an array of executive orders and policies from the previous three decades and transfers responsibility for any change to them to congressional authority. Title II compels the US to vote against Cuba's admission to international financial institutions until a free and democratic government is established on the island. It lays down eight major requirements and four additional factors that Cuba needs to address before the blockade is lifted, diplomatic relations are restored and negotiations over Guantánamo begin. The president is entrusted with monitoring Cuba's progress towards democracy. Title III allows US citizens to sue in US courts anyone trafficking in US property nationalized after 1959 (this right extends to those who were not yet citizens at the time of the expropriation). Property rights are to include any investment since nationalization. The president is allowed to suspend Title III for national security reasons or to promote Cuban democracy (this has been done regularly since 1996). Title IV bars entry to the US for foreign nationals involved in property trafficking. Helms–Burton additionally castigated Cuba for involvement in the international drugs trade and deemed it a threat to peace and security in the world. This sentiment was echoed by President George W. Bush after the 11 September 2001 attack on the World Trade Center in New York when he characterized Cuba as a rogue state and part of the 'axis of evil'.

Helms–Burton's provisions bear little resemblance to either reality or common sense and they are riddled with ideological hubris. Their political subtext is the removal of the Castro brothers and US control over a transition. Its detractors have seen annexation of the island as Helms–Burton's core objective. The legislation does not attempt to answer important questions such as how Cuban property would be returned to its 'rightful' owners or whether the social advances made since 1959 would be saved or dismantled (although one can hazard a guess). Furthermore, it violates international law as recognized by the UN and the OAS as well as contradicting Washington's espousal of free trade. It is suffused with notions of imperial reach; as Jesse Helms declared, 'all we're saying to these countries is, obey our law'.[19] This arrogant attitude did not impress its allies, many of whom had already resolved issues by negotiating compensation agreements with Cuba. The European Union threatened to protest to the new World Trade Organization, but amidst fears that the WTO would be undermined by what would be a major row, in 1997 the EU and Washington agreed upon a partial suspension of the Act. Under pressure from the Spanish premier, José María Aznar, the EU also established restrictions upon aid to and investment in Cuba so long as the latter failed to embark upon democratization. The matter was finally resolved in May 1998 when, under the terms of the Birmingham Agreement with the US, the EU agreed to the internationalization of the blockade. When Canada signed an agreement of cooperation with Cuba in February 1997, Washington was displeased but assuaged by the fact that Canada stressed it remained critical of Cuban domestic policy and was not setting itself against the United States. So although its allies were annoyed and showed their displeasure in statements critical of Washington, they were not prepared to break with it over its Cuba policy.

Helms–Burton was roundly criticized by supporters and opponents of Cuba. Ex-President Jimmy Carter described it 'one of the worst mistakes of the U.S.' whilst for Jorge Domínguez it constituted 'a godsend' for Castro as it would enable him to justify political control as a response to such overt aggression.[20] Others argued that it represented a profound shift in the nature of power within the US political system in that, whereas before the blockade had been based upon executive orders, it was now embedded in law. The executive had surrendered its constitutional right to conduct foreign policy and there could be no shift in Cuba policy until Helms–Burton was repealed. The hardline lobby was uninterested in such constitutional niceties. Newt Gingrich, then Republican House majority leader, hailed Helms–Burton as following in the tradition of the US intervention in Cuba in 1898 in that both had striven to eliminate dictatorships. Conservative commentator Michael Radu regarded the intensification of the blockade as 'still the best instrument for pressuring the Castro regime in the direction of democratisation, free markets, and respect for human rights'.[21] Not surprisingly, the Cuban government condemned Helms–Burton as 'a colonial reabsorption of the Republic of Cuba, a continuation of the application of the "manifest destiny", and the Platt Amendment, and of intervening in the internal affairs of Cuba'.[22]

A growing body of opinion within the United States sought to end the blockade. Members of USA Engage, a business lobby, began visiting Cuba in order to research investment opportunities there. Since Cuba had opened up to joint ventures, it was apparent that American firms were losing out to competitors. Writing in 1997, David R. Henderson argued that an acceleration of the dollarization of the Cuban economy and an investment and trading drive by US business would accomplish what the blockade had singularly failed to do.[23] Fidel's Cuba would succumb to the power of the dollar rather than be vanquished by Helms–Burton. The Chamber of Commerce, the National Association of Manufacturers and the National Trade Council all expressed their displeasure with Washington's continued use of economic sanctions and when prominent business people met Fidel at the fiftieth anniversary celebrations of the UN in New York in 1995, they condemned both the blockade and Helms–Burton.

Over recent years, many of the commanding names in the US economy including General Motors and Sears Roebuck have travelled to Cuba to explore future options and may have signed letters of intent to do business if the blockade is lifted. In 1997, a grouping of Cuban-American doctors and religious leaders and a bipartisan group of 30 Congressmen sponsored the Cuban Humanitarian Trade Act which became law in March 1998. This exempted some food and medicines from the blockade's remit. The legislation received strong support within the Cuban-American community, although prominent politicians such as Illeana Ros-Lehtinen (Republican, Florida), Lincoln Díaz Balart (Republican, Florida) and Robert Menéndez (Democrat, New Jersey) vehemently opposed it.[24] In 1998 there took place the launch of an umbrella organization called Americans for Humanitarian Trade with Cuba which embraced business, human rights and religious opinion and which included political notables such as former Treasury Secretary Lloyd Bentsen and Frank J. Carlucci, previously national security advisor to Ronald Reagan. In 1999 and 2000, Congress attempted to pass legislation in favour of all prohibitions on selling food and medicine to Cuba. Although the bills were either blocked or severely modified by Republicans in the House, it appeared that the momentum was slipping away from the diehards. In July 2002, Congress agreed to overturn restrictions on food, medicines and remittances and voted 262 to 167 to abandon the travel ban. However, the White House remained adamant with Secretary of State Colin Powell and Treasury Secretary Paul O'Neill writing a joint letter to Congress which maintained that Castro continued to show 'implacable hostility to the U.S.'.[25]

The issue of human rights

Throughout the 1990s, Washington dismissed Cuban overtures to negotiate over compensation for nationalized US properties, prisoners and human rights as not being in 'good faith'. Evidence of economic and political reform within Cuba was not viewed as the basis for bilateral discussions but rather as proof that its hostile policies were having effect and needed to be intensified. The Clinton administration sponsored a variety of interpersonal contacts between Cuban and American citizens with the aim of encouraging dissidents and putting pressure upon the Cuban government to begin democratization. This strategy became known as Track Two. In reality, it facilitated federal funding of hardline émigré groups. Thus, in December 1997, Jesse Helms, in his capacity as chair of the Senate Foreign Relations Committee, authorized the allocation of nearly $2 million to 'human rights' groups such as the ultraconservative Asociación de Ex-Hacendados (Association of Ex-Landowners) whose Instituto por la Democracia de Cuba (Institute for Cuban Democracy) worked to foment internal rebellion in Cuba.[26]

Human rights became the central strategy for émigré organizations, such as the Coordinating Body of Human Rights Organisations in Cuba, which forged institutional links with foreign bodies such as the Christian Democratic International in Brussels and the Hispanic Cuban Foundation based in Madrid. Spanish conservatives developed strong links with émigré organizations and spearheaded the anti-Castro lobby in Europe. There were close personal relations between Spanish prime minister, José María Aznar, and Mas Canosa and he was an enthusiastic supporter of Helms–Burton. Following the generally friendly relations between Havana and Madrid under the previous socialist government of Felipe González, the two countries then embarked upon a series of diplomatic quarrels. In early 1997, the activist Catholic group Pax Christi launched the European Platform for Democracy and Human Rights in Cuba in The Hague. Its objective was to encourage American NGOs to use their contacts in Cuba to destabilize the government although the majority ignored its appeal. A number of American and European NGOs (such as Oxfam-Solidarity, Belgium) have created their own version of Track Two by fostering links with their Cuban counterparts.[27] The American Pastors for Peace continue their annual Peace Caravans whilst Jewish Solidarity and Catholic Relief organize shipments of food and medicine to Cuba as well as spreading educational information and mobilizing public opinion against the blockade in the US.

Under the cover of a defence of human rights, an ideological offensive was attempting to interfere with Cuban sovereignty in a manner that would have not been countenanced within their own national borders by the states involved. A major site of contestation was the case of Elián Gonzaléz, a five-year-old Cuban boy who was rescued from a capsized motorboat in November 1999 and taken to Miami. As his mother had drowned at sea, his Cuban-American relatives asked that he be granted asylum. His father, who remained in Cuba, protested. As a quasi-religious iconography developed around the 'miracle boy' in Miami, the affair escalated with massive demonstrations both in Cuba and Florida and the involvement of the CANF, the US attorney general and President Clinton. Elián was eventually returned to Cuba in June 2000 with the US government admitting that his Cuban citizenship could not be taken from him and that his father was responsible for him. Whilst the majority of émigrés believed he should stay in the US, most Americans believed he should return to Cuba. The denouement of the affair was clearly a defeat for Cuban-American diehards, had negative electoral consequences for the Democrats, particularly presidential contender Al Gore and ex-Attorney General Janet Reno, and added to the further souring of relations between the two countries.

The Bush White House and Cuba

Both camps involved in the 2000 election campaign had close links with CANF. George W. Bush's brother Jeb was Governor of Florida whilst the Democratic Vice Presidential nominee Joe Lieberman was one of the top recipients of its funding. The role of Jeb Bush is significant. In 1984, he began a close relationship with Camilo Padreda, a former Batista intelligence officer, when Bush was chair and Padreda finance chairman of the Dade County Republican Party. Later Padreda pleaded guilty to defrauding the housing and urban development department of millions of dollars. Bush also worked as a lobbyist for Miguel Recarey's firm International Medical Centres which shipped free medical aid to the Contra; Recarey, who had been implicated in various plots to assassinate Fidel, later became a fugitive after charges of massive fraud. Bush was campaign manager for Illeana Ros-Lehtinen, one of the most intractable Cuban-American politicians, when she ran for Congress; at the time, his father was quoted as saying 'I am certain ... I will be the first American president to step foot on the soil of a free and independent Cuba.' Both Ros-Lehtinen and Jeb Bush were prominent in the campaign for Orlando Bosch's release. Amongst other terrorists released during the Bush administration were Jose Dionisio Suarez and Vigilio Paz Romero who were responsible for the Letelier assassination.[28]

These facts must clearly be taken into consideration when one considers the statesmanship of the Bush political dynasty. Both Al Gore and George Bush had pandered to CANF by arguing that Elián's case be sent to family court in south Florida (where the judgement was likely to go against the boy's father). Once in office following his tainted election (one in which the Cuban-American Florida vote was decisive) the president, mindful of Jeb's prospects in the November 2002 mid-term elections, was keen to show that he was tough on Cuba. The Treasury Department actively pursued Americans trying to do business on the island or visiting it as tourists. Only individuals who held licences to be in Cuba on religious, educational or journalistic grounds were exempt from prosecution. By February 2003, it was estimated that those sought for breaking the blockade had quadrupled since Bush's election and those taken to court faced large fines. Companies organizing holidays to Cuba were also liable to investigation. Many regarded this assault on ordinary Americans as unconstitutional. It was also a trend which seemed out of step with the burgeoning domestic campaign to end the blockade which itself reflected international opinion.

The hawkish members of the Bush administration would have liked to ignore adverse opinion be it at home or abroad. The president's appointment of veteran cold war warrior Otto Reich as Assistant Secretary of State for Inter-American Affairs in 2002 appeared to augur the way forward. Reich, Cuban-born, a Bacardí lobbyist and one of the authors of Helms–Burton, had once compared Castro's Cuba to Hitler's Germany. His selection was made without Senate confirmation because of a procedure known as a recess appointment. However, the new chairman of the Senate Foreign Relations Committee, Republican Richard Lugar, made it clear that he would not vote for Reich at confirmation hearings, and it was also known that Secretary of State Powell was uncomfortable with him as were a number of Latin American governments. Reich was roundly criticized for welcoming the abortive coup against Venezuelan President Hugo Chávez in April 2002. Faced with this degree of opposition, the White House had little choice but to demote him to a minor role at the National Security Council. However, its implacable approach persisted. Following 11 September, the US categorized Cuba as a terrorist state and accused it of espionage, trafficking in Chinese arms, harbouring Basque ETA terrorists and supporting the Colombian FARC.[29] In a speech in May 2002, Undersecretary of State John Bolton argued that Castro's recent visits to Iraq, Syria and Libya confirmed his complicity with these rogue states and in June of that year, the State Department's Head of Intelligence Carl Ford contended that the US had 'substantial information' that Cuba was developing biological weapons and that Iran had purchased dual-use equipment from the Cubans.[30] It does appear that Cuba has been placed on a triumphalist Washington's hit list following the war against Iraq in spring 2003.

Ideological shifts within Cuban-American opinion will also have repercussions for future policies towards Cuba. Más Canosa's death in November 1997 marked the passing of an era and CANF's public image was tarnished by Luis Posada Carriles's 1998 revelation that it had financed his operations including the notorious 1976 bombing of the Cubana de Aviación plane. There were challenges to CANF's hegemony from groups on the right and the left. Nonetheless, hard-liners continued to be the public representatives of the émigré community as liberal Cuban-Americans failed to make their mark electorally and were unable to unite politically. There was evidence that those groups seeking dialogue with the Cuban government shared concerns with many Cubans. Thus Cambio Cubano's 1996 Declaration of the 19th called upon Havana to 'continue with changes, honestly and with absolute transparency and with the certain goal that such economic changes be the carriers of political liberties and civil guarantees for the Cuban people who have the right to live free of any fear'. Attacking dollarization for creating privileged social sectors who felt no loyalty to the Revolution, it also called upon the Cuban government to ensure that foreign investment was not to the detriment of ordinary Cubans and to stop tourist resorts being exclusive and segregated enclaves.[31] Cuba has continued to sponsor conferences between Cuban-Americans and high-ranking officials (including Foreign Ministers Robaina and Pérez Roque) in New York. Divisions within the community are not just political but are also constructed around class, race, gender and age. Thus, many second- and third-generation Cuban-Americans hold distinctive views about their cultural identity and their relationship to the island. These differences create opportunities for continuing contacts and the possibility of reconciliation.[32]

Coming to terms with difference

> By tolerating a diversity of freely competing ... beliefs, the government's definition and practice of human rights could gain more acceptability and recognition abroad.[33]

The developing nature of the relationship between the state and its various social constituencies since the 1990s is of fundamental importance. I would argue that the deepening of *poder popular* (in all its manifestations) is essential to the survival of the Revolution. Reflection upon the evolution of those relationships produces both optimistic and pessimistic conclusions.

Women

Since 1959, Cuban women have become healthier, better educated and more assertive. The FMC now operates with a considerable degree of autonomy and no longer disassociates itself from feminist discourse. It has sponsored significant initiatives including the establishment of *casas de mujeres* (women's centres) which offer education and advisory services, support the start-up of small businesses and offer refuge from domestic violence and the *catedras de la mujer* (research centres) which are engaged in studying a wide variety of issues affecting women including the feminization of poverty, employment glass ceilings and the persistence of stereotypes in the media.[34] One of the major problems that Cuban women face is that of the resurgence of prostitution and what it says about the double standards of morality which still exist, although they are much weaker than before, in official attitudes and in society generally.

Prostitution and the double bind of tourism

Tourism has been courted vigorously by the Cuban state and its agency, Cubanacán, has sought to offer foreign visitors excellent facilities. Tourists enjoy a totally different quality of life from Cubans with the latter often excluded from hotels, beaches and resorts. The success of its tourism venture is intrinsic to the country's economic health but its expansion brings problems. One is the commodification of Cuban culture which reduces music, dance and religious ritual to mere spectacle and another is the impact of the incursion of the dollar on the lives of young women and men. Young women's bodies, in particular, are used in the construction of Cuba as a tourist paradise, much as they were in the 1950s. Sadly this is not a phenomenon exclusive to Cuba, but it is profoundly depressing given the inroads made towards women's emancipation. The state's approach to the existence of *jinterismo* (actually slang for hustling rather than prostitution) has been ambivalent, veering between denial in the early 1990s, blaming decadent Western men and castigating the *jinteras* themselves for shaming revolutionary morality. There has been little recognition of the fact that during the worst years of the Special Period, young girls from the provinces flocked to Havana and the beach resorts out of economic necessity (the cause of prostitution across the Third World) although as the economy recovered, the attraction for many would be the access to material goods afforded by the possession of dollars. In 1992, Fidel stated that 'Cuban women were *jinteras* not out of need but because they liked sex' whilst in 1995, Vilma Espín denounced them 'as decadent trash whose parents had lost control of them'.[35] The inference behind such statements was that this was an individual or family failing, not the result of state policies.

As the problem grew bigger, the state was compelled to respond with attempts to eliminate prostitution not by trying to curb the behaviour of tourists (which would have had a negative impact upon its foreign earnings) but by criminalizing the women. Those not resident in Havana were forcibly sent home and reoffenders were jailed. At this point, the FMC decided to intervene by suggesting education and retraining (the very policies it had first adopted in the 1960s), but the government has continued to introduce periodic crackdowns. It is interesting to note that the authorities have shown far less interest in regulating male prostitutes (*pingueros*) because there is far 'less political and cultural censure of male sex work than of its female counterpart'.[36] Research suggests that contemporary prostitution is quite different from that practised in the pre-revolutionary period in that many *jinteras* are darker-skinned women who do not benefit from remittances sent by Cuban-American relatives. Hence an unfortunate connection can be made between blackness and eroticism which serves to confirm continuing prejudices.

Afro-Cubans

Despite commitment to greater political representation, the 1997 Congress of the PCC elected a Central Committee that was whiter than that of 1991. In contrast to other social groups, the state has failed to allow Afro-Cubans institutional representation and they still cluster in the lower socio-economic categories. The riot in the heavily black neighbourhood of Centro Habana on the Malecón on 5 August 1994 must have been of serious concern to the government, particularly as Afro-Cubans had been seen as being amongst the most loyal constituents of the Revolution. There were growing demands that racial inequality be acknowledged as a pressing problem. Thus, in 1998, the Cuban Union of Writers and Artists called for greater representation of black Cubans in the media. There was growing Afro-Cuban involvement in activist and human rights groups and, in 1999, the creation of the Cofradía de la Negritude (the Black Brotherhood). It made frequent reference to Martí and Juan Gualberto Gómez in its attempts to shame the government into action. By January 1999, in a meeting with the US-based TransAfrica Forum, Fidel felt compelled to agree that discrimination persisted. The Cofradía has called upon Afro-Cubans to engage in self-help and denies being a political organization, but it is clear that it will continue to act as a powerful lobby, rejecting the official silence which has generally constituted government policy. Young Afro-Cubans are also challenging that silence particularly in the sphere of music where their politically charged rap lyrics talk about racism, police harassment and the tourism double standard. The latter has led Alejandro de la Fuente to speculate whether the 1997 reopening of the Havana Biltmore should be seen as symbolic. Its designation as a site catering exclusively for foreign investors and visitors offers a vivid contrast with the 1959 desegregation of public spaces.[37]

Gays

As well as seeing the *balseros* crisis, 1994 also saw the first small demonstration by the Gay and Lesbian Association of Cuba. Although this organization subsequently disappeared, other homosexual groupings emerged emboldened by the cultural and intellectual *apertura* (opening) in Havana and other cities. A sense of gay identity was emerging, facilitated by the fact that gay people could behave in a more relaxed fashion in public places and felt less (although not no) risk of harassment. Although police security checks continue, they tend to be focused upon upholding 'public order' rather than specifically targeting gays and lesbians. However, as Ian Lumsden had contended, oppression is 'still structured into the fabric of Cuban society and state institutions ...' and many individuals continue to feel marginalized.[38]

The Churches

The improving relationship between organized religion and the state suffered some setbacks in the 1990s. As its membership rose, the government feared that the Catholic Church would become more assertive and inspire disaffection. It was also concerned that as the Church was in receipt of donor funds, it could become an alternative source of authority. The Church responded by attempting to find common ground. Thus, its Second *Encuentro* (Meeting), held in 1996, diplomatically condemned the actions of the Hermanos as provocative whilst arguing that the official response (and particularly the harassment of Concilio Cubano activists) was disproportionate. It was important, the bishops concluded, that the Castro government and the émigrés seek reconciliation. The government continued to try to control local congregations through recourse to legal technicalities, but it was evident that it had come to accept what had become a 'state of civil coexistence'.[39]

Prospects for the Revolution

For Margaret Randall, 'the Cuban Revolution is extraordinary in its ability to admit mistakes and rectify them; it is slower to permit a critical discourse that encourages real debate and may help prevent such errors from being made'. Discussion has been allowed but only 'within a carefully delimited framework' and certain topics have been excluded from such discourse.[40] The major taboo has been upon challenges to the authority of the PCC. The problem with the Cuban system is that it has not facilitated the construction of boundaries between the party, the bureaucracy and society with a resulting diminution of the possibilities for individual expression. Juan Antonio Blanco (who, being a contributor to the journal *Pensamiento Crítico* in the 1960s, subscribed to a non-dogmatic Marxism) continues to be critical of the Soviet model of socialism which he argues failed 'to construct an alternative culture and ethical value system to the consumer societies of the West' and also 'never came to terms with accommodating dissent within the system'.[41] This is not to suggest that the system lacks legitimacy; it would not have survived the Special Period without popular endorsement. What I am saying is that that legitimacy would have been far more authentic if the political elite had embraced difference and debate rather than trying to suppress them. The 1990s was a decade in which Cuba experienced profound change. It did not mark the end of the Revolution but it certainly augured a new era within it. For C. Peter Ripley, the problem facing Cuba now 'was to redefine her proper place as a distinctive society ... a struggle of renewal and affirmation, involving more than just holding the line against decay and decline'.[42] Cuba's distinctiveness will inevitably diminish as it moves more fully into the world economy, as tourism continues to increase and global mass culture pervades the island. It will also diminish as the symbols of the Revolution leave the political stage no matter how reluctantly. This leads us, inevitably, to the question of what will Fidel do?

Fidel's charisma and his single-minded passion for Cuban independence has been the reason for the longevity of the government but also an inhibiting factor for necessary change. His 'omnipresence can and does retard progress ...' [His] 'ubiquity leaves little room for popular elements to decentralize power'.[43] To the question as to whether Fidel is essential to the survival of the Revolution, Liss argues that 'Cuba now has sufficiently strong institutions to permit it to run under a democratic form of socialist government without Castro'.[44] Younger political leaders need to come to the fore. They are doing so but very slowly. Thus in May 1999, the 34-year-old Felipe Pérez Roque (previously a personal aide to Fidel) surprisingly replaced Foreign Minister Robaina. Robaina, who had been in office since 1993, was widely credited with orchestrating the campaign against Helms–Burton and augmenting Cuba's diplomatic status.

There was speculation that Fidel was going to assume more direct responsibility for foreign policy. His personal diplomacy certainly increased in the 1990s, visiting every continent and virtually all international forums. Whether it be promoting trade, attacking environmental plundering and poverty or condemning global fiscal institutions (he has famously described the IMF as 'the kiss of evil'[45]), this might be an area of endeavour where he could concentrate his energies in the future. Given his extensive experience in world politics and the respect in which he is held in the Third World, he might also fulfil a role in international conflict resolution. On the domestic stage, it would be valuable if he withdrew from everyday government and concentrated on broader issues such as, for example, ensuring that the quality of the education and health systems is maintained. This would not be retirement but rather a recognition that his political life has entered a different stage. No matter what Fidel decides to do (and it may be that he has grown too accustomed to power to walk away from it), Cuba should embark upon a thorough democratization of power structures, breaking up party and government hierarchies, making institutions more representative with respect to gender and race and facilitating a real and effective empowerment of *poder popular*. A useful innovation would be the election of a prime minister responsible for economic development and other strategic areas. Stress should be placed upon increasing the dialogue with Cuban-Americans in order to circumvent the émigré intransigents and undermine Washington's strategies.

Cuba's development priorities should be to focus upon areas in which it has expertise (such as biotechnology and organic agriculture) and to address pressing problems such as the urgent need for urban regeneration with an improvement in the quality of housing stock and transport as priorities. It will be interesting to see the results of its 2002 commitment to restructuring the sugar industry. The objective is to reduce the land acreage used for the *zafra* by one-third and to concentrate resources upon those farms with superior yields in order to obtain high-quality sugar cane. If this policy is effected, it will have a massive impact upon rural communities and the state will need to address the consequences of this dislocation.[46] It will be extremely important that Cuba does not swap sugar dependency for a dependency upon tourism with its limited returns in terms of investment and its potentially corrosive impact upon the island's culture. Continued economic diversification will constitute a balance to the hegemony of tourism. Resilience is a word which can be applied to the Revolution's history. Another is ingenuity which is reflected in the ability of Cubans to recycle materials and to pursue intermediate technology solutions in the absence of spare parts. Both these qualities were exhibited in large measure during Hurricane Mitch which hit Cuba in November 2001. Starting at the Bahia de Cochinos and then travelling north, it affected five provinces. There was much destruction but the timely evacuation of some 700,000 people, advance planning and the involvement of trained local officials meant that a disaster was avoided. Such a successful example of community organization has lessons to offer to other countries.

Another characteristic of the Revolution has been its internationalism even if Cuba's capacity to send aid and expertise has been reduced during the difficult recent years. Cuba continues to see itself as an actor on the world stage and the US will not be able to prevent it from extending its economic and diplomatic relations nor will it inhibit its commitment to the creation of a system of global interdependence. In 2002, the Group of 77 (representing 120 of the world's poorest countries) met in Havana in order to press the WTO to resist Washington's efforts to gain endorsement of its corporate agenda. G 77 has also offered support to the World Development Movement and other anti-global organizations. Cuba continues to be a bulwark of the NAM and has wholeheartedly subscribed to its policy agenda which includes sustainable development, the security of small states and opposition to those economic blocs which exclude them, and the democratization of the UN.

Regionalism will also play an important role in Cuba's foreign policy. In contrast to its preoccupation in the 1980s with strengthening the states of the eastern Caribbean against the Cuban challenge, US interest in the region has declined. Its previous concern to create strong links with client states disappeared to the extent that it pressed the WTO to eliminate the trade preferences that the island economies enjoyed in Europe in order to protect its own farmers. Caribbean leaders began tentative contacts with Cuba and a number of bilateral agreements have been signed. Cuba, although not a member, was invited to CARICOM's 1998 summit and it was accepted into CARIFORUM, the association of Caribbean states which has institutional links with the EU and aims to create a free trade area. The US objected to these developments but failed to prevent them. Cuba needs access to markets; in return it is well placed to share knowledge and experience with its Caribbean neighbours. A member of the Latin American Parliament since 1985 (which involvement also facilitates links with the EU), Cuba also maintains close links with left-wing and progressive forces in Latin and Central America under the auspices of the São Paulo Forum.

This is not to suggest that future relations with its neighbours will be untroubled. Obviously the US continues to exert an excessive influence in the area. Thus, Cuba's relationship with Mexico (its oldest ally in the Americas) has been hampered by the latter's membership in NAFTA. Castro is also extremely sensitive to the idea of other nations interfering in Cuba's domestic affairs. Thus when President Vicente Fox visited Havana in February 2002, he was castigated for meeting dissidents. When a few weeks later a group of Cubans hijacked a bus and drove it into the compound of the Mexican embassy in Havana, the then Mexican Foreign Minister Jorge Castañeda was quoted as saying that the gates were 'open to all Cuban citizens'. In March, Fidel hastily departed a conference in Monterrey, claiming that Fox had pressed him to avoid meeting George W. Bush. The PRI-dominated Mexican Senate then voted to prevent Fox visiting the US. In April, Mexico delivered the crucial swing vote in favour of a UN resolution on human rights in Cuba. Fidel responded by releasing a tape which he claimed proved that Fox had asked him to leave Monterrey; when Fox demurred, Fidel called him a liar.[47] It may not be surprising that Cuba would find it difficult to maintain relations with a right-wing politician who has embraced neo-liberalism, but its foreign policy has always been pragmatic and it is unlikely that this crisis will produce a rupture in Cuban–Mexican relations.

In Latin and Central America, the promise of democratization in the 1990s raised huge expectations but has resulted in profound disillusionment. Democratic fatigue has been caused by the failure to bring repressive military hierarchies to justice for their human rights violations and, indeed, to prevent their continued brooding presence within the state; the continuation of guerrilla movements in Colombia and Peru; the failure to satisfy the land hunger of poor and indigenous communities; continuing discrimination against citizens on the basis of gender, ethnicity and sexuality; the impact of the political economy of neo-liberalism and its acceptance of poverty as a condition of political stability; an increase in movements of resistance to globalism and the perpetuation of a narrow, exclusive type of democracy. In the new century, the election of presidents with left-wing agendas (Luís Ignacio Lula da Silva in Brazil, October 2002) and Lucio Gutiérrez in Ecuador (November 2002) and the growth in influence of other potentially progressive forces (such as the Movimiento al Socialismo, led by the coca farmer Evo Morales, becoming the second largest party in the Bolivian Congress in July 2002) as well as the growth in anti-global sentiment may suggest that the foundations of political life are shifting. Wright has speculated that if 'current levels of poverty and marginalization continue into the new millennium, and if democracy loses its luster, might tomorrow bring another Fidel Castro, a new era of the Cuban

Revolution?'[48] The Cuban Revolution cannot happen again, but the causes which inspired it continue to beset Latin and Central America and much of the rest of the Third World and the principles to which it was, and remains, committed – egalitarianism and social justice, sovereignty and independence – continue to be fundamental to the futures of millions of world citizens.

Notes

1 Introduction

1 D. Parker, 'The Cuban Revolution. Resilience and Uncertainty', *NACLA Report on the Americas*, XXXII: 5 (March/April 1999), 20.

2 Cited by B. Weinberg, *Homage to Chiapas. The New Indigenous Struggles in Mexico* (London: Verso, 2000), p. 189.

3 Quoted by Y. LeBot, *Subcomandante Marcos: El Sueño Zapatista* (Barcelona: Plaza y Janés, 1997), p. 266.

4 The demonology literature is vast. To take one example, Nestor T. Carbonell, *And the Russians Stayed. The Sovietization of Cuba* (New York: William Morrow & Company, 1989) regards Castro as motivated by 'violence ... intransigence and insatiable ego' (pp. 35–6) and berates ' a confused and disjointed nation inexorably falling into a radical trap' (p. 66). His text is replete with self-aggrandizing references to his family's record of public service (ignoring the venality which characterized politics before 1959) and patronizing references to deferential servants and *guajiros* [peasants] on the family hacienda. The flight to exile of what he terms 'the freedom fighters' (p. 23) is described as a personal and national tragedy.

5 L. A. Pérez, Jr, 'Twenty Five Years of Cuban Historiography: Views from Abroad', *Cuban Studies* (1988) offers a valuable survey.

6 M. Radu, 'An Ocean of Mischief. Don't Reward Castro, Keep the Embargo', *Orbis*, 42: 4 (Fall 1998).

7 The two bills are discussed in Chapter 7.

8 W. E. Ratcliff (ed.), *The Selling of Fidel Castro. The Media and the Cuban Revolution* (New Brunswick: Transaction Books, 1987).

9 J. Arboleya, *The Cuban Counterrevolution* (Athens, Ohio: Ohio University Press, 2002), p. 2.

10 Quoted by T. G. Paterson, *Contesting Castro. The United States and the Triumph of the Cuban Revolution* (Oxford: Oxford University Press, 1995), p. 5.

11 Ibid., p. 12.

12 J. Petras, *The Left Strikes Back. Class Conflict in the Age of Neoliberalism* (Boulder, Colo.: Westview Press, 1999), p. 170.

13 T. C. Wright, *Latin America in the Era of the Cuban Revolution*, revised edn (Westport, Conn.: Praeger Publishers, 2001), p. xi.

14 Ibid., p. xii.

15 M. Randall, *Gathering Rage. The Failure of Twentieth Century Revolutions to Develop a Feminist Agenda* (New York: Monthly Review Press, 1992), p. 124.

16 A. de la Fuente, 'The Resurgence of Racism in Cuba', *NACLA Report on the Americas*, XXXIV (May/June 2001), 30.

17 *Santería*, the term commonly used to encompass all Afro-Cuban religions, is actually only one strand whose origins are largely based on the Lucumi (Yoruba) culture.

18   P. J. Smith, '*Fresa y Chocolate* [*Strawberry and Chocolate*]: Cinema as Guided Tour' in Smith, *Vision Machines. Cinema, Literature and Sexuality in Spain and Cuba, 1983–93* (London: Verso, 1996), p. 93.

19   J. Birringer, 'Homosexuality and the Revolution. An Interview with Jorge Perugorria', *CINEASTE*, XXI: 1–2 (1995), 21.

20   K. Cole, *Cuba from Revolution to Development* (London and Washington: Pinter, 1998), p. 60.

2   Encounters with 'the Monster' and Others

1   'Viví en el monstruo y le conozco las entrañas.' The quotation is taken from Martí's final, unfinished, letter written at the Dos Rios Camp to his friend Manuel Mercado. Quoted in D. Shnookol and M. Muñiz (eds), *José Martí Reader. Writings on the Americas* (Melbourne: Ocean Press, 1999), p. 234.

2   A. Hennessy and G. Lambie (eds), *The Fractured Blockade. West European–Cuban Relations during the Revolution* (Basingstoke: Macmillan – now Palgrave Macmillan, 1993), p. 11.

3   J. Domínguez, *To Make a World Safe for Revolution* (Cambridge, Mass.: Harvard University Press, 1989), p. 7.

4   F. Castro, 'Marxism-Leninism and the Cuban Revolution', *World Marxist Review*, 22: 1(January 1979), 17–18.

5   Domínguez, *To Make a World Safe*, p. 142.

6   The expedition, which very nearly became a suicidal mission, seemed to symbolize how the world viewed the rebels – adventurous, impulsive and youthful.

7   M. Morley, *Imperial State and Revolution. The United States and Cuba, 1952–1986* (Cambridge: Cambridge University Press, 1987), p. 2.

8   The huge base continues to dominate the bay with cargo ships using an international channel to reach Cuban ports. During the Missile Crisis, Fidel stated that US withdrawal would provide Cuba with a guarantee of friendlier intentions from its northern neighbour. Washington has consistently refused to discuss the issue. Over the years, there have been numerous violent clashes with some fatalities. In 1912, US marines were deployed from the base in order to crush the Afro-Cuban Partido Independiente de Color (PIC, Independent Party of Colour), whilst Batista's planes refuelled there before bombing the guerrillas in the Sierra Maestra. Following the attack on the World Trade Center on 11 September 2001, the base was used as an internment camp for Al Qaida and Taliban suspects, an action which was widely condemned as a blatant breach of the Geneva Convention on the rights of prisoners. For a history, see R. Ricardo, *Guantánamo. The Bay of Discord. The Story of the US Military Base in Cuba* (Melbourne: Ocean Press, 1994).

9   T. G. Paterson, *Contesting Castro. The United States and the Triumph of the Cuban Revolution* (Oxford: Oxford University Press, 1995), p. 241.

10   Ibid., p. 6.

11   Ibid., p. 248. Fidel was highly critical of the flamboyant actions of his younger brother, arguing that capturing American soldiers and engineers would only antagonize US public opinion. The most famous kidnap victim

was Juan Manuel Fangio, the Argentine racing driver, who regretted not competing in the 1955 Cuban Grand Prix but had only praise for his guerrilla hosts.

12 N. T. Carbonell, *And the Russians Stayed. The Sovietization of Cuba* (New York: William Morrow & Company, 1989), p. 56. Of the potential contenders for presidential power, Colonel Ramón Barquín had been imprisoned on the Isle of Pines in 1956 following a conspiracy against Batista. A member of the military group known as *los puros* ('the pure ones'), he had been military attaché at the Cuban embassy in Washington. Released on 1 January 1959, he was head of the army for 72 hours before going into exile. A last-ditch CIA attempt to send ex-Premier Manuel Antonio Varona to Cuba ended in disarray. Tony Varona would be an important figure in the émigré community in the United States in the 1960s. Jesús Arboleya argues that it is important to remember these pre-1959 contacts between the US authorities and anti-Batista groups when one considers the emergence of the anti-Castro movement after the Revolution (J. Arboleya, *The Cuban Counterrevolution* (Athens, Ohio: Ohio University Press, 2001), p. 36).

13 The Brazilian Escola Superior de Guerra (the School of Advanced War Studies) and the Peruvian Centro de Altos Estudios Militares (CAEM, the Centre for Higher Military Studies) educated officers in the social sciences and development theory as well as counter-insurgency. The objective was to make them understand the root causes of revolution in order to be able to contain it.

14 Nixon's political judgement was limited. Having met Castro, he reported to Eisenhower that 'his ideas as to how to run a government or an economy are less developed than those of almost any world figure I have met in fifty countries'. Quoted by S. Ambrose, *Nixon: the Education of a Politician, 1913–62* (New York: Simon and Schuster, 1987), p. 515. Clearly, Nixon should have schooled Castro in the art of unconstitutional and venal government.

15 Paterson, *Contesting Castro*, p. 244.

16 Ibid., p. 245.

17 Ibid., p. 254.

18 Morley, *Imperial State*, p. 56.

19 T. C. Wright, *Latin America in the Era of the Cuban Revolution*, revised edn (Westport, Conn.: Praeger, 2001), p. 58.

20 H. M. Erisman, *Cuba's International Relations. The Anatomy of a Nationalistic Foreign Policy* (Boulder, Colo.: Westview Press, 1985), p. 42.

21 A. Hennessy, 'Cuba, Western Europe and the US: an Historical Overview' in Hennessy and Lambie (eds), *Fractured Blockade*, p. 42. Fidel made his '*Soy un marxista leninista*' speech on 2 December 1961.

22 P. Gleijeses, *Conflicting Missions: Havana, Washington and Africa, 1959–1976* (Chapel Hill, NC: University of North Carolina Press, 2002), p. 95.

23 See W. M. Leogrande and W. S. Smith, 'Dateline Havana. Myopic Diplomacy', *Foreign Policy*, 48 (Fall 1982).

24 R. A. Pastor, 'Cuba and the Soviet Union. Does Cuba Act Alone?' in B. B. Levine (ed.), *The New Cuban Presence in the Caribbean* (Boulder, Colo.: Westview Press, 1983), p. 207.

25   J. I. Domínguez, 'The Nature and Uses of the Soviet–Cuban Connection' in
     E. Mujal Leon (ed.), *The USSR and Latin America. A Developing Relationship*
     (Boston: Unwin Hyman, 1989), p. 164.
26   E. Guevara, 'Cuba: Historical Exception?' in E. Guevara, *Obras, 1957–67*
     (Paris: Maspero, 1970), Vol. 2, p. 412.
27   E. Guevara, *Guerrilla Warfare* (Harmondsworth: Penguin, 1969), pp. 133–4.
28   J. Castañeda, *Utopia Unarmed: the Latin American Left after the Cold War*
     (New York: Vintage Books, 1994), p. 67.
29   R. Gott, *Rural Guerrillas in Latin America* (Harmondsworth: Penguin, 1970),
     p. 35.
30   Castañeda, *Utopia*, p. 4.
31   The circumstances were actually quite different. In 1945, the Western
     European economies were devastated but they still retained financial and
     technical expertise and institutional arrangements which facilitated rapid
     recovery. Western Europe did not resemble the political landscape of Latin
     America with its oligarchies and militaries which resisted the political and
     socio-economic transformations required to democratize and modernize the
     societies over which they presided.
32   S. G. Rabe, *The Most Dangerous Area in the World. John F. Kennedy Confronts
     Communist Revolution in Latin America* (Chapel Hill, NC: The University of
     North Carolina Press, 1999), p. 10.
33   Ibid., p. 8.
34   D. Deutschmann (ed.), *Che Guevara Reader. Writings on Guerrilla Strategy,
     Politics and Revolution* (Melbourne: Ocean Press, 1997), p. 220.
35   Quoted in R. J. Walton, *Cold War and Counterrevolution: the Foreign Policy of
     John F. Kennedy* (New York: Viking Press, 1972), p. 10.
36   Rabe, *Most Dangerous Area*, p. 159.
37   Ibid., p. 127.
38   Wright, *Latin America*, p. 70.
39   Rabe, *Most Dangerous Area*, p. 65.
40   A. Schlesinger, 'The Alliance for Progress: a Retrospective' in R. G. Hellman
     and H. J. Rosenbaum, *Latin America: the Search for a New International Role*
     (New York: Halstead Press, 1975), p. 74.
41   *Revolución* (1/4/62), 2.
42   Quoted by Hennessy and Lambie (eds), *Fractured Blockade*, p. 228.
43   Gleisejes, *Conflicting Missions*, p. 36.
44   Ibid., pp. 54–6.
45   Ibid., p. 78.
46   Che's experiences are discussed by W. Galvez, *Che in Africa. Che Guevara's
     Congo Diary* (Melbourne: Ocean Press, 1999); J. L. Anderson, *Che Guevara.
     A Revolutionary Life* (London: Bantam Books, 1997, Chs 26 and 27) and
     J. Castañeda, *Compañero. The Life and Death of Che Guevara* (London:
     Bloomsbury, 1997, Ch. 9).
47   E. Guevara, 'The Cuban Economy' in R. E. Bonachea and N. P. Valdes (eds),
     Che (Cambridge, Mass.: The MIT Press, 1969), p. 147.
48   J. A. Nathan, *Anatomy of the Cuban Missile Crisis* (Westport, Conn.:
     Greenwood Press, 2001), p. 34.
49   R. L. Millett, 'An Unclear Menace: U. S. Perceptions of Soviet Strategy in
     Latin America' in Mujal León (ed.), *The USSR*, p. 96.

50   Domínguez, *To Make a World Safe*, p. 33.
51   Although informed American opinion knew this to be true. A National Intelligence Estimate of March 1962 concluded that 'There are substantial numbers of Cubans ... who feel a surge of nationalistic pride in revolutionary Cuba, and who attribute all present short-comings to the implacable malevolence of Yankee imperialism.' Quoted by Gleisejes, *Conflicting Missions*, p. 17.
52   Morley, *Imperial State*, pp. 2–3.
53   A Cuban account is given by J. C. Rodriguéz in *The Bay of Pigs and the CIA* (Melbourne: Ocean Press, 1999). A fictional but compelling narrative is given by James Elroy in his novels, *American Tabloid* (London: Arrow Books, 1995) and *The Cold Ten Thousand* (London: Arrow Books, 2002).
54   'Inspector General's survey of the Cuban Operation, October 1961', pp. 143–5, The National Security Archive, The Gelman Library, George Washington University, Washington, DC.
55   W. S. Smith, *The Closest of Enemies. A Personal and Diplomatic Account of US–Cuban Relations since 1957* (New York: W. W. Norton & Company, 1987). Smith, a career diplomat, describes Playa Girón as beginning the profound disillusionment with US foreign policy which would eventually lead him to leave the Foreign Service in the 1980s.
56   J. G. Blight and P. Kornbluh (eds), *Politics of Illusion. The Bay of Pigs Reexamined* (Boulder, Colo.: Lynne Rienner, 1999), p. 152.
57   'Program of Covert Action Aimed at Weakening the Castro Regime' (CIA paper of 19/5/61), quoted by M. J. White (ed.), *The Kennedys and Cuba. The Declassified Documentary History* (Chicago: Ivan R. Dee, 1999), p. 56.
58   'Intelligence collection' is perhaps a misnomer. The release of FBI and CIA dossiers on Che Guevara offer illuminating reading including my particular favourite which is the report of several sightings of him in a 'yellow-painted pocket submarine' off the coast of the Dominican Republic. Quoted in M. Ratner and M. S. Smith (eds), *Che Guevara and the FBI. The US Political Police Dossier on the Latin American Revolutionary* (Melbourne: Ocean Press, 1997), p. 171.
59   Émigré groups also had links with organized crime. A Congressional inquiry failed to establish the nature of the involvement of the CIA – under Richard Helms's direction – in Mafia attempts on Fidel's life.
60   Nathan, *Anatomy*, p. 74.
61   White (ed.), *The Kennedys*, p. 36.
62   Memo from Goodwin to the President (22/8/61) quoted by Ratner and Smith (eds), *Che Guevara*, pp. 76–81.
63   Paterson, *Contesting*, p. 260.
64   Quoted in *The Guardian* (3/3/01), p. 12.
65   Nathan, *Anatomy*, p. xiv. The decision was made after the unexplained explosion of *La Coubre*, a French freighter carrying Belgian arms for Cuba in Havana Harbour in March 1960. A good source for the Missile Crisis are the documents displayed on the Cold War International History Project of the Woodrow Wilson International Center for Scholars website (http://cwihp.si.edu/cwihplib.nsf).
66   Ibid., p. 4.
67   The deal was made during a secret conversation between Robert Kennedy and the Soviet Ambassador Anatoly F. Dobrynin on 27 October. See

J. Hershberg, 'More on Bobby and the Cuban Missile Crisis (http.//cwihp.si.
edu/cwihplib.nsf), p. 2.

68　Nathan, *Anatomy*, p. 76.
69　P. Brenner and J. G. Blight, 'The Crisis and Cuban–Soviet Relations: Fidel
Castro's Secret 1968 Speech' (http.//cwihp.si.edu/cwihplib.nsf), pp. 2–3. This
Central Committee meeting was the one when the crimes of the Escalante
microfaction – chief amongst which was its closeness to the Soviet Union –
were condemned. However, the fact that Castro's speech was kept secret is
indicative that it would not be an irrevocable break and that Cuba was still
willing to accommodate Moscow. Escalante is discussed in Chapter 4.
70　Smith, *Closest of Enemies*, p. 90.
71　One of the more bizarre elements of the generally surreal period after 1959
was *Operación Pedro Pan* which engineered the exodus of thousands of
Cuban children to the US. The sensationalist Florida press relayed a rumour
that the Castro government was planning to strip parents of custody over
their children in order to indoctrinate the latter in godless values. A
network, set up by wealthy émigrés and the Catholic Church, took children
out of Cuba to host families and orphanages in the US. An extremely biased
account is given in V. A. Triay, *Fleeing Castro. Operation Pedro Pan and the
Cuban Children's Program* (Gainesville, Fla: University Press of Florida, 1999).
72　Most of the main figures of the old regime fled after the Rebel Army took
power, although lower-level collaborators remained in Cuba. Military
officers who were not accused of abuses of power were allowed to re-enlist
in the new army.
73　Camilo would die in a plane crash during one of his shuttles between
Havana and Camagüey. His death has been a subject of controversy, with
some insinuating that Fidel had removed a charismatic rival. It is far more
likely that it was an accident or a terrorist bomb. H. Matos, *Como llegó la
noche. Revolución y condena de un idealista cubano* (Barcelona: Tusquets, 2002)
offers his account of the degeneration of the Revolution.
74　Arboleya, *Cuban Counterrevolution*, pp. 61–5 offers an extensive survey of
the various Catholic organizations.
75　R. M. Levine and M. Asis, *Cuban Miami* (New Brunswick, NJ: Rutgers
University Press, 2000) give an evocative record of the physical look of Miami.

3　The Politics of National Identity

1　L. A. Pérez Jr, *On Becoming Cuban. Identity, Nationality and Culture* (Chapel
Hill, NC: University of North Carolina Press, 1999), pp. 5 and 9.
2　G. M. Joseph, 'Close Encounters. Towards a New Cultural History of US–Latin
American Relations' in G. M. Joseph, C. C. Legrand and R. D. Salvatore (eds),
*Close Encounters of Empire. Writing the Cultural History of US–Latin American
Relations* (Durham, NC: Duke University Press, 1998), p. 4.
3　Ibid., pp. 5 and 8.
4　Issuing his Protest of Baraguá, the black general Antonio Maceo refused to
sign the peace accord, arguing that Spain should have no role in the formation of a Cuban state. He continued fighting until lack of funds forced him
to leave Cuba.

5 Spain signed a treaty with Great Britain banning the slave trade to Cuba in 1835 but continued to flout the agreement until the pernicious trade finally ended in 1867. Slavery was itself abolished in 1886.

6 C. Schmidt-Nowara, *Empire and Antislavery. Spain, Cuba, and Puerto Rico, 1833–1874* (Pittsburgh, Pa: University of Pittsburgh Press, 1999), p. 19.

7 Pérez, *On Becoming Cuban*, p. 25.

8 Ibid., p. 84 and A. Kapcia, 'The Intellectual in Cuba: the National–Popular Tradition' in A. Hennessy (ed.), *Intellectuals in the Twentieth Century Caribbean*, vol. 11: *Unity in Variety: the Hispanic and Francophone Caribbean* (Basingstoke: Macmillan – now Palgrave Macmillan, 1992), p. 58.

9 Ibid., p. 59.

10 M. H. Morley, *Imperial State and Revolution. The United States and Cuba, 1952–1986* (Cambridge: Cambridge University Press, 1987), p. 31.

11 Jefferson, quoted in R. W. Van Alstyne, *The Rising American Empire* (Chicago: Quadrangle, 1960), p. 88 and Quincy Adams, quoted in P. Schwab, *Cuba. Confronting the US Embargo* (Basingstoke: Macmillan – now Palgrave Macmillan, 1999), vii.

12 B. Weinberg, *Homage to Chiapas. The New Indigenous Struggles in Mexico* (London: Verso, 2000), p. 40.

13 Quoted in D. Deutschmann (ed.), *Che Guevara Reader. Writings on Guerrilla Strategy, Politics and Revolution* (Melbourne: Ocean Press, 1997), p. 19.

14 L. A. Pérez Jr, *The War of 1898. The United States and Cuba in History and Historiography* (Chapel Hill, NC: University of North Carolina Press, 1998), p. 21.

15 Ibid., 29.

16 *The Platt Amendment*, US 5th Congress, Second Session, Chapter 3, 1901, 31 United States Statutes at Large, 897–8.

17 D. J. Fernández, *Cuba and the Politics of Passion* (Austin: University of Texas Press, 2000), p. 48.

18 C. D. Ameringer, *The Cuban Democratic Experience. The Auténtico Years, 1944–1952* (Gainesville, Fla: University Press of Florida, 2000), p. 2.

19 A. Kapcia, *Cuba: Island of Dreams* (Oxford: Berg, 2000), p. 60. It was also an extremely unstable politics with Liberal rebellions in 1905 and 1917. Such instability was seen as justifying further US military incursions under the terms of Platt.

20 Morley, *Imperial State*, p. 31. Jorge Ibarra, *Prologue to Revolution, Cuba, 1898–1958* (Boulder, Colo.: Lynne Rienner, 1998) offers a useful description of class structures, economic processes, differentiation by gender and ethnicity and rural–urban dichotomies during the period.

21 M. A. Figueras Pérez, 'Structural Changes in the Cuban Economy', *Latin American Perspectives*, 69: 18: 2 (Spring 1991), 69.

22 J. A. Arboleya, *The Cuban Counterrevolution* (Athens, Ohio: Ohio University Press, 2000), p. 19.

23 Quoted by E. Galeano, *Open Veins of Latin America. Five Centuries of the Pillage of a Continent* (New York: Monthly Review Press, 1973), p. 82.

24 C. J. Ayala, *American Sugar Kingdom. The Plantation Economy of the Spanish Caribbean 1898–1934* (Chapel Hill, NC: University of North Carolina Press, 1999), p. 2.

25 A. de la Fuente, *A Nation for All: Race, Inequality, and Politics in Twentieth Century Cuba* (Chapel Hill, NC: University of North Carolina Press, 2001), p. 105.

26 Morley, *Imperial State*, p. 32.

27 C. Brundenius, *Revolutionary Cuba: the Challenge of Economic Growth with Equity* (Boulder, Colo.: Westview Press, 1984), p. 10.

28 Ameringer, *Cuban Democratic Experience*, p. 135.

29 Arboleya, *Cuban Counterrevolution*, p. 11.

30 Ameringer, *Cuban Democratic Experience*, p. 124.

31 T. G. Paterson, *Contesting Castro. The United States and the Triumph of the Cuban Revolution* (Oxford: Oxford University Press), p. 35.

32 Ameringer, *Cuban Democratic Experience*, p. 5.

33 It might be said that the quota system was beneficial to Cuba in that the US paid above the world rate. The problem was that Cuba was never certain about the volume of demand or the price per ton and it was helpless in the face of US governmental decisions.

34 Pérez, *On Becoming Cuban*, p. 234.

35 O. Zanetti and A. García, *Sugar and Railroads: a Cuban History, 1837–1959* (Chapel Hill, NC: University of North Carolina Press, 1998), p. xvii.

36 De la Fuente, *A Nation*, p. 113.

37 Zanetti and García, *Sugar*, p. 374.

38 T. C. Wright, *Latin America in the Era of the Cuban Revolution*, revised edn (Westport, Conn.: Praeger, 2001), p. 2.

39 Arboleya, *Cuban Counterrevolution*, p. 24.

40 Pérez, *On Becoming Cuban*, p. 187.

41 R. Schwartz, *Pleasure Island. Tourism and Temptation in Cuba* (Lincoln, Neb.: University of Nebraska Press, 1997), p. 21.

42 Pérez, *On Becoming Cuban*, p. 141.

43 N. Miller, *In the Shadow of the State. Intellectuals and the Quest for National Identity in Twentieth-Century Spanish America* (London: Verso, 1999), p. 71.

44 W. H. Beasley and L. A. Curcio-Nagy, 'Introduction' in Beasley and Curcio-Nagy (eds), *Latin American Popular Culture. An Introduction* (Wilmington, Del.: Scholarly Books, 2000), p. xv.

45 An interesting account is given by G. Jacobs, 'CuBop! Afro-Cuban Music and Mid-Twentieth Century American Music' in L. Brock and D. Castañeda Fuertes (eds), *Between Race and Empire. African-Americans and Cubans before the Cuban Revolution* (Philadelphia, Pa: Temple University Press, 1998).

46 Arnaz, in his role as Ricky Ricardo in *I Love Lucy*, would become the archetypal Cuban to American television audiences in the 1950s with his macho posturing and strangled English.

47 L. Brock, 'Introduction' in Brock and Castañeda Fuertes (eds), *Between Race*, p. 5.

48 L. A. Pérez, Jr, 'Between Baseball and Bullfighting: the Quest for Nationality in Cuba, 1888–1898', *Journal of American History*, 81 (September 1994), 494.

49 Pérez, *On Becoming Cuban*, p. 266.

50 J. Martí, 'Plato de lentajes' (6/1/94), *Obras completas* (Havana, 1931), Vol. 1, p. 492.

51 This issue is discussed by R. Duharte Jiménez, 'The 19th Century Black Fear' in P. Pérez Sarduy and J. Stubbs (eds), *AfroCuba. An Anthology of Cuban Writing on Race, Politics and Culture* (Melbourne: Ocean Press, 1993).

52 G. Rénique, 'Review of Ada Ferrer, *Insurgent Cuba*', *NACLA Report on the Americas*, XXXIV (May/June 2001), 54.

53 A. Helg, *Our Rightful Share: the Afro-Cuban Struggle for Equality, 1886–1912* (Chapel Hill, NC: University of North Carolina Press, 1995), p. 47.

54 A. Ferrer, *Insurgent Cuba. Race, Nation and Revolution in Cuba, 1868–1898* (Chapel Hill, NC: University of North Carolina Press, 1999), p. 21.

55 These linkages are discussed by R. Scott, *Slave Emancipation in Cuba: the Transition to Free Labor, 1860–1899* (Pittsburgh, Pa: University of Pittsburgh Press, 2000).

56 Ferrer, *Insurgent Cuba*, p. 17.

57 Ibid., p. 3.

58 Ibid., p. 60.

59 Helg, *Our Rightful Share*, pp. 69–74 discusses the conspiracies against Maceo.

60 De la Fuente, *A Nation*, p. 25.

61 Universal male suffrage was granted in 1902.

62 An account of the rebellion and ensuing atrocities is given by Helg, *Our Rightful Share*, pp. 191–225.

63 De La Fuente, *A Nation*, p. 81.

64 E. Dore, 'Introduction' in D. Rubiera Castillo, *Reyita. The Life of a Black Cuban Woman in the Twentieth Century* (London: Latin American Bureau, 2000), p. 5.

65 For an account of the evolution of *santería* see M. Barnet, 'La Regla de Ocha. The Religious System of Santería' in M. Fernández Olmos and L. Paravisini-Gebert (eds), *Sacred Possessions. Vodou, Santería, Obeah and the Caribbean* (New Brunswick: Rutgers University Press, 1999).

66 Although the anthropologist Fernando Ortiz was the first writer to produce a serious analysis of Cuba's black society (in *Afro-Cuban Underworld, Negro Witchcraft* published in 1906) and to acknowledge what he termed the *ajiaco* (the 'stew') of Spanish, African and French cultural influences which contributed to Cuban identity, he has been criticized for perpetuating racial stereotypes and, thus, facilitating the repression of Afro-Cubans (Helg, *Our Rightful Share*, pp. 112–13).

67 De la Fuente, *A Nation*, pp. 146 and 157.

68 See R. Schwartz, 'Cuba's Roaring Twenties. Race Consciousness and the Column "Ideales de una raza"' in Brock and Castañeda Fuertes (eds), *Between Race*.

69 De La Fuenta, *A Nation*, p. 123.

70 Brock, 'Introduction' in Brock and Castañeda Fuertes (eds), *Between Race*, p. 19.

71 The concept of 'the black public space' is discussed by M. A. Neale, *What the Music Said. Black Popular Music and Black Popular Culture* (New York: Routledge, 1999).

72 See K. Kampwirth, *Women and Guerrilla Movements. Nicaragua, El Salvador, Chiapas, Cuba* (Pittsburgh, Pa: The Pennsylvania State University Press, 2002). Women largely managed the 26 July Movement whilst Castro and the other men were imprisoned on the Isle of Pines after Moncada. Espín

worked alongside Frank País in Santiago de Cuba whilst Santamaría raised funds in Miami. Women were also prominent in the Movimiento Resistencia Cívica (MRC, the Civic Resistance Movement), a broad front which provided money, medicine and supplies to the guerrillas.

73 This racism is discussed in N. R. Mirabel, 'Telling Silences and Making Community. Afro-Cubans and African-Americans in Ybor City and Tampa, 1899 –1915' in Brock and Castañeda Fuertes (eds), *Between Race*.

74 M. C. García, *Havana, USA: Exiles and Cuban Americans in South Florida, 1959–1994* (Berkeley: University of California Press, 1996), p. 94.

75 Quoted by Arboleya, *Cuban Counterrevolution*, p. 183.

4 Generations of Protest

1 T. C. Wright, *Latin America in the Era of the Cuban Revolution*, revised edn (Westport, Conn.: Praeger, 2001), p. 6.

2 A. Kapcia, 'Western European Influences on Cuban Revolutionary Thought' in A. Hennessy and G. Lambie (eds), *The Fractured Blockade. West European–Cuban Relations during the Revolution* (Basingstoke: Macmillan – now Palgrave Macmillan, 1993), p. 76.

3 R. Saumell-Muñoz, 'Castro as Martí's Reader in Chief' in J. Rodríguez-Luis (ed.), *Re-reading José Martí [1853–1895]. One Hundred Years Later* (New York: Albany State University of New York Press, 1999), p. 99.

4 Martí served as the New York consul for Uruguay, Argentina and Paraguay as well as representing Uruguay at international conferences and travelling extensively in Central America and the Caribbean.

5 G. E. Poyo, 'José Martí: Architect of Social Unity in the Émigré Communities of the United States' in C. Abel and N. Torrents (eds), *José Martí. Revolutionary Democrat* (London: Athlone Press, 1986), p. 28.

6 J. Martí, 'The Monetary Congress of the American Republics' in P. S. Foner (ed.), *Inside the Monster* (New York: Monthly Review Press, 1975), pp. 371–3.

7 J. Ibarra, 'Martí and Socialism' in Abel and Torrents (eds), *José Martí*, p. 99.

8 Ibid., pp. 88–9.

9 Cuban students were part of a wider Latin American movement for university reform which began in Córdoba in Argentina in 1918. The Popular University in Havana was inspired by the Universidad Popular González Prada set up in Lima in 1921. The popular universities provided free education for workers.

10 M. Caballero, *Latin America and the Comintern, 1919–1943* (Cambridge: Cambridge University Press, 1986), p. 48.

11 Mella joined in ideological debate with Víctor Raúl Haya de la Torre, leader of the Peruvian Alianza Popular Revolucionaria Americana (APRA, the American Popular Revolutionary Alliance), lambasting his influential organization as adventurist, opportunistic and petty bourgeois. Haya responded to Mella's *¿ Que es el ARPA?* (Lima: Libreria Editorial Minerva, 1975) [*APRA* was misspelt in the original] with his 1928 work, *El Antiimperialismo y el APRA* (Lima: Editorial Amauta, 1970). Haya contended that imperialism not capitalism was the main enemy and that communist parties, which sought their bases of support amongst the urban proletariat, had little chance of

success in societies which were predominantly agricultural. The American Revolution would only be victorious if its political leadership sought a multi-class constituency. In Peru, Haya's views were hotly contested by the Marxist José Carlos Maríategui, although he also resisted Comintern's attempts to take over the nascent socialist movement.

12 Born Nicanor MacPhelland of Scottish–Santo Dominican parents, Mella went into exile in Mexico where he worked for the Mexican communist newspaper, *El Machete*. Increasingly at odds with the Comintern which accused him of Trotskyism because of his contacts with Andrés Nin and other members of the Left Opposition, he was hunted down by Machado's agents who assassinated him on 10 January 1929. There is a need for a proper biography of Mella. Details of his life can be found in the biography of his lover, M. Hook, *Tina Modotti. Radical Photographer* (New York: Da Capo Press, 1993).

13 A. de la Fuente, *A Nation for All: Race, Inequality and Politics in Twentieth Century Cuba* (Chapel Hill, NC: University of North Carolina Press, 2001), p. 80.

14 Caballero, *Latin America*, p. 129.

15 As a university student, Castro had been attracted by the *Ortodoxo* campaign against political corruption and joined the party in 1947, although he led a splinter group out of it which called for direct action. He was likely to have won a congressional seat in 1953 had Batista's coup not interrupted the constitutional process.

16 S. B. Liss, *Fidel! Castro's Political and Social Thought* (Boulder, Colo.: Westview Press, 1994), p. 17.

17 Fidel's political identity is discussed by M. Azicri, 'Twenty-Six Years of Cuban Revolutionary Politics: an Appraisal' in S. Jones and N. Stein (eds), *Democracy in Latin America. Visions and Reality* (New York: Bergin & Garvey, 1990), pp. 177–8.

18 In a 1968 article commemorating Che's death. Quoted by Wright, *Latin America*, p. 16.

19 There are many accounts of the revolutionary war. Guevara's *Episodes of the Revolutionary War* (New York: Pathfinder, 1996) is the most famous. It has recently been criticized for providing the official view which tended to exaggerate the guerrilla army's role. See J. E. Sweig, *Inside the Cuban Revolution: Fidel Castro and the Urban Underground* (Harvard: Harvard University Press, 2002).

20 E. Galeano, *Days and Nights of Love and War* (London: Pluto Press, 2000), p. 59.

21 Quoted by R. Gott, *Rural Guerrillas in Latin America* (Harmondsworth: Penguin, 1970), p. 241.

22 The conspiracy theory model was first posited by Carlos Franqui, Fidel's close friend turned opponent, in *Retrato de familia con Fidel* (Barcelona: Seix Barral, 1981).

23 This was not always the case. Fidel's dismissal of Soviet aid to Colombia was couched in the following fashion: 'loans in dollars to an oligarchical government that is ... persecuting and murdering guerrillas. ... This is absurd' (*Granma* 11/8/67: 4). One of the occasions when he was openly annoyed with Che was after the latter's speech to the Second Economic Seminar of the Organization of Afro-Asian Solidarity in Algeria in February 1965 when

he castigated Moscow for contributing to the imperialist suffocation of the Third World through its unjust terms of trade. It was not in Che's nature not to be a straight talker.

24 A. Kapcia, *Cuba: Island of Dreams* (Oxford: Berg, 2000), p. 196.

25 In the immediate aftermath of the seizure of power, he was in charge of political security at La Cabaña fortress in Havana; then head of the industrial department of the National Institute of Agrarian Reform; director of the National Bank and minister for industry. In addition, he did many hours of voluntary labour. It may be argued that Che's personal standards and his expectations of others were too high. They certainly led to his sacrificing both himself and his family to the greater good of the Revolution and stimulated criticism of authoritarianism and even ruthlessness.

26 Anibal Escalante had condemned Che for wishing to move Cuba to a Eurocommunist viewpoint as espoused by the French, Italian and Spanish parties. His 'microfaction' was purged in 1968, accused of conspiracy, subversion and secret meetings in the Soviet embassy.

27 J. Castañeda, *Utopia Unarmed: the Latin American Left after the Cold War* (New York: Vintage Books, 1994), p. 80.

28 The Armed Forces of National Liberation and the Revolutionary Army of the People of Argentina. Both Marighela in *For the Liberation of Brazil* (Harmondsworth: Pelican, 1971) and Guillén (*Strategy of the Urban Guerrilla: Basic Principles of Revolutionary War* (Montevideo: Ediciones de Liberación, 1966)) argued that urban warfare brought guerrillas into a direct assault upon state power whereas rural *focos* ran the risk of isolation and annihilation by regular armies.

29 The Farabundo Marti National Liberation Front and the Revolutionary Armed Forces of Colombia.

30 'Revolutionary Ideas are not Obsolete', quoted in G. Mina, *An Encounter with Fidel Castro* (Melbourne: Ocean Press, 1991), p. 263.

31 J. I. Domínguez, *To Make A World Safe for Revolution: Cuba's Foreign Policy* (Harvard, Mass.: Harvard University Press, 1989), p. 250.

32 Liss, *Fidel!*, p. 23.

33 Ibid., p. 25.

34 M. Piñeiro, *Che Guevara and the Latin American Revolutionary Movements* (Melbourne: Ocean Press, 2001), p. 40.

35 Castañeda, *Compañero*, p. 129.

36 'Mensaje a los pueblos del mundo a través de la Tricontinental' in E. Guevara, *Obras, 1957–1967*, 2 vols (Paris: Maspero, 1970), pp. 584 and 598 [author's translation].

37 F. Claudin gives a succinct account of Moscow's dealings with the early communist movement in *The Communist Movement: From Comintern to Cominform* (Harmondsworth: Penguin, 1973).

38 A stimulating account of the break between the Old and New Lefts is given by J. Rodríguez Elizando, *Las Crisis de las Izquierdas en América Latina* (Caracas: Editorial Nueva Sociedad, 1990). The dichotomy between the two lefts was as much about style and generation as it was about revolutionary strategy. The romantic image of the Cuba of the 1960s fitted perfectly into the New Left's utopian vision.

39   Malcolm was sceptical of the Cubans' enthusiasm for the empowerment struggles of African-Americans, although other militants, such as Stokeley Carmichael, were more impressed. Fidel's speech to the UN stressed that Cuba and Africa were linked by slavery, underdevelopment and decolonization and that it was Cuba's duty to support national liberation movements there. Carlos Moore contends that such rhetoric was directed more to forging a spurious national integration at home and was, thus, hypocritical (C. Moore, *Castro, the Blacks and Africa* (Los Angeles: UCLA, Center for Afro-American Studies, 1988), pp. 88–91).

40   The column was destroyed in April 1964. Masetti had previously been the first editor-in-chief of Prensa Latina, the Cuban news agency.

41   Castañeda, *Utopia*, p. 63.

42   H. Béjar, *Perú, 1965. Apuntes sobre una Experiencia Guerrillera* (Lima: Editorial Campodónico-Moncloa, 1969), p. 51 [author's translation].

43   'La influencia de la Revolución cubana en la América Latina' in Guevara, *Obras*, p. 473 [author's translation].

44   Debray's role in Che's murder has long been an issue for the Cubans. His daughter, Aleida Guevara, is convinced that Debray's naivety was indirectly responsible for leading the Bolivian army to her father because of comments he made after his own capture. See C. Vilas, 'Fancy Footwork: Regis Debray on Che Guevara', *NACLA Report on the Americas*, XXX: 3 (November/December 1996).

45   Quoted by Gott, *Rural Guerrillas*, p. 29.

46   E. Guevara, 'Cuba: ¿ Excepción histórica o vanguardia en la lucha anti-imperialista?' in Guevara, *Obras*, p. 404 [author's translation].

47   Ibid., p. 407.

48   Quoted in G. Reed, *Island in the Storm* (Melbourne: Ocean Press, 1992), pp. 78 and 89.

49   Useful assessments of the dependency writers are offered by R. A. Packenham, *The Dependency Movement* (Cambridge, Mass.: Harvard University Press, 1992) and I. Roxborough, *Theories of Underdevelopment* (Basingstoke: Macmillan – now Palgrave Macmillan, 1994).

50   Liss, *Fidel!*, p. 51.

51   They were named after the place where Che was recuperating following a physical breakdown.

52   Kapcia, *Cuba*, p. 134.

53   Ibid.

54   E. Guevara, 'Speech given at the closing session of a seminar on "Youth and Revolution" ' cited by C. Tablada, *Che Guevara. Economics and Politics in the Transition to Socialism* (New York: Pathfinder, 1987), p. 163.

55   Che later admitted that although the government had been correct to concentrate upon income distribution and social needs, it had done so without 'sufficiently taking the state of our economy into consideration'. Quoted by C. Brundenius, *Revolutionary Cuba: the Challenge of Economic Growth with Equity* (Boulder, Colo.: Westview Press, 1984), p. 107.

56   K. Cole, *Cuba from Revolution to Development* (London and Washington: Pinter, 1998), p. 29.

57   Wright, *Latin America*, p. 37.

58   R. L. Harris, *Marxism, Socialism, and Democracy in Latin America* (Boulder, Colo.: Westview Press, 1992), p. 146.
59   Ibid.
60   Wright, *Latin America*, p. 37.
61   R. Fagan, 'Continuities in Cuban Revolutionary Politics' in P. Brenner, W. M. Leogrande, D. Rich and D. Siegel (eds), *The Cuban Reader: the Making of a Revolutionary Society* (New York: Grove Press, 1989), p. 57.
62   L. M. Smith and A. Padula, *Sex and Revolution: Women in Socialist Cuba* (New York: Oxford University Press, 1996), p. 85.
63   Harris, *Marxism*, p. 54.
64   Brundenius, *Revolutionary Cuba*, p. 43.
65   Kapcia, *Cuba*, p. 114.
66   The *Lucha contra Bandidos* (Struggle against bandits) which took place between 1962 and 1966 targeted recalcitrant peasants and counter-revolutionary armed groups.
67   Liss, *Fidel!*, p. 60.
68   Ibid., p. 63.
69   Cole, *Cuba*, p. 31.
70   Castañeda, *Utopia*, p. 74.

5   The Revolution Matures

1   In a speech given in May 1970, Fidel admitted: 'We can say with absolute certainty that the people didn't lose the battle. ... The administrative apparatus and the leaders of the Revolution are the ones who lost the battle' (*Granma Weekly Review*, 31/5/70: 10).
2   S. Eckstein, *Back from the Future. Cuba under Castro* (Princeton, NJ: Princeton University Press, 1994), p. 135.
3   E. Cardoso and A. Helwege, *Latin America's Economy. Diversity, Trends and Conflicts* (Cambridge, Mass.: MIT Press, 1992), p. 244.
4   Trade with market economies rose from 22.8 per cent of total trade in 1965 to 28.1 per cent (in 1970) and 40.1 per cent in 1975 but later shrank to 12.9 per cent in 1988. Cited by M. Azicri, *Cuba Today and Tomorrow: Reinventing Socialism* (Gainesville, Fla: University Press of Florida, 2000), p. 32.
5   This section is indebted to G. Lambie, 'Western Europe and Cuba in the 1970s: the Boom Years' in A. Hennessy and G. Lambie (eds), *The Fractured Blockade. West European–Cuban Relations during the Revolution* (Basingstoke: Macmillan – now Palgrave Macmillan, 1993).
6   Cuba also depended upon Soviet oil to meet more than 90 per cent of its needs. Oil was sold at a pegged price so that when the world price declined in 1986 and thereafter, Cuba lost $3.1 billion between 1986 and 1990. Cuba also paid over world prices for Soviet machinery (Azicri, *Cuba Today*, p. 34).
7   J. I. Domínguez, *To Make a World Safe For Revolution. Cuba's Foreign Policy* (Cambridge, Mass.: Harvard University Press, 1989), p. 66. Mechanization of the *zafra* reached 50 per cent of production in 1980 with an accompanying falling demand for labour.
8   Eckstein, *Back from the Future*, pp. 41–6.

9 C. Mesa-Lago, 'The Economic Effects on Cuba of the Downfall of Socialism in the USSR and Eastern Europe' in C. Mesa-Lago (ed.), *Cuba. After the Cold War* (Pittsburgh, Pa: University of Pittsburgh Press, 1993), p. 133.

10 Domínguez, *To Make a World Safe*, p. 92.

11 Pensions and social-security schemes have been privatized across Latin and Central American states to the detriment of the middle and working classes. This has contributed to an even more skewed distribution of wealth to the benefit of the domestic rich and their foreign allies. The impact of this transnationalization of capital upon one country, Chile, is discussed by S. Rosenfeld and J. L. Marré, 'How Chile's Rich Got Richer', *NACLA Report on the Americas*, XXX: 6 (May/June 1997).

12 Piñeiro and his team of professional revolutionaries at Liberación remained active into the 1990s. Increasingly bypassing official channels, there was speculation that they had become involved in rogue operations and, possibly, the drugs trade. See J. Castañeda, *Utopia Unarmed: the Latin American Left after the Cold War* (New York: Vintage Books, 1994), p. 65.

13 In 1975, at the behest of Henry Kissinger, $24.7 million of covert military assistance was approved for UNITA (*The Guardian*, 25/2/02, 18). The reason why so much importance was attached to Angola was that it was the richest of Portugal's ex-colonies (its wealth based upon diamonds and oil) and also had the largest white population. The country's racial and ethnic complexity was reflected in the fact that each guerrilla group was based upon a particular tribe.

14 P. Gleisejes, *Conflicting Missions. Havana, Washington, and Africa, 1959–1976* (Chapel Hill, NC: University of North Carolina Press, 2002) offers an in-depth account of Cuba's involvement in Angola. It is particularly interesting because he was permitted access to Cuban state archives which had been hitherto closed to foreign scholars.

15 Ibid., p. 345.

16 M. C. García, *Havana, USA: Exiles and Cuban Americans in South Florida, 1959–1994* (Berkeley: University of California Press, 1996), p. 45.

17 Ibid., p. 139.

18 The FBI estimated that Bosch had masterminded more than 70 armed actions against Cuba. Allowed to return to the US in 1988, the Justice Department wanted to deport him but leading Cuban-Americans organized a campaign on his behalf and he was allowed to remain. A 1977 *United Press* report contended that the CIA was also involved in a deliberately introduced epidemic of African swine fever into Cuba in 1971. The Agency refused to comment although a former agent, Eduardo Arocena, admitted to a US court in 1984 that this had happened.

19 W. S. Smith, *The Closest of Enemies. A Personal and Diplomatic Account of US–Cuban Relations since 1975* (New York: W. W. Norton & Company, 1987), p. 148.

20 Ibid., p. 139.

21 C. Vance, *Hard Choices* (New York: Simon and Schuster, 1983), p. 88.

22 H. M. Erisman, *Cuba's International Relations. The Anatomy of a Nationalistic Foreign Policy* (Boulder, Colo.: Westview Press, 1985), p. 91.

23 R. Dugger, *Reagan: the Man and His Presidency* (New York: McGraw-Hill, 1983), p. 360.

24   This was despite the fact that Havana insisted that the Salvadorean guerril-las seized most of their arms from the enemy or bought them in the open market and that the vast majority of Cubans in Nicaragua were teachers and doctors and not military personnel. See S. B. Liss, *Fidel! Castro's Political and Social Thought* (Boulder, Colo.: Westview Press, 1994), p. 105.

25   Ibid., p. 122. The marked differences between the paths taken by Cuba after 1959 and Nicaragua after 1979 are discussed by M. Azicri, 'Comparing Two Social Revolutions', *Journal of Communist Studies*, 5: 4 (1989).

26   C. M. Vilas, *Between Earthquakes and Volcanoes. Market State and the Revolutions in Central America* (New York: Monthly Review Press, 1995) offers a depressing account of the aftermath of the 1987 Central American Peace Accords. They did not represent a consensual settlement given that the military establishments continue to enjoy untrammelled power; there is continued abuse of human rights, particularly within indigenous communi-ties, and there has been no resolution of the causes of the insurgencies. These centred upon demands for political democracy, structural economic reform and social justice.

27   F. Castro, *This is the Battle for Latin America's Real Independence* (Havana: Editoro Política, 1985), p. 11. He argued that the International Monetary Fund's refusal to allow debtor countries to negotiate collectively instead opting for one-to-one discussions inhibited cooperative efforts to resolve the problem. An evaluation of Fidel's views on the debt crisis can be found in P. O'Brien, ' "The Debt Cannot Be Paid": Castro and the Latin American Debt', *Bulletin of Latin American Research*, 5: 1 (1986).

28   The odyssey of the Latin America left from armed struggle and Marxism to an embrace of parliamentary democracy is described in a number of texts including R. Munck, 'Farewell to Socialism? A Comment on Recent Debates', *Latin American Perspectives*, 65: 17: 2 (Spring 1990); B. Carr and S. Ellner (eds), *The Latin American Left. From the Fall of Allende to Perestroika* (Boulder, Colo.: Westview Press, 1993) and G. Lievesley, *Democracy in Latin America. Mobilization, Power and the Search for a New Politics* (Manchester: Manchester University Press, 1999), ch. 3.

29   Castañeda, *Utopia*, p. 342.

30   García, *Havana, USA*, p. 147.

31   J. Arboleya, *The Cuban Counterrevolution* (Athens, Ohio: Ohio University Press, 2001), p. 172.

32   Cuban-Americans were also involved in Operation Condor by which Pinochet sought to extend his reign of terror in Chile (1973–89) to other countries. Members of the fascist Movimiento Nacionalista Cubana (MNC, the Cuban Nationalist Movement) were implicated in the assassinations of Allende loyalist and Pinochet's predecessor as army chief, General Carlos Pratts, and his wife Sofia in Argentina in 1974 and of Orlando Letelier and Ronnie Moffatt in Washington in 1976. See H. O'Shaughnessy, *Pinochet: the Politics of Torture* (London: Latin American Bureau, 1999) and P. Verdugo, *Chile, Pinochet and the Caravan of Death* (Miami: University of Miami North-South Center, 2001).

33   The racist profile of the *marielitos* was reflected in Brian de Palma's remake of Howard Hawks's 1932 film *Scarface*. Al Pacino's Tony Camonte switches profession from bootlegger in Cuba to drugs dealer in Miami and, challeng-

ing Colombian monopoly over the industry, establishes a bloody empire. The Miami city commissioner was so outraged by the cinematic imagery that he tried to prevent filming.

34 These relations and their consequences for urban politics are examined in A. Portes and A. Stepnick, *City on the Edge. The Transformation of Miami* (Berkeley: University of California Press, 1993). It is particularly insightful in its discussion of the class and racial divisions within the Cuban-American communities and the absence of a coherent or united view on their role in the world.

35 Smith, *Closest of Enemies*, p. 213.

36 In 1984, Cuba signed a protocol with the Reagan administration which allowed 20,000 Cubans into the US annually whilst the Cuban government agreed to take back those criminal and mentally ill persons who had arrived during Mariel. However, later events, such as the start of Radio Martí's transmissions in 1985, resulted in the suspension of the agreement.

37 Quoted García, *Havana, USA*, p. 147. Calle Ocho is the major street in Little Havana in Miami.

38 Arboleya, *Cuban Counterrevolution*, p. 222.

39 The third tendency included Cambio Cubano which was formed by Eloy Gutiérrez Menoyo in 1992 and the Comité Cubano para la Democracia (Arboleya, *Cuban Counterrevolution*, pp. 278–83).

40 It claimed 121 prisoners. In 1991, the UN finally voted to appoint a human rights monitor for Cuba but this was resisted by the Cuban chief delegate, Raúl Róa Kouri, on the grounds that it violated the country's sovereignty (*Amnesty International Report on Prisoners of Conscience*, 1990, http://www.amnesty.org).

41 Quoted by Liss, *Fidel!*, p. 106.

42 Erisman, *Cuba's International Relations*, p. 174. See also W. M. Leogrande and W. S. Smith, 'Dateline Havana: Myopic Diplomacy', *Foreign Policy*, 48 (Fall 1982).

43 F. T. Fitzgerald, *The Cuban Revolution in Crisis. From Managing Socialism to Managing Survival* (New York: Monthly Review Press, 1994), p. 171.

44 G. Suárez Hernández, 'Political Leadership in Cuba: Background and Current Projections', *Latin American Perspectives*, 69: 18: 2 (Spring 1991), 55. At the time of writing, she was a professor of philosophy at the Escuela Superior del Partido Comunista de Cuba 'Nico López' so this may be taken as an official view.

45 Azicri, *Cuba Today*, p. 98.

46 Ibid., p. 100.

47 R. L. Harris, *Marxism, Socialism, and Democracy in Latin America* (Boulder, Colo.: Westview Press, 1992), p. 111.

48 Further regulations which stipulated that failing state enterprises would no longer automatically be rescued by the National Bank appeared to herald a more hard-headed approach to business dynamics.

49 K. Cole, *Cuba from Revolution to Development* (London and Washington: Pinter, 1998), p. 46.

50 Eckstein, *Back from the Future*, p. 63.

51 'In 1989, 80 per cent of cereals, 99 per cent of beans, 21 per cent of meat, 38 per cent of milk and dairy products and 94 per cent of cooking oil and

lard were imported', P. Rosset and M. Benjamin, *The Greening of the Revolution* (Melbourne: Ocean Press, 1994), p. 19.

52 J. Carranza Valdés, 'Economic Changes in Cuba: Problems and Challenges' in J. S. Tulchin, A. Serbin and R. Hernández (eds), *Cuba and the Caribbean. Regional Issues and Trends in the Post-Cold War Era* (Wilmington, Del.: Scholarly Resources, 1997), p. 201.

53 J. M. Blanco and M. Benjamin, *Talking about Revolution* (Melbourne: Ocean Press, 1994), p. 29.

54 Cole, *Cuba*, p. 40.

55 Ibid., p. 50.

56 *Granma Weekly Review*, 18/10/87, 5.

57 J. L. Domínguez, 'The Political Impact on Cuba of the Reform and Collapse of Communist Regimes' in C. Mesa-Lago (ed.), *Cuba. After the Cold War* (Pittsburgh, Pa: University of Pittsburgh Press, 1993), p. 106.

58 P. Monreal, 'Sea Changes. The New Cuban Economy', *NACLA Report on the Americas*, XXX11: 5 (March/April 1999).

59 Opening address to the Fourth Congress of the Cuban Communist Party (10/10/91). Quoted by G. Reed, *Island in the Storm* (Melbourne: Ocean Press, 1992), p. 33. He continued: 'The only situation in which we would have no future would be if we lost our homeland, the revolution and socialism.'

60 J. Stubbs, 'Social Equity, Agrarian Transition and Development in Cuba, 1945–90' in C. Abel and C. M. Lewis (eds) *Welfare, Poverty and Development in Latin America* (Basingstoke: Macmillan – now Palgrave Macmillan, 1993), p. 293.

61 L. M. Smith and A. Padula, *Sex and Revolution: Women in Socialist Cuba* (New York: Oxford University Press, 1996), p. 61.

62 W. S. Smith, 'An Ocean of Mischief. Our Dysfunctional Cuban Embargo', *Orbis*, 42: 4 (Fall 1998), 536.

63 The 2001 vote was 167 to 3 with Israel and the Marshall Islands voting with the US and Latvia, Micronesia and Nicaragua abstaining (*CubaSi*, Winter 2001–2, 18).

64 Liss, *Fidel!*, p. 124.

6 The Cuban State and the Cuban People

1 W. M. Leogrande, 'Participation in Cuban Municipal Government: from Local Power to People's Power' in D. E. Schulz and J. S. Adams, *Political Participation in Communist Countries* (New York: Pergamon Press, 1981), p. 277.

2 S. B. Liss, *Fidel! Castro's Political and Social Thought* (Boulder, Colo.: Westview Press, 1994), p. 52.

3 F. Castro, *Granma Weekly Review* (12/12/71), 13.

4 R. Hernández and H. Dilla, 'Political Culture and Popular Participation in Cuba', *Latin American Perspectives*, 69: 18: 2 (Spring 1991), 41.

5 'Between Vision and Reality: Democracy in Socialist Theory and Practice: the Cuban Experience', PhD dissertation, Massachusetts Institute of Technology, 1985, p. 209. Quoted by P. Roman, *People's Power: Cuba's Experience with Representative Government* (Boulder, Colo.: Westview Press, 1999), p. 69.

6 J. A. Blanco, 'Cuba: Utopia and Reality Thirty Years Later' in Centro de Estudios Sobre América (ed.), *The Cuban Revolution into the 1990s. Cuban Perspectives* (Boulder, Colo.: Westview Press, 1995) p. 27.

7 G. Suárez Hernández, 'Political Leadership in Cuba', *Latin American Perspectives*, 69: 18: 2 (Spring 1991), 52.

8 F. Castro, speech of 26/7/74; quoted by Roman, *People's Power*, p. 90; H. Dilla, G. González and A. T. Vincentelli, *Participación popular y desarrollo en los municipios cubanos* (Havana: Centro de Estudios Sobre América, 1993), p. 91 [author's translation].

9 T. C. Dalton, *'Everything within the Revolution.' Cuban Strategy for Social Development since 1960* (Boulder, Colo.: Westview Press, 1993), p. 133.

10 Hernández and Dilla, 'Political Culture', p. 53.

11 F. Martínez Heredia, 'Cuban Socialism: Prospects and Challenges', *Latin American Perspectives*, 69: 18: 2 (Spring 1991), 32.

12 S. Eckstein, *Back from the Future. Cuba under Castro* (Princeton, NJ: Princeton University Press, 1994), p. 21.

13 Liss, *Fidel!*, p. 71.

14 E. Guevara, *Che Guevara and the Cuban Revolution* (New York: Monthly Review Press, 1987), p. 197.

15 M. Lowy, 'Mass Organisation, Party and State: Democracy in the Transition to Socialism' in R. Fagan, C. Deere and J. L. Corragio (eds), *Transition and Development: Problems of Third World Socialism* (New York: Monthly Review Press, 1986), p. 270.

16 Eckstein, *Back from the Future*, p. 24.

17 Lowy, 'Mass Organisation', p. 271.

18 T. Kapcia, *Cuba. Island of Dreams* (Oxford: Berg, 2000), p. 220.

19 H. Dilla, 'The Virtues and Misfortunes of Civil Society', *NACLA Report on the Americas*, XXXII: 5 (March/April 1999), 30.

20 J. M. Bunck, *Fidel Castro and the Quest for a Revolutionary Culture in Cuba* (Philadelphia, Pa: Pennsylvania State University Press, 1994), p. 113.

21 L. M. Smith and A. Padula, *Sex and Revolution: Women in Socialist Cuba* (New York: Oxford University Press, 1996), p. 43.

22 Ibid., p. 95.

23 Bunck, *Fidel Castro*, p. 88; S. Kaufman Purcell, 'Modernizing Women for a Modern Society: the Cuban Case' in A. Pescatello (ed.), *Female and Male in Latin America* (Pittsburgh, Pa: University of Pittsburgh Press, 1973), p. 258.

24 In 'Notes on Man and Socialism in Cuba', Che painted a stark picture of family life. He argued that revolutionary leaders 'have children just beginning to talk, who are not learning to call their fathers by name; wives, from whom they have to be separated as part of the general sacrifice of their lives to bring the revolution to its fulfilment. ... There is no life outside of the revolution' (New York: Pathfinder Press, 1968), p. 20. Despite the evident love between Che, Aleida March and their children, his commitment to the Revolution came at tremendous personal cost. One wonders how many others could have emulated this Spartan code?

25 Bunck, *Fidel Castro*, p. 93.

26 Ibid., p. 115.

27 Smith and Padula, *Sex*, p. 46.

28 E. Guevara, 'Speech made during Investiture with Honorary Doctorate in the Central University of "Martha Abréu" ', *Hoy* (1/1/60), 2.

29 C. Moore, *Castro, the Blacks and Africa* (Los Angeles: UCLA Center for Afro-American Studies, 1988), p. 50. Bitterly anti-Castro and anti-communist, Moore argued that black Cubans were duped by the government's Afrocentric foreign policy and his courting of African-American activists such as Angela Davis and Huey Newton (whilst simultaneously repressing Afro-Cuban intellectuals such as Walterio Carbonell who were critical of its domestic policies).

30 For the next two years, he broadcast Radio Free Dixie to the southern states of his homeland before growing disillusioned with the growing Soviet presence in Cuba and the persistence of racism: 'I had a choice of remaining in Cuba ... but I don't see any difference in being a socialist Uncle Tom than being an Uncle Tom in capitalist and racist America' (T. B. Tyson, *Radio Free Dixie: Robert F. Williams and the Roots of Black Power* (Chapel Hill, NC: University Press of North Carolina, 1999), p. 294). Other militants, including Eldridge Cleaver, would also depart Cuban exile having complained about prejudice.

31 Smith and Padula, *Sex*, p. 170. A charge of prevailing homophobia is problematic. Traditionally, gay men were tolerated as long as they kept a low public profile so as not to bring shame to their families. There was contempt for effeminate males; the word used for them – *maricón* – also means coward. This celebration of aggressive male sexual activity chimes well with the *machista* devaluation of women. Ian Lumsden, *Machos, Maricones and Gays. Cuba and Homosexuality* (Philadelphia, Pa: Temple University Press, 1996) offers a fascinating account of the gay experience.

32 Quoted by D. West, 'Strawberry and Chocolate, Ice Cream and Tolerance. Interviews with Tomás Gutiérrez Alea and Juan Carlos Tabío', *CINEASTE*, XXI: 1–2 (1995), 16. Whilst Che was very hostile towards gays, Fidel appears to have been far less judgemental; indeed, Alfredo Guevara, one of his closest friends and the head of the Cuban Film Institute, was openly gay. Despite the strongly homophobic attitudes demonstrated by successive Soviet governments, leading communists Carlos Rafael Rodríguez and Blas Roca were disturbed by the thought of the Cuban state following suit.

33 For a critique of the documentary's failure to offer a historical or social context for its talking heads, see 'Néstor Almendros/Reinaldo Arenas: Documentary, Autobiography and Cinematography' in P. J. Smith, *Vision Machines. Cinema, Literature and Sexuality in Spain and Cuba, 1983–93* (London: Verso, 1996). Arenas, whose autobiographical *Antes que anochezca* (*Before Night Falls*, published in 1992) offered a flamboyant and graphic account of queer Cuba, left during the Mariel exodus and later died of Aids in New York.

34 There has been a similar evolution within the émigré community. Historically as staunchly homophobic as it was anti-communist, there is now an active although small homosexual movement which has opposed the introduction of discriminatory practices. Thus, for example, in 2002 it mobilized against the Take Back Miami–Dade campaign which was backed by the Christian Coalition and right-wing pressure groups (*The Guardian*, 9/9/2002, 3).

35 P. Schwab, *Cuba, Confronting the US Embargo* (Basingstoke: Macmillan – now Palgrave Macmillan, 1999), p. 113.

36 In his conversations with the radical Catholic Frei Betto, Fidel contended that there was no incongruity in being Marxist and Christian in that both traditions were committed to ending exploitation and fighting for social justice. See Frei Betto, *Fidel y la religión: Conversaciones con Frei Betto* (Havana: Oficina de Publicaciones de Estado, 1985).

37 Schwab, *Cuba*, p. 117.

38 M. Azicri, *Cuba Today and Tomorrow: Reinventing Socialism* (Gainesville, Fla: University Press of Florida, 2000), p. 261.

39 At the same time, the Cuban government turned down CANF's proffered $100 million in aid as an insult.

40 'Cuba Libre' in W. J. Harris (ed.), *The LeRoi Jones/Amiri Baraka Reader* (New York: Thunder's Mouth Press, 1991), p. 160.

41 N. Miller, 'The Intellectual in the Cuban Revolution' in A. Hennessy (ed.), *Intellectuals in the Twentieth Century Caribbean. Vol. II. Unity in Variety: the Hispanic and Francophone Caribbean* (Basingstoke: Macmillan – now Palgrave Macmillan, 1992), p. 84.

42 C. Wright Mills, *Listen Yankee* (New York: Ballantine Books, 1960); J. P. Sartre, *Sartre on Cuba* (New York: Ballantine Books, 1961) and S. de Beauvoir, *Force of Circumstance* (New York: Putnam, 1965).

43 A. Salkey, *Havana Journal* (Harmondsworth: Penguin, 1971). Salkey was critical of creeping bureaucratization and uncomfortable with the privileges accorded visitors but was generally elated by what he found on the island.

44 Quoted in J. Castañeda, *Utopia Unarmed: the Latin American Left after the Cold War* (New York: Vintage Books, 1994), p. 185.

45 A. Kapcia, 'Western European Influences on Cuban Revolutionary Thought' in A. Hennessy (ed.), *Intellectuals*, p. 74. The protagonist of *Memorias* is a cultured middle-class man, self-centred, spoilt and misogynistic. He is indecisive about his life, the revolution and the question of exile.

46 E. Guevara, *Obras, 1957–1967* (Paris: Maspero, 1970), p. 636.

47 Speech at the UNEAC awards ceremony in December 1969. Quoted by Miller in Hennessy (ed.), *Intellectuals*, p. 92.

48 Speech at the First Congress of Education and Culture, April 1970. Quoted by Miller in Hennessy (ed.), *Intellectuals*, p. 94.

49 J. I. Domínguez, *To Make a World Safe for Revolution: Cuba's Foreign Policy* (Harvard, Mass.: Harvard University Press, 1989), p. 280.

50 J. Duncan, *In the Red Corner. A Journey into Cuban Boxing* (London: Yellow Jersey Press, 2000), p. 19.

51 *The Guardian* (2/9/2000), 6.

52 'Son for my Cuba', composed by Mario Fernández and published on the *Estrellas de Areita–Los Heroes* album, recorded at the Egrem Studios, Havana in 1979.

53 Y. Daniel, *Rumba, Dance and Social Change in Contemporary Cuba* (Bloomington, Ind.: Indiana University Press, 1995), pp. 127, 125.

54 Ibid., p. 142.

55 K. Thompson and D. Bordwell, *Film History. An Introduction* (New York: McGraw-Hill, 1994), p. 620.

56 R. P. Kolker, *The Altering Eye. Contemporary International Cinema* (Oxford: Oxford University Press, 1983), p. 277.

57 'For an Imperfect Cinema'; quoted in Thompson and Bordwell, *Film History*, p. 617.

58 D. West, 'Reconciling Entertainment and Thought. An Interview with Julío García Espinosa' *CINEASTE*, XVI: 1–2 (1987–88), 20.

59 Discussed by T. Barnard, 'Death is not True. Form and History in Cuban Film' in J. King, A. M. López and M. Alvarado (eds), *Mediating Two Worlds. Cinematic Encounters in the Americas* (London: British Film Institute, 1993), p. 233.

60 T. Gutiérrez Alea, 'I Wasn't Always a Filmmaker', *CINEASTE*, XIV: 1 (1985), 37.

61 Ibid., p. 38.

62 M. D'Lugo, 'Transparent Women. Gender and Nation in Cuban Cinema' in King, López and Alvarado (eds), *Mediating Two Worlds*, p. 279.

63 Kolker, *Altering Eye*, p. 298.

64 M. Chanan, *The Cuban Image* (London: British Film Institute, 1985), p. 248.

65 In his autobiography, Almendros describes objecting to the Cuban market being flooded by unimaginative and dogmatic Soviet and East European films at the expense of radical European ones.

66 D. West, 'Alice in a Cuban Wonderland. An Interview with Daniel Díaz Torres', *CINEASTE*, XX: 1 (1993), 24–7.

67 Quoted in A. Hennessy and G. Lambie (eds), *The Fractured Blockade. West European–Cuban Relations during the Revolution* (Basingstoke: Macmillan – now Palgrave Macmillan, 1993), p. 38.

68 D. J. Fernández, *Cuba and the Politics of Passion* (Austin: University of Texas Press, 2000), p. 92.

7 Conclusion

1 The Cuban human rights group Concilio Cubano had planned to hold a public meeting on the day the planes were shot down but its activists were arrested before this could happen.

2 This figure did not include immediate relatives of US citizens but did cover all those Cubans currently on the waiting list for visas. Washington's intransigence on the blockade is ironic given that it now enthusiastically pursues trading relations with erstwhile enemies, China and Vietnam.

3 Quoted by K. Cole, *Cuba from Revolution to Development* (London and Washington: Pinter, 1998), p. 54. At the time of writing, Lage was Vice President of the Council of State with special responsibility for the economy.

4 M. Azicri, *Cuba Today and Tomorrow: Reinventing Socialism* (Gainesville, Fla: University Press of Florida, 2000), p. 306.

5 H. Dilla, 'The Virtues and Misfortunes of Civil Society', *NACLA Report on the Americas*, XXX11:5 (March/April 1999), 36.

6 P. Schwab, *Cuba. Confronting the US Embargo* (Basingstoke: Macmillan – now Palgrave Macmillan, 1999), pp. 93–5.

7 A. Aitsiselme, 'Despite U. S. Embargo Cuban Biotech Booms', *NACLA Report on the Americas*, XXXV: 5 (March/April 2002), 38–9.

8 The institute is named after the doctor who pioneered the cure for yellow fever during the Cuban–Spanish–American War.

9 Aitsiselme, 'Despite US Embargo', p. 39.

10 *The Guardian* (2/10/2000), 2. Cuba has 21 medical schools to the UK's 12, more practice nurses and more GPs per head of population.

11 P. Rosset, 'The Greening of Cuba', *NACLA Report on the Americas*, XXVIII: 3 (November/December 1994), 94.

12 L. Davies, 'Nothing to Lose but Their Spades', *The Independent on Sunday* (8/4/2002), 32.

13 W. Schwarz, 'The Future is Orange', *Guardian Society*, 19/12/2001, 9.

14 K. Cole's review of a UNICEF Report, *The Guardian* (22/4/1997), 8. Cuba regards such liberalization programmes as creating human and social misery and has been adamant that it would never take such a road.

15 J. Carranza Valdés, L. Gutiérrez Urdaneta and P. Monreal González, *Cuba: la Restructuración de la Economía* (Havana: Editorial de Ciencias Sociales, 1995), p. 6.

16 J. Petras, *The Left Strikes Back. Class Conflict in the Age of Neoliberalism* (Boulder, Colo.: Westview Press, 1999), p. 172.

17 Its sponsors were Indiana Representative Dan Burton and Jesse Helms (Republican, North Carolina), veteran red baiter and chair of the Senate Foreign Relations Committee until his retirement in 2002.

18 Bacardí left Cuba in 1957. In the 1960s, it provided financial backing for armed groups including the *brigadistas* and the RECE whilst CANF leaders were shareholders in the company. Bacardí enjoyed close relations with the CIA and right-wing politicians such as Helms and Jeanne Kirkpatrick, Ambassador to the UN, and also participated in Reagan's Project Democracy. Bacardí's CEO, Manuel J. Cutillas, supported UNITA in Angola and the Nicaraguan Contra. Since the 1990s, it has been heavily involved in preparations for a Cuban transitional government along with other multinationals such as Coca Cola, General Sugar and Chiquita. Part of the strategy is to sell off all public assets on the island. See H. Calvo Ospina, *Bacardí. The Hidden War* (London: Pluto, 2000).

19 Quoted by W. S. Smith, 'An Ocean of Mischief. Our Dysfunctional Cuban Embargo', *Orbis*, 42: 4 (Fall 1998), 537.

20 Quoted by J. Roy, *Cuba, the United States, and the Helms–Burton Doctrine. International Reactions* (Gainesville, Fla: University Press of Florida, 2000), pp. 4 and 29.

21 M. Radu, 'An Ocean of Mischief. Don't Reward Castro, Keep the Embargo', *Orbis*, 42: 4 (Fall 1998), 546.

22 Ricardo Alarcón, quoted by Roy, *Cuba*, p. 84.

23 *Fortune* (13/10/97), 48.

24 There were growing fissures within the community. The Clinton administration acknowledged the decline of the hardliners when the president met with moderates such as Eloy Gutiérrez Menoyo and Alfredo Durán, former chair of the Cuban Democracy Committee. Clinton was criticized for this shift in relations as well as for the concessions he made after the Pope's visit to Cuba. His worst crime was undoubtedly shaking hands with Castro at the UN Millennium Conference in September 2000 although that was unintentional.

25   *The Guardian* (25/7/2002), 13.

26   H. Calvo Ospina and K. Declercq, *Dissidents or Mercenaries? The Cuban Exile Movement* (Melbourne: Ocean Press, 2000), p. 76. Dissident groups within Cuba are small, beset by factionalism and vulnerable to state harassment and are wholly dependent upon external funding.

27   The head of mobilization and political action at Oxfam-Solidarity, Belgium stated that working with the Cubans was 'different because ... they are more aware of their historic process, as a result of which both the government and the people have a great sense of dignity and won't allow anything to be imposed on them'. Quoted by Calvo and Declercq, *Dissidents*, p. 153.

28   *The Guardian* (2/12/2002), 14.

29   In fact, terrorism was being conducted but against Cuba rather than by it. There were assassination attempts on diplomats, bombings in Havana's tourist hotels and attacks upon Cuban ships and planes. The most recent case of Cubans charged with spying in the US is that of the 'Miami Five' convicted in 2001. The Cuban government insisted that the men were investigating the activities of right-wing groups operating in Florida including the infamous Orlando Bosch. Tried in a flawed trial with tainted evidence and a jury selected from hard-core anti-Castro districts in Miami, they received long sentences.

30   *The Guardian* (6/6/2002), 15. Ex-President Jimmy Carter immediately countered this claim, contending that he had not been briefed about the allegations before his visit to Cuba in May 2002. Carter called upon President Bush to initiate a process of engagement with Cuba, the first step of which should be discussions about the blockade, but his advice was snubbed by the White House.

31   Quoted by T. M. Leonard, *Castro and the Cuban Revolution* (Westport, Conn.: Greenwood Press, 1999), p. 147.

32   G. Peréz Firmat, *Life on the Hyphen: the Cuba–American Way* (Austin: University of Texas Press, 1994) discusses the evolution of the Cuban-American identity but is criticized for idealizing the community by M. J. Castro, 'The Trouble with Collusion. Paradoxes of the Cuban-American Way' in D. J. Fernández and M. Cámara Betancourt, *Cuba. The Elusive Nation. Interpretations of National Identity* (Gainesville, Fla: University Press of Florida, 2000).

33   Azicri, *Cuba*, p. 18.

34   A. O'Halloran, 'Questioning the Primacy of Autonomy in the Women's Movement: the Case of Cuba', *Central America Women's Network*, 16 (Winter 2002/3), 16.

35   C. Fusco, 'Hustling for Dollars. *Jinterismo* in Cuba', in K. Kempadoo and J. Doezema, *Global Sex Workers. Rights, Resistance, and Redefinition* (New York: Routledge, 1998), p. 161.

36   G. D. Hodge, 'Colonization of the Cuban Body. The Growth of Male Sex Work in Havana', *NACLA Report on the Americas*, XXXIV: 5 (March/April 2001), 23.

37   A. de la Fuente, 'The Resurgence of Race in Cuba', *NACLA Report on the Americas*, XXXIV (May/June 2001).

38   I. Lumsden, *Machos, Maricones and Gays. Cuba and Homosexuality* (Philadelphia, Pa: Temple University Press, 1996), p. 146.

39 S. T. Malone, 'Conflict, Coexistence and Cooperation: Church–State Relations in Cuba' at www.georgetown.edu/sfs/programs/clas/caribe: 16.

40 M. Randall, *Gathering Rage. The Failure of Twentieth Century Revolutions to Develop a Feminist Agenda* (New York: Monthly Review Press, 1992), pp. 138–9.

41 J. A. Blanco, 'Cuba: Crisis, Ethics and Viability' in S. Jonas and E. J. McCaughan (eds), *Latin America Faces the Twenty-First Century. Reconstructing a Social Justice Agenda* (Boulder, Colo.: Westview Press, 1995), pp. 190 and 192.

42 C. P. Ripley, *Conversations with Cuba* (Athens: University of Georgia Press, 1999), p. 139.

43 S. B. Liss, *Fidel! Castro's Political and Social Thought* (Boulder, Colo.: Westview Press, 1994), p. 178.

44 Ibid., p. 179.

45 *The Financial Times* (19/9/1998), 3.

46 B. Pollit, ' "Restructuring" Cuba's Sugar Economy – the End of an Era', *Cuba Si* (Winter 2002–3), 27.

47 *The Financial Times* (27/4/2002), 5. The opposition Partido Revolucionaria Institucional dominated Mexican politics until Fox's election in July 2000.

48 T. C. Wright, *Latin America in the Era of the Cuban Revolution*, revised edn (Westport, Conn.: Praeger, 2001), p. 205.

Bibliography

Abel, C. and N. Torrents (eds) *José Martí. Revolutionary Democrat* (London: Athlone Press, 1986)

Ameringer, C. D. *The Cuban Democratic Experience. The Auténtico Years, 1944–1952* (Gainesville, Fla: University Press of Florida, 2000)

Anderson, J. L. *Che Guevara. A Revolutionary Life* (London: Bantam, 1997)

Arboleya, J. *The Cuban Counterrevolution* (Athens, Ohio: Ohio University Press, 2001)

Arenas, R. *Before Night Falls* (London: Serpent's Tail, 1993)

August, A. *Democracy in Cuba and the 1997–98 Elections* (Havana: Editorial José Martí, 1999)

Ayala, C. J. *American Sugar Kingdom. The Plantation Economy of the Spanish Caribbean 1898–1934* (Chapel Hill, NC: University of North Carolina Press, 1999)

Azicri, M. 'Twenty-six Years of Cuban Revolutionary Politics: an Appraisal' in S. Jonas and N. Stein (eds), *Democracy in Latin America. Visions and Reality* (New York: Bergin & Garvey, 1990)

Azicri, M. *Cuba Today and Tomorrow: Reinventing Socialism* (Gainesville, Fla: University Press of Florida, 2000)

Barnet, M. 'La Regla de Ocha. The Religious System of Santería' in M. Fernández Olmos and L. Paravisini-Gebert (eds) *Sacred Possessions. Vodou, Santería, Obeah and the Caribbean* (New Brunswick: Rutgers University Press, 1999)

Beasley, W. H. and L. A. Curcio-Nagy 'Introduction' in W. H. Beasley and L. A. Curcio-Nagy (eds) *Latin American Popular Culture. An Introduction* (Wilmington, Del.: Scholarly Books, 2000)

Béjar, H. *Perú 1965: Apuntes sobre una Experiencia Guerrillera* (Lima: Editorial Campodónico-Moncloa, 1969)

Belnap, J. and R. Fernández (eds) *José Martí's 'Our America'* (Durham, NC: Duke University Press, 1999)

Bernard, T. 'Death is Not True. Form and History in Cuban Film' in J. King, A. M. Lopez and M. Alvarado *Mediating Two Worlds. Cinematic Encounters in the Americas* (London: British Film Institute, 1993)

Birringer, J. 'An Interview with Jorge Perugorria', *CINEASTE*, XXI: 1–2 (1995)

Blackburn, R. 'Prologue to the Cuban Revolution', *New Left Review*, 21 (1963)

Blanco, J. A. 'Cuba: Utopia and Reality Thirty Years Later' in Centro de Estudios Sobre América (ed.) *The Cuban Revolution into the 1990s. Cuban Perspectives* (Boulder, Colo.: Westview Press, 1992)

Blanco, J. A. 'Cuba, Crisis, Ethics and Viability' in S. Jonas and E. J. McCaughan (eds) *Latin America Faces the Twenty-First Century. Reconstructing a Social Justice Agenda* (Boulder, Colo.: Westview Press, 1995)

Blanco, J. A. and M. Benjamin *Talking about Revolution* (Melbourne: Ocean Press, 1994)

Blight, J. G. and P. Kornbluh (eds) *Politics of Illusion. The Bay of Pigs Reexamined* (Boulder, Colo.: Lynne Rienner, 1999)

Bonachea, R. E. and N. P. Valdes (eds) *Che* (Cambridge, Mass.: The MIT Press, 1969)

Bonachea, R. E. and N. P. Valdes (eds) *Cuba in Revolution* (New York: Doubleday, 1972)

Brenner, P. and P. Kornbluh 'Clinton's Cuba Calculus', *NACLA Report on the Americas*, XXIX: 2 (September/October 1995)

Brenner, P., W. M. Leogrande, D. Rich and D. Siegel (eds) *The Cuba Reader: the Making of a Revolutionary Society* (New York: Grove Press, 1989)

Brock, L. and D. Castañeda Fuertes (eds) *Between Race and Empire. African-Americans and Cubans before the Cuban Revolution* (Philadelphia, Pa: Temple University Press, 1998)

Brundenius, C. *Revolutionary Cuba: the Challenge of Economic Growth with Equity* (Boulder, Colo.: Westview Press, 1984)

Bunck, J. M. *Fidel Castro and the Quest for a Revolutionary Culture in Cuba* (Philadelphia, Pa: Pennsylvania State University Press, 1994)

Burbach, R. 'Clinton's Latin America Policy: a Look at Things to Come', *NACLA Report on the Americas*, XXVI: 5 (May 1993)

Caballero, M. *Latin America and the Comintern, 1919–1943* (Cambridge: Cambridge University Press, 1986)

Cabezas, A. L. 'Discourses of Prostitution. The Case of Cuba' in K. Kempadoo and J. Doezema *Global Sex Workers. Rights, Resistance, and Redefinition* (New York: Routledge, 1998)

Calvo Ospina, H. *Bacardi. The Hidden War* (London: Pluto Press, 2002)

Calvo Ospina, H. and K. Declercq *Dissidents or Mercenaries? The Cuban Exile Movement* (Melbourne: Ocean Press, 2000)

Carbonell, N. T. *And the Russians Stayed. The Sovietization of Cuba* (New York: William Morrow & Co., 1989)

Carr, B. and S. Ellner *The Latin American Left. From the Fall of Allende to Perestroika* (Boulder, Colo.: Westview Press, 1993)

Carranza Valdés, J. 'The Current Situation in Cuba and the Process of Change', *Latin American Perspectives*, 69: 18: 2 (Spring 1991)

Castañeda, J. *Utopia Unarmed: the Latin American Left after the Cold War* (New York: Vintage Books, 1994)

Castañeda, J. *Compañero. The Life and Death of Che Guevara* (London: Bloomsbury, 1997)

Centeno, M. A. and M. Font (eds) *Towards A New Cuba? Legacies of a Revolution* (Boulder, Colo.: Lynne Rienner, 1997)

Centro de Estudios Sobre América (ed.) *The Cuban Revolution into the 1990s. Cuban Perspectives* (Boulder, Colo.: Westview Press, 1992)

Chanan, M. *The Cuban Image* (London: British Film Institute, 1985)

Claudin, F. *The Communist Movement. From Comintern to Cominform* (Harmondsworth: Penguin, 1973)

Cole, K. *Cuba from Revolution to Development* (London and Washington: Pinter, 1998)

Cook, P. and M. Bernink (eds) *The Cinema Book*, 2nd edn (London: British Film Institute, 1999)

Crowdus, G. 'Up to a Point: an Interview with Tomás Gutiérrez Alea and Mirta Ibarra', *CINEASTE*, XIV: 2 (1985)

Crowdus, G. and D. Georgakas 'Spread a Little Sunshine. An Interview with Jack Lemmon in Havana', *CINEASTE*, XIV: 3 (1986)

Dalton Thomas, C. *'Everything within the Revolution': Cuban Strategies for Social Development* (Boulder, Colo.: Westview Press, 1993)

Daniel, Y. *Rumba. Dance and Social Change in Contemporary Cuba* (Bloomington, Ind.: Indiana University Press, 1995)

Debray, R. *Strategy for Revolution* (Harmondsworth: Penguin, 1970)

Debray, R. *The Revolution on Trial* (Harmondsworth: Penguin, 1978)

De la Fuente, A. *A Nation for All: Race, Inequality, and Politics in Twentieth Century Cuba* (Chapel Hill, NC: University of North Carolina Press, 2001)

De la Fuente, A. 'The Resurgence of Racism in Cuba', *NACLA Report on the Americas*, XXXIV (May–June 2001)

Deutschmann, D. (ed.) *Che Guevara Reader. Writings on Guerrilla Strategy, Politics and Revolution* (Melbourne: Ocean Press, 1997)

Dilla, H. (ed.) *La democracia en Cuba y el diferendo con los Estados Unidos* (Havana: Centro de Estudios Sobre América, 1995)

Dilla, H. *La participación en Cuba y los retos del futuro* (Havana: Centro de Estudios Sobre América, 1996)

Dilla, H., G. González and A. T. Vincentelli *Participación popular y desarrollo en los municipios cubanos* (Havana: Centro de Estudios Sobre América, 1993)

D'Lugo, M. 'Transparent Women. Gender and Nation in Cuban Cinema' in J. King, A. M. Lopez and M. Alvarado (eds) *Mediating Two Worlds. Cinematic Encounters in the Americas* (London: British Film Institute, 1993)

Domínguez, F. 'Political Issues in Cuba's Economic Reform'. Paper presented to the Society of Latin American Studies Conference, University of Cambridge (April 1999)

Domínguez, J. I. *To Make a World Safe for Revolution. Cuba's Foreign Policy* (Cambridge, Mass.: Harvard University Press, 1989)

Domínguez, J. I. 'US–Cuban relations: From the Cold War to the Colder War', *Journal of Interamerican Studies and World Affairs* (Fall 1997)

Duncan, J. *In the Red Corner. A Journey into Cuban Boxing* (London: Yellow Jersey Press, 2000)

Dye, A. *Cuban Sugar in the Age of Mass Production* (Cambridge: Cambridge University Press, 1998)

Eckstein, S. *Back from the Future. Cuba under Castro* (Princeton, NJ: Princeton University Press, 1994)

Elizondo, J. R. *La crisis de las izquierdas en América Latina* (Madrid and Caracas, Instituto de Cooperación Iberoamericana: Editorial Sociedad, 1990)

Elliston, J. (ed.) *Psywar on Cuba* (Hoboken, NJ: Ocean Press, 1999)

Erisman, H. M. *Cuba's International Relations. The Anatomy of a Nationalistic Foreign Policy* (Boulder, Colo.: Westview Press, 1985)

Erisman, H. M. *Cuba's Foreign Relations in a Post-Soviet World* (Gainesville, Fla: University Press of Florida, 2000)

Fagan, R. 'Continuities in Cuban Revolutionary Politics' in P. Brenner, W. M. Leogrande, D. Rich and D. Siegel (eds) *The Cuba Reader: the Making of a Revolutionary Society* (New York: Grove Press, 1989)

Feinsilver, J. 'Can Biotechnology Save the Cuban Revolution?', *NACLA Report on the Americas*, XXVI: 5 (May 1993)

Fernández, D. J. *Cuba and the Politics of Passion* (Austin: University of Texas Press, 2000)

Fernández, D. J. and M. Cámara Betancourt *Cuba, the Elusive Nation. Interpretations of National Identity* (Gainesville, Fla: University Press of Florida, 2000)

Fernández Olmos, M. and L. Paravisini-Gebert (eds) *Sacred Possessions. Vodou, Santería, Obeah and the Caribbean* (New Brunswick: Rutgers University Press, 1999)

Fernández Retamar, R. 'The Modernity of Martí' in C. Abel and N. Torrents (eds) *José Martí. Revolutionary Democrat* (London: Athlone Press, 1986)

Ferrer, A. *Insurgent Cuba. Race, Nation and Revolution in Cuba, 1868–1898* (Chapel Hill, NC: The University of North Carolina Press, 1999)

Ferrer, A. 'The Silence of Patriots: Race and Nationalism in Martí's Cuba' in J. Beltrap and R. Fernandez (eds) *José Martí's 'Our America'* (Durham, NC: Duke University Press, 1999)

Figueras Pérez, M. A. 'Structural Change in the Cuban Economy', *Latin American Perspectives*, 69: 18: 2 (Spring 1991)

Fitzgerald, F. T. *The Cuban Revolution in Crisis. From Managing Socialism to Managing Survival* (New York: Monthly Review Press, 1994)

Foreign Policy Research Institute, 'Cuba Libre! A Century On', *Orbis*, 42: 4 (Fall 1998)

Freeman Smith, R. (ed.) *Background to Revolution. The Development of Modern Cuba* (Huntington, NY: Robert E. Krieger Publishing Company, 1979)

Fusco, C. 'Hustling for Dollars. *Jinterismo* in Cuba' in K. Kempadoo and J. Doezema *Global Sex Workers. Rights, Resistance, and Redefinition* (New York: Routledge, 1998)

Galeano, E. *Open Veins of Latin America. Five Centuries of the Pillage of a Continent* (New York: Monthly Review Press, 1973)

Gálvez, W. *Che in Africa* (Hoboken, NJ: Ocean Press, 1999)

García, M. C. *Havana, USA: Exiles and Cuban Americans in South Florida, 1959–1994* (Berkeley: University of California Press, 1996)

García-Perez, G. M. *Insurrection and Revolution. Armed Struggle in Cuba, 1952–1959* (Boulder, Colo.: Lynne Rienner, 1998)

Garthoff, R. L. *Reflections on the Cuban Missile Crisis* (Washington: The Brookings Institute, 1989)

Gillespie, R. (ed.) *Cuba after Thirty Years: Rectification and Revolution* (London: Frank Cass, 1990)

Gleisejes, P. *Conflicting Missions: Havana, Washington and Africa, 1959–1976* (Chapel Hill, NC: University of North Carolina Press, 2000)

Gott, R. *Rural Guerrillas in Latin America* (Harmondsworth: Penguin, 1970)

Guevara, E. *Reminiscences of the Cuban Revolutionary War* (New York: Monthly Review Press, 1968)

Guevara, E. *Guerrilla Warfare* (Harmondsworth: Penguin, 1969)

Guevara, E. *Obras, 1957–1967*, 2 vols (Paris: Maspero, 1970)

Guevara, E. *Che Guevara and the Cuban Revolution* (New York: Pathfinder Press, 1987)

Gutiérrez Alea, T. 'I Wasn't Always a Filmmaker', *CINEASTE*, XIV: 1 (1985)

Habel, J. *Cuba* (London: Verso, 1991)

Halebsky, S. and J. Kirk *Cuba: Twenty Five Years of Revolution* (New York: Praeger, 1985)

Halebsky, S. and J. Kirk *Cuba in Transition* (Boulder, Colo.: Westview Press, 1992)

Harris, R. L. *Marxism, Socialism, and Democracy in Latin America* (Boulder, Colo.: Westview Press, 1992)

Helg, A. *Our Rightful Share: the Afro-Cuban Struggle for Equality, 1886–1912* (Chapel Hill, NC: University of North Carolina Press, 1995)

Hennessy, A. (ed.) *Intellectuals in the Twentieth Century Caribbean*. Vol. II. *Unity in Variety: the Hispanic and Francophone Caribbean* (Basingstoke: Macmillan – now Palgrave Macmillan, 1992)

Hennessy, A. and G. Lambie (eds) *The Fractured Blockade. West European–Cuban Relations during the Revolution* (Basingstoke: Macmillan – now Palgrave Macmillan, 1993)

Hernández, R. 'Frozen Relations. Washington and Cuba after the Cold War', *NACLA Report on the Americas*, XXXV: 4 (January/February 2002)

Hernández, R. and H. Dilla, 'Political Culture and Popular Participation in Cuba', *Latin American Perspectives*, 69: 18: 2 (Spring 1991)

J. Hill and P. Church Gibson (eds) *The Oxford Guide to Film Studies* (Oxford: Oxford University Press, 1998)

Huberman, L. and P. Sweezy *Cuba. Anatomy of a Revolution* (New York: Monthly Review Press, 1960)

Huberman, L. and P. Sweezy (eds) *Regis Debray and the Latin American Revolution* (New York: Monthly Review Press, 1969)

Ibarra, J. 'Martí and Socialism' in C. Abel and N. Torrents (eds) *José Martí. Revolutionary Democrat* (London: Athlone Press, 1986)

Ibarra, J. *Prologue to Revolution. Cuba, 1898–1958* (Boulder, Colo.: Lynne Rienner, 1998)

Joseph, G. M., C. C. Legrand and R. D. Salvatore (eds) *Close Encounters of Empire. Writing the Cultural History of US–Latin American Relations* (Durham, NC: Duke University Press, 1998)

Kampwirth, K. *Women and Guerrilla Movements. Nicaragua, El Salvador, Chiapas, Cuba* (Pittsburgh, Pa: The Pennsylvania State University Press, 2002)

Kapcia, A. 'Cuban Populism and the Birth of the Myth of Martí' in C. Abel and N. Torrents (eds) *José Martí. Revolutionary Democrat* (London: Athlone Press, 1986)

Kapcia, A. 'The Intellectual in Cuba: the National-popular Tradition' in A. Hennessy (ed.) *Intellectuals in the Twentieth Century Caribbean*. Vol. II. *Unity in Variety: the Hispanic and Francophone Caribbean* (Basingstoke: Macmillan – now Palgrave Macmillan, 1992)

Kapcia, A. 'Western European Influences on Cuban Revolutionary Thought' in A. Hennessy and G. Lambie (eds) *The Fractured Blockade. West European–Cuban Relations during the Revolution* (Basingstoke: Macmillan – now Palgrave Macmillan, 1993)

Kapcia, A. *Cuba: Island of Dreams* (Oxford: Berg, 2000)

Kaplowitz, D. R. *Anatomy of a Failed Embargo. US Sanctions against Cuba* (Boulder, Colo.: Lynne Rienner, 1997)

Kaufman Purcell, S. and D. Rothkopf (eds) *Cuba: the Contours of Change* (Boulder, Colo.: Lynne Rienner, 2000)

King, J., A. M. Lopez and A. Alvarado, *Mediating Two Worlds. Cinematic Encounters in the Americas* (London: British Film Institute, 1993)

Kolker, R. P. *The Altering Eye. Contemporary International Cinema* (Oxford: Oxford University Press, 1983)

Landau, S. 'Clinton's Cuba Policy: a Low-priority Dilemma', *NACLA Report on the Americas*, XXVI: 5 (May 1993)

Leogrande, W. M. 'A Policy-driven Policy. Washington's Cuba Agenda is Still in Place – for Now', *NACLA Report on the Americas*, XXXIV: 3 (November/December 2000)

Leogrande, W. M. and W. S. Smith, 'Dateline Havana: Myopic Diplomacy', *Foreign Affairs*, 48 (Fall 1982)

Leonard, T. M. *Castro and the Cuban Revolution* (Westport, Conn.: Greenwood Press, 1999)

Levine, R. M. and M. Asís *Cuban Miami* (New Brunswick, NJ: Rutgers University Press, 2000)

Lightfoot, C. *Havana. A Cultural and Literary Companion* (Oxford: Signal Books, 2002)

Liss, S. B. *Fidel! Castro's Political and Social Thought* (Boulder, Colo.: Westview Press, 1994)

Lowy, M. *The Marxism of Che Guevara* (New York: Monthly Review Press, 1977)

Lumsden, I. *Machos, Maricones and Gays. Cuba and Homosexuality* (Philadelphia, Pa: Temple University Press, 1996)

Macdonald, T. *Schooling the Revolution. An Analysis of Developments in Cuban Education since 1959*, 2nd edn (London: Praxis Press, 1996)

McEwan, A. *Revolution and Economic Development in Cuba* (New York: St Martin's Press, 1981)

McManus, J. *Cuba's Island of Dreams. Voices from the Isle of Pines and Youth* (Gainesville, Fla: University Press of Florida, 2000)

Martínez Heredia, F. 'Cuban Socialism: Prospects and Challenges', *Latin American Perspectives*, 69: 18: 2 (Spring 1991)

Matthews, H. I. *Castro. A Political Biography* (Harmondsworth: Penguin, 1969)

Mesa Lago, C. *Revolutionary Change in Cuba* (Pittsburgh, Pa: Pittsburgh University Press, 1971)

Mesa Lago, C. *Cuba in the 1970s. Pragmatism and Institutionalisation* (Alburquerque, NM: University of New Mexico Press, 1978)

Mesa Lago, C. (ed.) *Cuba. After the Cold War* (Pittsburgh, Pa: University of Pittsburgh Press, 1993)

Mesa Lago, C. *Are Economic Reforms Propelling Cuba to the Market?* (Miami: University of Miami North-South Center, 1994)

Miller, N. *In the Shadow of the State. Intellectuals and the Quest for National Identity in Twentieth-century Spanish America* (London: Verso, 1999)

Mina, G. *An Encounter with Fidel Castro* (Sydney: Ocean Press, 1991)

Moore, C. *Castro, The Blacks and Africa* (Los Angeles: UCLA, Center for Afro-American Studies, 1988)

Morley, M. H. *Imperial State and Revolution. The United States and Cuba, 1952–1986* (Cambridge: Cambridge University Press, 1987)

Moses, C. *Real Life in Castro's Cuba* (Wilmington, Del.: Scholarly Resources, 1999)

Mujal León, E. *The USSR and Latin America. A Developing Relationship* (Boston: Unwin Hyman, 1989)

Nathan, J. A. *Anatomy of the Cuban Missile Crisis* (Westport, Conn.: Greenwood Press, 2001)

O'Reilly Herrera, A. *ReMembering Cuba. Legacy of a Diaspora* (Austin: University of Texas Press, 2001)

Parker, D. 'The Cuban Crisis and the Future of the Revolution: a Latin American Perspective', *Latin American Research Review*, 33: 1 (1998)

Paterson, T. G. *Contesting Castro. The United States and the Triumph of the Cuban Revolution* (Oxford: Oxford University Press, 1995)

Peck, J. (ed.) *The Chomsky Reader* (New York: Pantheon, 1987)

Pérez Firmat, G. *Life on the Hyphen: The Cuba–American Way* (Austin: University of Texas Press, 1994)

Pérez, L. A. Jnr 'Twenty-five Years of Cuban Historiography: Views from Abroad', *Cuban Studies* (1998)

Pérez, L. A. Jnr *The War of 1898. The US and Cuba in History and Historiography* (Chapel Hill, NC: University of North Carolina Press, 1998)

Pérez, L. A. Jnr *On Becoming Cuban. Identity, Nationality and Culture* (Chapel Hill, NC: University of North Carolina Press, 1999)

Pérez Sarduy, P. and J. Stubbs (eds) *Afrocuba. An Anthology of Cuban Writing on Race, Politics and Culture* (Melbourne: Ocean Press, 1993)

Petras, J. *The Left Strikes Back. Class Conflict in the Age of Neoliberalism* (Boulder, Colo.: Westview Press, 1999)

Petras, J. and M. Morley, 'Cuban Socialism: Rectification and the New Model of Accumulation' in J. Petras and M. Morley *Latin America in the Time of Cholera: Electoral Politics, Market Economies and Permanent Crisis* (New York: Routledge, 1992)

Piñeiro, M. *Che Guevara and the Latin American Revolutionary Movements* (Melbourne: Ocean Press, 2001)

Portes, A. and A. Stepick *City on the Edge. The Transformation of Miami* (Berkeley: University of California Press, 1993)

Poyo, G. E. 'José Martí: Architect of Social Unity in the Émigré Communities of the United States' in C. Abel and N. Torrents (eds) *José Martí. Revolutionary Democrat* (London: Athlone Press, 1986)

Rabe, S. G. *The Most Dangerous Area in the World. John F. Kennedy Confronts Communist Revolution in Latin America* (Chapel Hill, NC: University of North Carolina Press, 1999)

Randall, M. *Gathering Rage. The Failure of Twentieth Century Revolutions to Develop a Feminist Agenda* (New York: Monthly Review Press, 1992)

Ratliff, W. E. (ed.) *The Selling of Fidel Castro. The Media and the Cuban Revolution* (New Brunswick, NJ: Transaction Books, 1987)

Ratner, M. and M. S. Smith (eds) *Che Guevara and the FBI. The US Political Police Dossier on the Latin American Revolutionary* (Melbourne: Ocean Press, 1997)

Reed, G. *Island in the Storm* (Melbourne: Ocean Press, 1992)

Ricardo, R. *Guantánamo. Bay of Discord* (Melbourne: Ocean Press, 1993)

Ripley, C. P. *Conversations with Cuba* (Athens, Ga: University of Georgia Press, 1999)

Rodríguez, J. C. *Bay of Pigs and the CIA* (Melbourne: Ocean Press, 1999)

Rodríguez-Luis, J. (ed.) *Re-reading José Martí [1853–1895]. One Hundred Years Later* (New York: Albany State University of New York Press, 1999)

Roman, R. 'Reviewing the Cuban Revolution', *Latin American Perspectives*, 96: 24: 5 (1997)

Roman, R. *People's Power: Cuba's Experience with Representative Government* (Boulder, Colo.: Westview Press, 1999)

Roy, J. *Cuba, the United States and the Helms–Burton Doctrine* (Gainesville, Fla: University Press of Florida, 2000)

Roy, M. *Cuban Music* (Princeton, NJ: Markus Wiener Publishers, 2002)

Rubeira Castillo, D. *Reyita. The Life of a Black Cuban Woman in the Twentieth Century* (London: Latin American Bureau, 2000)

Schmidt-Nowara, C. *Empire and Antislavery. Spain, Cuba, and Puerto Rico, 1833–1874* (Pittsburgh, Pa: University of Pittsburgh Press, 1999)

Schwab, P. *Cuba. Confronting the US Embargo* (New York: St Martin's Press, 1998)

Schwartz, R. *Pleasure Island: Tourism and Temptation in Cuba* (Lincoln, Neb.: University of Nebraska Press, 1997)

Shnookal, D. and M. Muñiz (eds) *José Martí Reader. Writings on the Americas* (Melbourne: Ocean Press, 1999)

Smith, L. M. and A. Padula *Sex and Revolution: Women in Socialist Cuba* (New York: Oxford University Press, 1996)

Smith, P. J. *Vision Machines. Cinema, Literature and Sexuality in Spain and Cuba, 1983–93* (London: Verso, 1996)

Smith, W. S. *The Closest of Enemies. A Personal and Diplomatic Account of US–Cuban Relations since 1957* (New York: W. W. Norton & Company, 1987)

Stubbs, J. 'Social Equity, Agrarian Transition and Development in Cuba, 1945–90' in C. Abel and C. M. Lewis (eds) *Welfare, Poverty and Development in Latin America* (Basingstoke: Macmillan – now Palgrave Macmillan, 1993)

Suárez Hernandez, G. 'Political Leadership in Cuba', *Latin American Perspectives*, 69: 18: 2 (Spring 1991)

Sweeney, P. *The Rough Guide to Cuban Music* (London: Rough Guides Ltd, 2001)

Tablada, C. *Che Guevara. Economics and Politics in the Transition to Socialism* (New York: Pathfinder, 1987)

Tablada, C. 'The Creativity of Che's Economic Thought' in Centro de Estudios Sobre América (ed.) *The Cuban Revolution into the 1990s* (Boulder, Colo.: Westview Press, 1992)

Thomas, H. *Cuba or the Pursuit of Freedom* (London: Eyre & Spottiswoode, 1971)

Thompson, K. and D. Bordwell *Film History. An Introduction* (New York: McGraw-Hill, 1994)

Triay, V. A. *Fleeing Castro. Operation Pedro Pan and the Cuban Children's Program* (Gainesville, Fla: University Press of Florida, 1999)

Tulchin, J. S., A. Serbin and R. Hernández (eds) *Cuba and the Caribbean. Regional Issues and Trends in the Post-Cold War Era* (Wilmington, Del.: Scholarly Resources, 1997)

Vilas, C. 'Fancy Footwork: Regis Debray on Che Guevara', *NACLA Report on the Americas*, XXX: 3 (November/December 1996)

Weinberg, B. *Homage to Chiapas. The New Indigenous Struggles in Mexico* (London: Verso, 2000)

West, D. 'Reconciling Entertainment and Thought. An Interview with Julio García Espinosa', *CINEASTE*, XVI: 1 and 2 (1987–88)

West, D. 'Alice in a Cuban Wonderland. An Interview with Daniel Díaz Torres', *CINEASTE*, XX: 1 (1993)

West, D. '*Strawberry and Chocolate*, Ice Cream and Tolerance: Interviews with Tomás Gutiérrez Alea and Juan Carlos Tabio', *CINEASTE*, XXI: 1–2 (1995)

White, M. J. (ed.) *The Kennedys and Cuba. The Declassified Documentary History* (Chicago: Ivan R. Dee, 1999)

Wright, T. C. *Latin America in the Era of the Cuban Revolution*, revised edn (Westport, Conn.: Praeger, 2001)

Yglesias, J. *In the Fist of the Revolution* (London: Penguin, 1968)

Zanetti, O. and A. García *Sugar and Railroads, 1837–1959* (Chapel Hill, NC: University of North Carolina Press, 1998)

Index